ROME
AGAINST CARATACUS

The Roman Campaigns in Britain
AD 48–58

ROME
AGAINST CARATACUS

The Roman Campaigns in Britain
AD 48–58

B. T. BATSFORD LTD LONDON

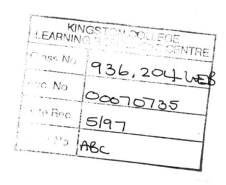
To George Counsell Boon
in gratitude for many years of help and friendship

© Graham Webster 1981

First published 1981
Revised edition 1993

Photoset in Monophoto Apollo by
Servis Filmsetting Ltd, Manchester
and printed in Great Britain by
The Bath Press, Avon
for the publishers
B.T. Batsford Ltd
4 Fizhardinge Street London W1H 0AH

British Library Cataloguing in Publication Data

Webster, Graham
    Rome against Caratacus.
    1. Great Britain – History – Roman period,
    55 B.C.–449A.D.
    2. Great Britain – Politics and government –
    to 1485
I. Title
936.2'04   DA 145

Cover illustration: Mansell Collection

ISBN 0 7134 7254 5

Contents

Acknowledgments

The Author and Publisher wish to thank the following for permission to reproduce photographs and plans appearing in the book:

Mr Arnold Baker for pl. 5, 6, 11, 13 and 15
The Committee for Aerial Photography, University of Cambridge for pl. 14, 16, 17, 21 and 22
Dr Kevin Greene for fig 38
Dr W. Manning for allowing me to adapt fig 3
The National Museum for Wales for pl. 1 and 2
Professor W. Ravenhall for fig 35
The West Yorkshire Metropolitan County Council for pl. 19

The Plates

Between pages 62 and 63

Line Illustrations

Preface

This volume follows on from *The Roman Invasion of Britain* (published 1980) which dealt with the invasion of 43 and the governorship of Aulus Plautius. The present volume takes up the story from the advent of the second governor, P. Ostorius Scapula, in the winter of 47/48 and his subsequent campaigns against Caratacus. The events which followed his sudden death cover the period of the third governor A. Didius Gallus. The final years of Claudius were marked with indecision. The state of Britain remained unresolved until Nero and his advisers decided on a new advance to settle the problem of the Welsh frontier, and sent Q. Veranius in 56/57 to implement his new policy. He had only one campaign season, but his unexpected death brought Suetonius Paullinus and, with him, the bursting of the great dam of British resentment in the revolt of Boudica, an account of which I have published in a separate volume (*Boudica*, 1979).

The campaigns of the present volume took the army from the south-east into the West Midlands and the Welsh Marches. The former is my own territory, but, in dealing with the events and sites of the Principality, I have been dependent on the help of many old friends and colleagues. First and foremost is George Boon, the Keeper of the Department of Archaeology and Numismatics of the National Museum of Wales, to whom I am delighted to have the honour of dedicating this volume. Other scholars and archaeologists to whom I am greatly indebted are Professor Mike Jarrett, Dr Bill Manning, Dr Jeffrey Davies, Professor Barri Jones, Peter Webster and Chris Musson. For information about Caerleon, I am also grateful to Vivienne Metcalfe and David Zienkiewicz. The campaigns of Scapula also embraced the south-west peninsula of Devon and Cornwall and here I am grateful for the help of Dr Valerie Maxfield.

Didius Gallus, as I have endeavoured to demonstrate, had to face a new threat created by Queen Cartimandua. To study the changes he made to the northern frontier, I have received the help and advice of specialists in this area, in particular Dr Derrick Riley, who has contributed so much to aerial archaeology in the lower Trent and South Yorkshire. Others to whom I am much indebted are Brian Hartley, Herman Ramm and Phil Mayes.

The outstanding contribution over many years to our knowledge of the Roman military sites and campaigns has been Professor J.K. St Joseph, until recently Director of the Committee for Aerial Photography, University of Cambridge. Without the great mass of evidence he has discovered and published, this book could not have been started. We all owe an enormous debt to him and I am pleased also to acknowledge the help of David Wilson, who was his assistant and now the Director. But the solid foundation stone on which my study is based was laid a long time ago by Cornelius Tacitus; for without his account of the events in Britannia in his *Annals*, all indeed would be in darkness.

For a new and perceptive translation of the appropriate passages, I am grateful to Mary Beard and Chloe Chard. I am also much indebted to Professor Barrett for writing a note on Cogidubnus, which appears as Appendix 2. Once more, my friend Barrie Eccleston has produced a set of maps and plans with his accustomed skill and artistry. My own patient Diana has endeavoured to remove blemishes and inconsistencies from the text and also provide fine drawings of equipment. I am most grateful also to Peter Kemmis Betty who has done much to improve the text. My hard-worked secretary Mary Pinder deserves special praise for coping with my illegible hand and for the constant reworking of mangled text. Errors and omissions seems always to be unavoidable and I would be grateful to readers who would kindly inform me, so that any future editions can be improved. This book remains merely a statement of the present portion. Fresh evidence is continuously pouring out of excavations and from aerial observation which in turn changes theories and ideas – so that one progresses slowly and painfully towards historical truth.

Finally I must express my deep gratitude to Professor Barrett and Peter Jennings for their considerable help with the proof reading.

Preface to the revised edition

The most important additions to knowledge since 1981 are summarized in *Fortress into City*, 1988 which I edited and to which I contributed. There are now also the full excavation reports on the work at Usk by Professor Manning who sees it as a legionary fortress.[1] But his plan of the area of the *via principalis* is far more like a legionary storebase. There is also the discovery of an early fortress below Silchester by Professor M. Fulford,[2] which is evidence that this is the fortress of *Leg.* II *Aug.* rather than Chichester which must have been held by an auxiliary unit. My excavation at Wroxeter finished in 1985 and the military report (AD 56-90) is almost complete and publication is within the foreseeable future. Another forward base fort has been investigated by Professor S. S. Frere at an Iron Age fort, Brandon Camp, Herefordshire, which produced ample dating evidence of this period.[3]

[1] *The Fortress Excavations 1968-71*, 1981, *The Fortress Excavations 1972-1974*
[2] Personal communication
[3] *Brit.* 13 (1982), pp. 360-1; 15 (1984), pp. 294-5; 17 (1986), pp. 292-3; 18 (1987), p. 11

Historical Chart

AD	EVENTS IN BRITAIN	GOVERNOR	EMPEROR
43	Invasion of Britain and creation of the province of Britannia	Aulus Plautius	Claudius (41–54)
47/48	Incursion into Britannia by Caratacus Founding of the *colonia* at Camulodunum and creation of the two client kingdoms of Cogidubnus and Prasutagus	P. Ostorius Scapula	
50	Defeat of Caratacus		
51/52		Death of Scapula	
52		A. Didius Gallus	
52/56	Consolidation of Welsh frontier Trouble with Cartimandua Adjustments to northern frontier		Nero (54–68)
57/58		Q. Veranius (died within the year)	
58	Campaign against the Silures		
58/59	Continued and completed, then against the Ordovices	C. Suetonius Paullinus	
60/61	Attack in Anglesey Revolt of Boudica		

Introduction

The invasion of Britain by the Roman army had taken place late in the summer of AD 43. It had been in response to the sudden rise to power by the anti-Roman faction of the royal house of the Trinovantes, following the death of its King, Cunobelinus. The task of the first governor, Aulus Plautius, had been to land his forces without serious opposition and defeat the Britons. The latter he had achieved with remarkable success at the decisive battle of the Medway; thereafter he was able to spread out and occupy the rest of the new province with little difficulty, except for fierce resistance in the south-west, which was overcome by the future emperor Vespasian, then in command of *Legio II Augusta*.

The area selected by Rome for the creation of the province of Britannia embraced the lowlands which contained most of the rich agricultural land and the mineral wealth then known. The latter comprised the silver ores of the Mendips, the iron of Kent, and the limestone belt crossing modern Oxfordshire, Northants and Lincolnshire. The major factor in limiting the conquest may have been that the tribes occupying these lands were those most likely to yield to the policy of urbanisation, which was such a necessary part of Roman life. Certainly most of these tribes had migrated from the Continent in the centuries preceding the invasion, and some of those in the Thames Estuary had only arrived recently, as a direct consequence of Caesar's advent into Gaul. The frontier of the province stretched from the Humber along the Trent Valley to the lower Severn and the Bristol Channel, and then cut across country to the Estuary of the Exe. Significantly, only the tribes to the south and east of this line had their own coinage. A glance at the map of Roman Britain shows clearly the density of sites and close network of roads in contact with the areas beyond.

Rome's interest in these outer barbarian lands was confined at this time to the safety of their new province. The practice, continued from an earlier period, had been to seek protection of frontiers through friendly states. A special arrangement under the Roman method of patronage visualised the creation or recognition of kingdoms, the rulers of which had a client relationship with the Senate and people of Rome and, after Augustus, with the Emperors. It was the primary duty of the client rulers to prevent peoples beyond the frontier from invading Roman territory. This was a highly convenient system since security could be maintained along the difficult frontiers at minimal cost.

Having secured the province, Plautius had the immediate task of looking for protection of this nature. But his one and only success, although a considerable one, was to place Queen Cartimandua on the throne of Brigantia, so bringing together a large number of small tribes living in the river valleys of what are now the vast counties of Yorkshire and Lancashire, straddling the Pennines. (We are not sure of Cartimandua's northern boundary, since additional security was achieved by a dynastic marriage with Venutius, thought to have been a ruler of a tribe to the north of Brigantia.) Thus, Rome secured the most difficult and vulnerable frontier. Doubtless similar arrangements were sought to the west to protect the province from raids by the wild mountain peoples of the country now known as Wales. Here Plautius failed, and he must soon have realised that the sole reason for this failure was the presence there of Caratacus. But so long as this warrior remained quiet, Plautius may not have been over-concerned, since he had first to ensure that the area of the province was pacified and that the British rulers who had surrendered were totally subservient to the Roman Government. His term of office came to an end in the winter of 47/48 and he returned to Rome to receive his well-deserved *ovatio*.

The new governor, Publius Ostorius Scapula, arrived to find the province in turmoil. Caratacus had timed his strike well. Having quietly built up his strength on the west bank of the lower Severn, he had waited for the brief, but significant interval between the departure of the out-going governor and the arrival of the replacement (since there could have been difficulties in protocol had two governors been in a province at the same time). Before, however, we consider the fierce struggle that Scapula was to face, the two protagonists must be introduced and their characters assessed.

Caratacus

The British prince was a son of Cunobelinus who reigned over the two kingdoms of the Trinovantes and Catuvellauni, both tribes having migrated from Gaul sometime in the first century BC. Their large territories stretched from the Colne peninsula to the Chilterns, in the south bounding the River Thames and in the north the Kingdom of the Iceni (Norfolk). Cunobeline, a great statesman, had maintained throughout his long reign (c. AD 10–40) a skilful balance between the two bitterly opposing factions, those for, and those against, Rome. The eldest son Togodumnus inherited the throne and took his place at the side of Caratacus against Rome, but a third brother, Adminius, had been given the north-east tip of Kent, which included the only land-locked harbour along the south-east coast and the Wansum Channel into the Thames Estuary. It appears to have been Roman policy to ensure that the main landing points would remain in friendly hands; it was the enfeeblement, or death, of Cunobeline (c.40) which changed this and caused the new British rulers to adopt a policy of hostility towards Rome.

The first result was the flight of Adminius to Gaius (Caligula) to seek his aid in restoring the *status quo ante*. The schemes of that wayward emperor are obscured by his apparently wanton acts, but it is evident that an invasion was under consideration, but was deferred. Meantime, in Britain, Togodumnus took over the kingdom of his father and Caratacus began to invade the lands south of the Thames. Within a year another British ruler was a suppliant at the Imperial Court. This time it was Verica of the Atrebates beseeching Claudius, who had only just been thrust into power. This time the plea was taken more seriously, since Claudius needed a diversion from Rome where his relationship with the Senate was charged with suspicion and hostility. There were other reasons why the time was ripe for a full-scale invasion, and these have been considered in detail in the first volume of this trilogy (*The Roman Invasion of Britain*, 84–5).

Caratacus had by now acquired a kingdom and was issuing coins, but un-fortunately not enough have been found for them to offer a satisfactory dis-tribution pattern which might show the extent of his power. It does, however, give some indication of his forceful personality, leadership and organising ability, that he was able in such a short time to reduce and dominate a powerful neighbouring tribe. He may have exercised control by means of allies over the whole of his lands south of the Thames from the Solent to the east coast of Kent. The Kings of Kent had never been a powerful force and had no coins of their own; possibly as a result of their crushing defeat suffered under Caesar or their own internal divisions. They were dominated throughout this period and between the invasions by rulers from without, and this, together with their anti-Roman feelings, would have made it easy for Caratacus to gain their sympathy and later control over them. Further to the west were the Durotriges, a tribe which, for unknown reasons, had become bitterly hostile to Rome. Their hill-forts were to be stormed by Vespasian's legionaries, but as yet they were far from pacified. As will be seen later, they probably had assistance from their neighbours to the north, the southern section of the Dobunni. Thus, Caratacus had solid support from the west, and had he been left alone might have started to move towards the tribes in the midlands and north-west and on to those distant parts of Britain where the Druids, as priests and mediators, would have spread his fame to all the tribes.

Publius Ostorius Scapula[1]

Very little is known about the man appointed by Claudius as the second governor of Britain; almost the whole account of his period of office in Britain comes from the *Annals* of Tacitus. Yet to be given such a difficult and important command of a province so recently conquered, with the large force of four legions, demanded strong leadership and diplomacy. This shows that he was highly regarded in Rome, not only for the abilities needed for such a position, but also for his known loyalty to the Imperial house. His father, or more probably his grandfather, was Q. Ostorius Scapula, who had reached the top of the equestrian tree as Prefect of Egypt, after being appointed by Augustus as one of the first pair of Praetorian Prefects in 2 BC. Ronald Syme has conjectured that the mother, or wife, of Scapula was Sallustia Calvina.[2] If so, then there was a family connection with Lucius Vitellius, whose daughter-in-law Junia Calvina was the brother of the ill-fated Silanus, one of the two young men who brought the despatch of Claudius to the Senate after his victories in Britain (Dio, lxii. 22). He had been a suffect consul[3] with P. Suillius Rufus, the son of Vistilia (whose fecundity was a matter of comment by Pliny the Elder).[4] She was also the mother of Domitius Corbulo. The year of Scapula's consulship is not known, but Ronald Syme has suggested AD 45 as the most likely.[5] This prompts him to hazard the guess that Scapula may have distinguished himself in the invasion of Britain as one of the *comites* and thus brought himself to the notice of Claudius. An experience of Britain would certainly have been an advantage, but, following Syme's tenuous line of argument, had he been connected with L. Vitellius, this great weight of influence would have been all that was necessary, since he was the power behind Claudius at this time (Suet., *Vitellius* 2). It would, nevertheless, have been extraordinary if Scapula had not had any military experience before this command, and it is reasonable to suppose that he must have been at least a legionary commander in the earlier part of his career.[6]

15

The character of Scapula emerges from his actions against Caratacus, some of which were hasty and ill-considered even by the standards of military expediency. His growing frustration and anger, which led to his death, prompts the view that he was a sick man on entering office. But clearly his ailment cannot have been either too obvious or too serious at the time of his appointment.

The Lands and Peoples of the West

The geology of Britain varies enormously as one travels from the south-east to the north-west. The reason for this is that the rock stratum is tilted; but apart from the river valleys erosion has more or less levelled the earth's surface. As a result, narrow bands of different rocks are found at the surface in the form of strips stretching across the country in diagonal lines from the south-west to the north-east, thus creating a most varied sequence of landscape for the traveller. This general pattern is, however, abruptly broken by the older and harder rocks in the west, into which have penetrated even harder volcanic intrusions.

The western part of Britain was occupied by peoples who had arrived by different routes from those in the east. Some had been forced to move westwards by more recent migrants who landed and settled on the east and south coasts, either conquering or displacing the tribes already there. So a kind of shunting action had taken place which tended to push those on the edge of the lowland zone into the hill-lands beyond. But there were already folk who had come by water up the Bristol Channel and the Severn. The hill country beyond the Severn was not very suitable for arable farming since the valleys were as yet undrained marsh, subject to seasonal flooding. The uplands had already been farmed by pastoral folk with sheep and goats. By the third and fourth centuries BC any newcomers wou'd have been faced with serious opposition. The determination of the hill-folk to hold their territories is amply shown by the great concentration of their strongly defended forts stretching along the marcher country. Their resistance to penetration and conquest was strengthened by the knowledge that to the west were the mountains, even less friendly to settlement. Consequently the tribes of these areas were fiercely independent and very wary of the peoples of the lowlands.

So far the name of Wales has not been introduced. The *Walas* or *Wealas* was a name used by the Saxons for the Britons, and, as it means serfs or slaves, it must have been generally applied to the rural population. But it was also used in the sense of 'foreigner', i.c. someone who was not a Saxon or other people from the continent. To the Saxons the Welsh were the British and Wales was the country inhabited by them. Although it perpetrates an anachronism, the words Wales and the Welsh will be used in this volume to avoid confusion.

The Tribes

Our knowledge of the tribes of Britain comes from a variety of sources, road books like the Antonine Itinerary, the Ravenna Cosmography, the Geography of Ptolemy and the Roman historians. Added to these are a few epigraphic items and the survival of names into early medieval records. There must have been small tribes or parts of larger ones which lost their identity when Roman officials organised the main administrative units of the British *civitates*. Since these were designed for administration, taxation and justice, it was convenient to create larger tribal areas and for the most part it is only the names of these which have survived.

The two main border tribes east of the Severn were the Dobunni and the Cornovii. More is known of the former since the tribal area came within contact range of the Gallo-Belgic tribes of the south-east and so, directly or indirectly, with the Roman traders. A study of their coins indicates that the Dobunni were divided into two groups in a state of mutual hostility. The northern tribal centre was the large *oppidum* at Bagendon, near Cirencester, and this section of the tribe was said by Dio to have been subject to the Catuvellauni (lx. 20). He stated also that part of the Dobunni surrendered to Aulus Plautius soon after the landing in 43. The presumption is that this submission on behalf of the tribe was made by a group of levies due to join the forces of Caratacus at the Medway. The distribution of coins shows that the western boundary of this tribe at this time was most probably the Severn, although later in the Roman reorganisation of the *civitas* for judicial and administrative purposes, it may have extended westwards into what is now Herefordshire.[7] The presence of an ally on this part of the frontier zone must have been a great advantage to Scapula in his preparation for a campaign into southern Wales.

Between the Dobunni and the Cornovii to the north, there appears to be a gap and it is possible that the identity of a small tribe has been lost in the Roman planning of the territories of the *civitates*. Unfortunately, very little can be said of the Cornovii since they had no coins, or any distinctive pottery or metalwork.[8] The little which can be deduced from a study of the artefacts and details of the construction of the hill-forts, points to this tribe as a northern group of peoples with a similar ethnic origin to those which occupied the Severn valley, and the lands to the west. Nor is it possible to identify their centre from the several large hill-forts, and there may have been no dominant ruler, with the tribe divided into small groups or septs under their own rulers. All that can be said at present is that one of them at least, based on the Wrekin, offered resistance to the Roman army, and had to be stormed and destroyed.

The southern group, occupying what is now Herefordshire, has produced more evidence of artefacts. It has been claimed that its centre was Credenhill Camp,[9] near the later Roman town at Kenchester. But again, the name of these people has not survived. In the lands of the Welsh the names of only four tribes are known with any certainty, the Silures, Demetae, Ordovices, Deceangli, but there are hints of others.[10]

The Silures occupied an area on the north shore of the Bristol Channel and it was this tribe which became the main enemy of Scapula. Their name appears several times in Tacitus, in the road itineraries[11] and on an inscription from Caerwent (*RIB* 311). There is a hint from Tacitus (*Agricola* 11) that these people may originally have migrated from Spain by the Atlantic route. Apart from the fact that Caerwent (Venta Silurum) became their capital, there are no indications of the boundaries of their territory. The obvious western and northern boundary is the River Wye, and to the west they faced their neighbours the Demetae of Pembroke and Cardiganshire. The name of the Demetae is given by Ptolemy and was also known to Gildas,[12] the Briton who wrote a kind of religious tract in the early sixth century; the name survives in the modern Dyfed. Their capital was Carmarthen (Moridunum) and Ptolemy included Loughor (Leucarum) in their territory. The boundary between them and the Silures was, therefore, either the Tame or the Mellte.

The only other major known tribe is the Ordovices, recorded by Tacitus (*Annals* xii. 33) and Ptolemy (ii. 3, 11). It survives in modern Dinorwig and Rhyd Orddwy, near

Rhyl. The name of the tribe seems to mean 'the hammer fighters',[13] and it may be worth noting that at Graig Lwyd on the slopes of Penmaer Mawr was one of the most important prehistoric stone axe factories in Britain.[14] It is not suggested, of course, that these later warriors were still using such weapons, but the axe-hammer may have been their symbol. There are serious difficulties in attempting to define the territory of this tribe. Place-name evidence suggests it may have extended as far east as the Vale of Clwyd. Ptolemy, whose source may have been a Neronian survey map,[15] includes two places under the tribe, Brannogenium and Mediolanum. The former has been

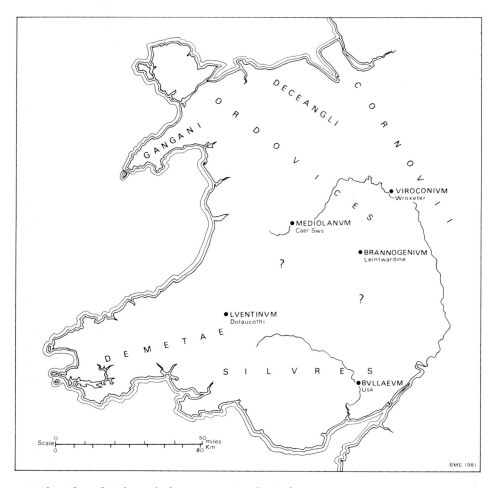

1   The tribes of Wales and place-names given by Ptolemy

identified with 'Bravonio' in the Antonine Itinerary, and this places it at Leintwardine in north Herefordshire. This however, seems too far to the south, and suggests to Rivet and Smith (120 and 143) an error in Ptolemy's figures. The site of Mediolanum is generally agreed as Whitchurch, halfway between Wroxeter and Chester. It is fixed in

18

position by the road lists and the place suits its name which is a very common one, meaning in 'the middle of the plain'. But this is also remote from Ordovician lands and would appear to have been in the territory of the Cornovii. There is however, the possibility, first suggested by Richmond and Crawford,[16] that there may have been another Mediolanum included as No. 81 in the Ravenna list, which places it west of Wroxeter, and a suitable site would be Caersws. This theory is strengthened by an obvious boundary along the watershed of the central mountains running down to the Dovey Estuary. Continued east, it could almost include Brannogenium, which would then have been in the very south-east corner of the tribal territory. This would have left a gap in central Wales, north of the Wye, for an unknown tribe which would have occupied much of Herefordshire. There is another name to be considered in Ptolemy under Ganganorum Promontorium, which can be identified as the headland of the Lleyn Peninsula. (But the Gangani also appears as a tribe in Ireland, so it is possible that there may be a confusion here.)[17]

There is finally a well-attested name, that of the Deceangli, which appears stamped on the lead pigs from Flintshire.[18] It survives into the Middle Ages as Tegeingl, one of the cantreds of the county.[19] The problem is whether this is the equivalent to the name in Tacitus which appears in the text[20] as Cangos, normally amended to Decangos. A case has been made for this tribe to have been in Herefordshire but, as will be seen below, it would not fit very well with the route taken by the punitive expedition sent in this direction by Scapula. But to complicate matters, there is another possibility of a tribal name surviving in Deganwy on the Conway Estuary. This could have been derived from Decanti, a name which can hardly be the same as Deceangli;[21] so there remains the possibility that this was a coastal tribe which was subject to and a sept of the Ordovices.

The Military Organisation of Britannia under Plautius

Rome's success had been partly military and partly political. The great victory at the Medway had been a crushing blow for the anti-Roman faction, but many of the levies must have escaped to the south-west since the main aim of Plautius seems to have been to prevent Caratacus and his brother from crossing the Thames. The British tribes had not yet fully accepted conquest, but as always Rome's aim was to divide the Britons and secure alliances which would place responsibility for law and order in the hands of the tribal rulers. Eleven kings are said to have made subjection to Claudius at Camulodunum, the only tribe whose submission was recorded is the presumably northern section of the Dobunni (Dio, lx. 20). It is difficult even to guess at the names of the other ten since some of the smaller ones became absorbed into the later large administrative units, and their names have vanished. There could, for example, have been three or four Kentish tribes apart from the well-known Regni, Atrebates, Catuvellauni,. Trinovantes, Iceni, Brigantes, etc. It is probable that all the eleven belonged to the area of the province, and they were certainly unlikely to include any beyond the western frontier.

In his military dispositions, Plautius would have taken into account the potential hostility of different peoples, but precisely how this was done is far from clear. Our present sparse information, as seen in the maps in my earlier study, *The Roman Invasion of Britain* (116–21), shows an even spread of forts holding the main means of communication. It is evident from the limited amount of detailed excavation that some units were split, and each legion had to give up at least two cohorts for out-post garrison duties to provide for adequate cover over the whole of the province. The sites chosen for the four legions may be significant. *Legio XX* held the British capital Camulodunum, *Legio II Aug.* was at Silchester, where it could strike quickly by sea against any trouble in the south-west, yet protected in its rearward fortress. *Legio IX* occupied a forward position at Longthorpe, near Peterborough on the Nene; and a case has been made for *Legio XIV* having been at Leicester with a direct line of communication with headquarters at Camulodunum. If this is a correct assumption, it would suggest that Plautius had his most serious doubts about the Corieltauvi (of Leicestershire and Lincolnshire). During his three-and-a-half years in office the governor would have had time for an accurate appraisal of the attitude and strength of all the tribal rulers and may have adjusted the sites and positions of his units accordingly. But one thing is certainly clear, that AD 48 was hardly a time to mount a major offensive which would remove troops from the greater part of the province. Yet this was the challenge facing Ostorius Scapula.

First, however, he had to deal with the serious emergency created by Caratacus. The phrases used by Tacitus underly the gravity of the crisis, *turbidae res excepere, effusis in agrum sociorum hostibus eo violentius* . . . (xii. 31), i.e. Scapula was faced with 'serious disruption, hostile tribes had irrupted violently into the lands of our allies'. As Professor Anthony Barrett had pointed out, the word *turbidae* could mean far more than 'disturbance' which is used by most translators. Tacitus elsewhere uses this word when he refers to a mutiny (*Hist.* i. 5) and to internal disorder (*Ann.* iii. 27). It could mean that hostile Britons within the province had combined with the forces of Caratacus to cause the maximum damage over a wide area. The allies must have been the southern Dobunni, but, as previously noted, they were one of the opposing branches of the tribe. The northern half had submitted to Plautius prior to the Medway battle, and this would have given rise to great bitterness felt by the southern section which had allied itself to the Durotriges. It would also help to explain why Caratacus chose to invade their territory as revenge for their 'defection' as well as an assault against Rome. The Durotriges could have struck to the east into the lands of the Atrebates, which would have brought a large area of the south-west into a state of chaos in mid-winter.

Scapula had to move quickly, deploying his mounted cohorts to break up the bands of rebels and raiders, and cut them down with typically Roman brutality and decisiveness. Once order had been restored, he needed to consider how to prevent Caratacus from striking again. He presumably summoned the legionary commanders and senior advisers to a conference at his headquarters at Camulodunum. The problems he faced were indeed daunting. He could not afford to leave the initiative to Caratacus, since the frontier was long and vulnerable and gave the British leader great scope to infiltrate his men into the Midlands, as well as the south-west, and strike at any point without warning. Yet to deal with his enemy, Scapula was obliged to mount a large search-and-find operation and force him into a battle where the anti-Roman forces would be completely annihilated. But the province was still in an unsettled state and the Roman troops must have felt uneasy about the Britons wherever they were stationed, wondering how far they could be trusted, should the opportunity to rise against them occur. As Tacitus says, inaction would have resulted in a false armed peace (*infida pax*) which allowed no rest either to the commander or his troops. Obviously Scapula could not order his troops westwards and leave large areas without any garrisons, but to be effective against Caratacus he needed at least half his army in the field. Tacitus gives us the solutions arrived at to deal with a seemingly intractable problem. Although it is tempting to change the Tacitean order of events, this would impose our own thinking on the situation. The benefit of 1,930 years' hindsight is quite inadequate in the face of our ignorance of the state of mind of Scapula and of the information available to him. As Tacitus is our only guide, it is vital that we do not stray from his text.

The first Roman action is a surprising one. Unfortunately, it is buried in a corrupt sentence in the text, but the brilliant emendation reported by the Victorian scholar, Dr H. Bradley[22] has made excellent sense of it; *detrahere arma suspectis cunctaqua cis Trisantonam et Sabrinam fluvios cohibere parat*, i.e. 'he prepared to disarm all the suspect tribes on our side of the rivers Trent and Severn'. The first point to note is that this gives us the key to the frontier line linked on the ground with its lateral communication route, the Fosse Way (see *The Roman Invasion of Britain*, 123). The next aspect is an attempt to appreciate the motive behind this decision. Under Roman law no one was allowed to carry arms except the troops and officers in the state service, though knives and hunting swords were exempt. One of the consequences of an act of submission by a tribe would have been the handing over of all weapons. There would naturally have been a great reluctance to do this on the part of those not yet convinced of Rome's intentions of bringing peace to Britain. Many indeed still remained totally hostile and would have carefully concealed their weapons and handed in old and scrap items if public occasion demanded. If the conjecture that tribes in the south-west joined Caratacus in the winter rising is correct, it would have shown the Roman authorities how easily the Britons took to arms. Even had they been forced to surrender all their swords after a battle, each family only needed a small cache of currency bars[23] and a local blacksmith.

The Disarming of the Tribes

However, Scapula was not concerned with the retrieval of arms so much as with instilling terror into the hearts and minds of the Britons by means of an organised search for hidden weapons. To ask for arms to be given up would have been a futile gesture; a more positive approach was needed. One can imagine units of the army descending upon the villages and farmsteads, lining up all the inhabitants and searching meticulously in the houses and yards, turning out everything, beds, haystacks, heaps of rubbish, delving into storage pits, tearing the thatch of the roof apart. The slightest sign of protest would have been a hostile act, promptly followed by stripping and beating the whole family or a good proportion of the local population. The Roman soldiers would have enjoyed this, as many had had to live with sullen folk whose fierce defiance was so near the surface. They may have lost some of their comrades in the unrest or by being knifed on a dark night. Beating up the Britons would have released much tension and frustration, but Scapula's main object was to reduce the tribes to silent acquiescence until Caratacus had been crushed.

This is admittedly only a conjectural interpretation of a difficult sentence of Tacitus, but it appears to be substantiated by the immediate refusal by a branch of the Iceni to submit to this kind of treatment. That they are stated by Tacitus to be 'the first' to react (*quod primi Iceni abnuere*) implies that there were others who also showed open defiance. It may have been the aim of Scapula to produce this effect of

21

identifying potential trouble-spots and remove them immediately. Tacitus does not weary his readers with other examples, but selected this particular one for several reasons. The Iceni, a powerful and undefeated tribe, were especially angered by Scapula since they had voluntarily become allies of Rome; in fact this alliance dated back to Julius Caesar. They were joined in their revolt by neighbouring tribes, presumably the Corieltauvi, and chose a position to defend with some care, with a narrow approach so that the Romans could not use cavalry. Scapula assembled a force of auxiliary cohorts, and all the mounted troopers were ordered to fight on foot. The Romans burst through the defences. The Britons, finding themselves trapped within them, fought hard since they knew they had already forfeited their lives. But they were overcome by the superior arms. During this battle, the governor's son, Marcus Ostorius, was rewarded for saving the life of a fellow citizen.[24]

This revealing passage raises the question of why Scapula had no legionaries available and was obliged to use his *auxilia*. There are two possible answers. They were already engaged in risings elsewhere or they were still busy in the search for hidden arms. Regretfully, Tacitus was highly selective in the material he included. This particular incident was of interest to him, since it involved an old ally of Rome and a man who was later to be a victim of Nero's psychotic condition in his final years.[25] The crushing of the revolt persuaded others hovering on the brink of unrest to remain quiet. Scapula was now satisfied that the Britons within the province were unlikely to give any trouble in the immediate future. In the longer term, however, what may have been justified as military expediency was to leave a deep-seated sense of grievance which was to develop into a determined hatred of Rome.

A Reconnaissance Raid to North Wales

In the same sentence Tacitus dramatically switches to a forward move, not, however, against the Silures, but, oddly as it may seem at first, towards the 'Decangi'. This would appear to refer to the Deceangli, a tribe known to have occupied Flintshire (see above p. 19). This would agree with what follows in Tacitus, since he states that 'Ostorius was not far from the sea which faces Ireland'. The land was devastated and booty taken but the tribesmen would not risk an open battle, limiting their hostility to harassing skirmishes. Then comes another revealing incident – reaction from a section of the Brigantes (*discordiae apud Brigantas*) which reminded Scapula of the danger of being diverted from his main aim: he was, Tacitus states, firm in his resolve not to start a new conquest before he had secured his present priorities. The rising died away quickly; there were a few executions but the rest were pardoned.

The whole of this passage needs careful thought and interpretation. One has to consider firstly what lay behind this sudden attack on north Wales. There could have been several purposes. Scapula needed information about the geography of this region for the planning of his campaign against Caratacus, but he also probably wanted to seal off any possibility of aid from Brigantia. Although Cartimandua was firmly in control, her kingdom was so large and contained so many different tribal units that there were inevitably some anti-Roman elements among them. This is how it appears from Tacitus, but he may have been using official phrases from dispatches and the choice of the word *discordia* may be significant. It is normally used to mean internal dissension and one has to reconcile the timing of a move by dissidents in Brigantia with Scapula's long-range reconnaissance. It is possible that there were tribal affinities between the people of the Clwyd Valley and those of the Cheshire Plain, and even beyond to the north. As Sir Ian Richmond pointed out in 1954,[26] there is a similarity in the styles of hill-fort building. A movement of people and spread of cultural links seems inevitable along the range of low hills skirting the eastern edge of Cheshire Plain, dominated by the hill-forts at Maiden Castle and Eddisbury, and provides a link with the Pennines of the Mersey watershed. It may not, therefore, be surprising that the Roman drive provoked such a sharp reaction which produced a typically enigmatic Tacitean statement about Scapula not wishing to enlarge the war. Had a group of Brigantes attacked the Romans, this would have been an act of war, but it would have placed Scapula in a very difficult position with Cartimandua, who had the responsibility for the behaviour of her people. There could, therefore, have been a diplomatic face-saver in calling the incident *discordia* and merely executing the leaders, so that the client relationship would have remained unimpaired. Obviously, any anti-Roman faction in Brigantia would have wished to maintain a communication link with Caratacus. This was neatly severed, thus making it impossible for any large war party to join him. But it was a clear warning to Rome that Brigantia could become a problem if the firm control of her queen ever lessened. There were people in Brigantia who were sympathetic to Caratacus and this fact has a bearing on later events.

There were advantages gained by Scapula. A tribe had been demoralised sufficiently for it to be of little use as an ally of Caratacus. He could now envisage naval patrols along the north coast of Wales operating from the Dee estuary. In the light of all this (but maybe with the advantage of hindsight), the Roman action would seem to have been a brilliant piece of strategy. Knowledge of the actual lines of advance on the ground is at present sparse, although the possibilities can be listed, without, at this stage, considering the archaeological evidence in detail. A route which immediately suggests itself is the line of Watling Street[27] which offers the most direct approach to the Dee Estuary. It has been conjectured in the first volume that Leicester was the site of the fortress of *Legio XIV* in the Plautian phase. There is evidence of a large early military establishment at Mancetter (see p. 47 below), but it could be that this legion was moved forward on to this route at this stage and provided the cohorts for the task force. To secure this route, the left flank of such a line of advance, a second thrust may have been directed towards the important river crossing at Worcester, via Alcester, an out-post fort in the Plautian frontier zone. The Severn Valley north of Worcester is difficult broken country but a route is discernible as far as Greensforge, near Wolverhampton, where there is evidence of considerable military activity during this period. Thence north-west to the key site on the Severn at Wroxeter, which was to develop into a major establishment. The earliest hint of a military presence is the 20-acre Eye Farm fort which appears to be linked with the reduction of the hill-fort on the Wrekin.[28] Whether it was at this early stage, or later, that the task force moved towards the Welsh foot-hills and secured the Perry and Dee valley is not clear, but an early fort is known at Rhyn Park, near Oswestry (see p. 84 below). One cannot however date any of these sites to any of the campaign years of 49–52, since archaeological evidence does not allow such precision.

The Camulodunum Colonia

The next statement by Tacitus suggests that a campaign had already been directed across the lower Severn at the Silures, the tribe which held much of south-east Wales.

'Neither severity nor clemency changed the Silures who continued to wage war.' This would seem to indicate that the units called out in the winter extended their field of operations beyond the Severn with some success and that diplomatic mediation had been attempted. Or it may have been taken from one of Scapula's dispatches to Rome when he needed approval for his plans to mount a large campaign against Caratacus. The sentence about the Silures is linked by Tacitus to Scapula's next move – the redeployment of a legion. He chose the lowest crossing point of the Severn, which is at Gloucester, and where there is evidence of a fortress on the Kingsholm site (see p. 42 below). Tacitus even tells us which legion was moved: 'To promote this, a colony was founded in the conquered lands at Camulodunum by a strong detachment of veterans.'

So *Legio XX* was transferred from the British capital to block the lower Severn and became the main force for the planned attack. It was common practice in preparation for a new campaign to weed out the old soldiers and replace them with fitter younger men. At this time there was no regular annual discharge when men reached their required twenty years' of service, so it was inevitable that there would have been men in the ranks who were no longer capable of the rigours of front-line warfare. Those discharged veterans were given land allotments in areas where they could continue to serve the State as a reserve force. It was necessary for Scapula to have such a body at Camulodunum, the capital of Togodumnus, who had led the Britons at the Medway battle. The necessary land was the confiscated estates of the royal household and the new *colonia* was built on the side of the legionary fortress.[29] In other parts of the Empire it is not difficult to identify the presence of the land allotments since they were laid out over large tracts of country on a strict geometric pattern,[30] but such a system has not yet been observed in Britain. Tacitus is clear about the duties of the veterans: 'a military support against rebellion and to imbue our allies with a sense of their legal duties'; in other words, to maintain a close watch on the natives, stifle any rising and force them to accept the Roman legal code. They had another responsibility, that of being model citizens, demonstrating to the Britons the qualities of urban life. But this latter refinement was rather too much to ask of these ex-legionaries, most of whom had themselves been recruited from frontier lands and had spent all their adult lives in the army. They took the other duties all too seriously and soon gained a reputation for callous brutality against the Trinovantes living in and around the *colonia*.

The Client Kingdoms

Could Scapula now afford to strip the whole of eastern Britain of the troops he needed for his large-scale campaign? He had probably decided that his force required at least two legions, *XIV*, and *XX*, and there would have been cohorts of the other two (*II Aug.* and *IX*). With an equivalent strength of auxiliaries his campaign army would have amounted to about half his total troops. To have removed such a large number of soldiers to the required forward positions would have stripped half the province of its garrisons; all the land to the east of a line from the Wash to the Solent was now to be virtually deprived of troops. It would seem to have been such an enormous risk that it leaves one to consider if there were no other measures he could have taken to improve the security of this large area.

There has been a general assumption that the two client kingdoms of Prasutagus and Cogidubnus were created by Claudius as a reward for the services of these two rulers at the time of the invasion. But even accepting some quirkiness in the Emperor's behaviour,[31] the founding of the two independent kingdoms which occupied so much of the territory of the new province seems very odd. There would appear to have been no valid reasons for their creation at the time of the visit of Claudius, nor is there any evidence for it in Dio or Tacitus. The latter may have recorded the event in one of his lost books, but when he mentions the Iceni on the occasion of the revolt of 48 (xii. 31, see above) he merely describes them loosely as allies (*socii: quia societatem nostram volentes accesserant*). Had the tribe been part of a client kingdom, it would have deserved some comment, since its king would have been held responsible. The first notice of Prasutagus is at his death, prior to the Boudican revolt. Tacitus merely states 'Prasutagus, King of the Iceni, celebrated for his wealth of long duration' (*Ann.* xiv. 31).

Tiberius Claudius Cogidubnus (see Appendix 2)

Apart from Caratacus, the most interesting British character of this period is Cogidubnus, who was presumably given Roman citizenship by Claudius and took his name. Since there are no references to him before the conquest and there are no coins bearing his name, some have assumed that he must have belonged to the royal household of the Regni. He is known to us only from Tacitus and an inscription found in Chichester in 1723 (*RIB* 91), which refers to him as the great King of Britain or the Britons – REG(IS) MAGNI BRIT(ANNIAE) or (ANNORVM).[32] This must indicate that he was a client King and that Chichester was a town in his kingdom. From its name in Ptolemy and Ravenna NOVIOMAGVS REG(I)NORVM was also the cantonal capital of the Regni. The inscription is a dedication to a temple of Minerva and Neptune, erected by a guild of iron-workers, COLLEGIVM FABROR(VM). Although the word, when unqualified, means only artisans, it normally refers to iron-smiths. The combination of these two particular deities strongly implies ship-building, which is hardly surprising with the proximity of Bosham Harbour and the Roman naval base at Fishbourne, and also the large-scale iron production on the Weald, closely associated with the British Fleet.[33] The guild members must have gained their prestige as ship-building and repairing contractors to the Roman Army to become sufficiently wealthy in the first century to fund the building of the temple.

All this was done with the authority of Cogidubnus, although the precise date of the dedication is a matter of debate. The only clue is the dedication which is combined with the well-being of the Divine House, PRO SALVTE DO(MVS) DIVINAE; the ruling Emperor must, therefore, have belonged to a dynasty which included a deified member. This could only have applied to Claudius, or Nero, Titus or Domitian, and not Vespasian.[34] The probability is that it was dedicated under Nero and, therefore, before 68; twenty-five years would presumably have been adequate for the founding of the guild and the accumulation of its wealth, perhaps with the help of artisan settlers from Gaul after the conquest.

Cogidubnus is otherwise only recorded in the *Agricola* of Tacitus, in his brief review of the state of Britain before Agricola's governorship (*Agricola* 14). The phrase he uses is intriguing: *quaedam civitates Cogidubno regi donatae*, i.e. 'certain tribes were given to King Cogidubnus' – of which more below. The founding of the two kingdoms would seem a logical part of Scapula's plan to provide for the safety of his rear, once his garrisons had been removed from the eastern part of the province.[35] Troops may have been left behind to protect the vital supply route from Richborough to London.

The phrase used by Tacitus *quaedam civitates* implies that Cogidubnus was given more than one tribe, and it has further been assumed by some that this refers to an addition to his original kingdom. The one certain tribe he ruled was the Regni (or Regini)[36] of Sussex, the evidence for which comes from the Chichester inscription. But which of the other *civitates* did he control? This question has been the subject of speculation by several archaeologists and historians. There is general agreement that the Atrebates are a very possible choice and George Boon has suggested that this is supported by the Imperial stamped tiles found at Calleva.[37] This is a circular stamp bearing the name of Nero (NER CL CAE AVG GER)[38] and two similar, but not identical, examples have been found at Calleva; one in 1902, on the site of the bath-house,[39] the other at Little London about two miles from the Roman town on the site of a tile-factory which has not been investigated.[40] If, as would appear, this is the site of an Imperial tile factory, the inference is that the Emperor had given his client ruler technical assistance in a building programme launched in the fulfilment of the Romanised urban ideal. Another suggestion has been advanced by Professor Applebaum that Nero would have received the estates of Cogidubnus on his death.[41] So it is possible that this was before 68, although this is difficult to reconcile with the date of the great palace at Fishbourne, thought to be associated with him. However, one tile from a modest civic bath-house offers too little evidence to form any accurate assessment on the early development of Calleva, but the gridded street pattern would appear, on present evidence, to be of later construction.[42] Professor Frere has linked Cogidubnus with Calleva on the evidence of the early defences,[43] but there are problems over the date and functions of these earthworks.[44]

The extent of the kingdom towards the west and south-west is more difficult to assess. The eastern limit of the territory of the Durotriges, clearly defined by the distribution of their coins, has been shown by Derek Allen[45] to have been the River Avon. Winchester, known as Venta Belgarum, was the capital of a tribe known as the Belgae. Ptolemy includes Bath and Ischalis, of uncertain identification (see fig 23 below), within their territory, and if this is correct, it would have created a strange-shaped area with its capital far from its centre. There is a strong possibility that this was an artificial authority created by the Romans[46] in the late first century in their reorganisation of the tribes of Britain. One of the small tribes that disappeared altogether was the southern section of the Dobunni, and another may have been a tribe between the Regni and the Durotriges. The southern Dobunni probably suffered extinction by their hostility, while the Durotriges retained their identity, losing only part of their lands on the northern boundary, which their coins seem to show was a separate sept with closer links with the Dobunni.[47] However, Professor Cunliffe considers that Winchester was at one time under the control of the Atrebates,[48] and this may well have been the case in the fluctuation of power from Commius to Caratacus. It is not inconceivable that Cogidubnus may have been given the territories from which troops had been withdrawn as far west as the Itchen or the Test, but this would have been regarded as a temporary measure made necessary by Scapula's need for a large campaign force. But this possible extension of the King's authority would help to explain the need for the creation of the *civitas* of the Belgae in the later local government reorganisation.[49]

Whatever may be the truth behind all these speculations, by the spring of 49 Scapula had to be ready for his advance. The depth of his misgivings about that part of the province, now virtually free of troops, cannot be assessed, but he may have felt that his terror tactics, associated with the arms search, would have stamped out any ideas some Britons may have had of taking advantage of the absence of the army and of staging a rising. In justifying his harsh action as a military expedient, he gave little thought for the future. His two decisions, disarming the tribes and founding the *colonia*, were to sow the seeds of distrust and bitterness, which were to ripen into the great tragedy of 60.

CHAPTER TWO

The Last Stand of Caratacus

Without more ado, Tacitus plunges straight into his description of the battle which was to be so decisive to both Caratacus and Scapula. The lines of advance and the preliminary battles and skirmishes are ruthlessly excised by the historian, ever anxious to move onwards towards a dramatic climax. He offers only a hint of the direction of the campaign when he states that the British leader 'moved the war into the territory of the Ordovices' (*transfert bellum in Ordovicas*) (*Ann*, xii. 33) but, in an equally terse phrase, Tacitus tells us that Caratacus was 'inferior in military strength' (*vi militum inferior*) and that, having set up his standard, he was 'joined by those who dreaded our (i.e. Roman) peace'. This clearly implies that the purpose of the move was to bring more warriors to his standard especially from the large and important tribe of the Ordovices which he could expect to join him.

But there could be far more than is suggested here. Had he been assisted by the Druids, it was in their interests he should have protected the approach to their main sanctuary on Anglesey. The Druids would have had an intelligence service to keep them fully informed of Roman army movements and intentions. They may even have appreciated the limitations within which Scapula was forced to operate and have realised that he had one objective only – the elimination of Caratacus. Even so, any advance into the central area of Wales would have been a serious threat to them, since they would have seen the next stage as being directed against them. The Druids' efforts would thus have been concentrated not only on preventing the army from penetrating into central Wales, but also on making life hazardous for the Roman troops constructing and holding any positions beyond the Severn. Caratacus needed to increase the size of his forces, but this move may have served another purpose. The build-up of Roman strength on the lower Severn would suggest that Scapula's first aim was to attack Caratacus in his Silurian stronghold. A swift advance up the Wye, accompanied by coastal landings along the Bristol Channel, would have encircled the British leader and cut him off from any assistance from the north. This would also have been a typical Roman military strategy of dividing the enemy and reducing each part separately. But we have no inkling of these early stages of the campaign which must have developed over three seasons. Tacitus takes his readers immediately to the place selected by Caratacus for his stand.

The Site of the Battle

Caratacus had by now some experience of Roman battle tactics and he must have thought deeply about the most effective way of using his ill-equipped levies against such discipline and professionalism. He had witnessed the enormous weight and power of the legionaries carving their paths through the packed mass of Celts. He knew too of the heavy losses his men would suffer in a standing fight. No doubt he would have preferred a different kind of war where his tribesmen could suddenly emerge from the forests and hills and attack small bodies of Romans, and by sheer surprise and ferocity do brisk execution before disappearing as rapidly as they came. In a terrain they knew so well this was possible, but not when the army was massed together and could not be attacked in this way. He could only plan guerilla tactics when the Romans were spread out over a large area in their separate units as construction and foraging parties; but if he was clever enough to choose a place to put them at the most serious disadvantage, he could inflict serious damage. It was essential, however, to be able to extract his tribesmen before they were cut down or forced to surrender. The site had to be deep into the British territory so as to lure the Roman force far from its bases, and in country suitable for his men to escape by melting into the forests and mountains where they could not easily be hunted by cavalry. His site must be one not capable of being surrounded so that the legions would be forced to a frontal assault at a carefully fixed narrow front.

Antiquarians of past generations, in their attempts to identify this famous site, have been more inspired by local patriotism than a close study of the words of Tacitus, and there are many hills which bear the name Caer Caradoc – none of which fit the qualifications given by the historian. Firstly, it must be in Ordovician territory and by a river with a difficult crossing (*praefluebat amnis vado incerto*). This implies a sizeable river and the only possible one is the Severn. The earlier antiquarians have always chosen a hill-fort, but only a rampart of stones is mentioned as defending the steep slope and this was at one point only; the rest of the hill rose sheer (*hinc montibus arduis*). So the site could be one of a number of hills close to the Severn in its upper stretches, probably in the narrow valley below Caersws. The most likely hills would be those above Newtown, since this is where the old E-W trackway meets the Severn and this is the route that would probably have been that followed by the Roman army.

There is another factor to be considered when searching for a site – the changes which have taken place in the landscape in the intervening centuries. The countryside today is the result of man's efforts to exploit the land for agriculture and forestry, so that the landscape we see now is virtually all man-made. It is difficult to imagine the terrain as it would have appeared to the advancing Roman soldiers. There would have been a little cultivation here and there round the settlements, and the flocks and herds would have cleared large areas of the hills by grazing; but the peoples of the late Iron Age were unable to embark on large-scale drainage schemes. Thus the river valleys would have been subject to flooding and there would rarely have been clear edges to the rivers. Water would have flowed through an expanse of marsh and sand-banks and this would have applied especially to the narrow valley of the Severn, thus making it all the more important to find river crossings where firm ground approached the edges on both sides. These crossing points would have been known and well used by the local people, but they would have been inadequate for a large army. The Roman army would naturally seek these places, and their engineers and their construction teams were trained to cut routes across difficult country. They would clear forests and build causeways across the marshes with the use of timber piles and log and brushwood roads raised above the water level, and the rivers themselves would be easily bridged with the assistance of pontoons. To this extent, the Romans were independent of the local routes and could circumvent heavily defended passages through otherwise inaccessible terrain. Whether the army could have cut its way up the Severn at this period is doubtful, and the prehistoric route is quite certainly on the high ground to the south, along 'The Sarn' (see p. 84–5).

The Strength of the Two Armies

The account of the battle is unusual in that no figures are given for the number of participants or casualties. The reason for this omission by Tacitus is perhaps a credit to the skill of Caratacus in his carefully planned withdrawal, which prevented the Romans from inflicting heavy losses on the Britons. While the size of the British forces is purely guesswork, those of Rome can be roughly estimated. Scapula would have had the fighting strength of two legions *XIV Gemina* and *XX Valeria* and doubtless cohorts of the other two – probably some 10,000 to 12,000 legionaries in all, to which must be added an equivalent strength of *auxilia*, making a total army of 20,000 to 25,000 men. Had the Britons been four or five times that number, it would not have caused Scapula any serious qualms. He had now successfully achieved his primary objective. After a considerable march into hostile territory, he had located his enemy, and, at this stage, the total defeat and elimination of Caratacus must have been a foregone conclusion. The British leader, however, had other plans, and, as Tacitus reminds us, he had, by then, inspired his warriors with a total confidence of the outcome.

The Battle

Tacitus begins his account with Caratacus and his tribal chiefs raising the spirits of their men with the usual pre-battle addresses, but the opportunity is not taken on this occasion to put suitable pieces of rhetoric directly into the mouths of the two commanders. Caratacus, according to Tacitus, called up the ancestors of the Britons who had repulsed the dictator Caesar and so avoided Roman law and the paying of tribute, and then retained their freedom. The Roman historian may have considered such sentiments as suitable propaganda for the occasion, but it contains questionable statements. The tribes of Wales had never known Caesar nor had he been repulsed by the people of the south-east, who after their defeat had been forced to pay a large annual tribute. The ancestors of Caratacus himself had in all probability been allies of Caesar.

Although all this fervour and shouting may have disconcerted Scapula, he was probably more worried about the physical difficulties facing his troops: the new rampart (*additum vallum*), the towering heights (*inminentia iuga*) and the dense throng of defiant Britons at every point (*nihil nisi atrox et propugnatoribus frequens terrebat*). The Roman soldiers must have been eager for the fray, but a kind of fiction was maintained so that Scapula had almost to be persuaded to give orders for the attack. There may well have been a delay since the Roman commander would first have ordered a careful survey of the position to seek out any weakness which could be exploited. Most hills have an easy route to the top, but Caratacus had chosen well and Scapula was forced to the conclusion that there was only one way – a frontal assault across the river of unknown depths and difficulty, edged by marsh. Any commander could be forgiven for pausing, and possibly a delay might have forced the Britons to some rash act which he could have turned to his advantage. But the temper of his troops had been aroused, the enemy was in view after weeks of hard foot-slogging through hills, marsh and forest, and it was clearly the moment to strike.

Scapula placed himself at the head of his men and crossed the river without difficulty. Before them were the steep slopes stiffened with a stone rampart and crowded with defenders. As the Romans advanced, they came under a constant hail of missiles. The legionaries were well trained to cope with such a problem. They grouped together and held their shields above their heads to form the familiar *testudo* (pl 3). Under this protective covering, soldiers, with their hands and picks free, began to prise out the stones of the rampart, loosening it until by its weight it began to disintegrate. They gradually edged their way up the rocky ascent and, as soon as they came within reach of the Britons plunged headlong into them. Such was their discipline and ferocity of attack that they drove the Britons up the hill. As the ground evened out, the battle spread and Tacitus paints a picture of the Britons scattered in complete confusion – the legionaries advancing in close order, with the auxiliaries round their flanks darting here and there with their light javelins. Against this, the Britons with little body armour to protect them stood no chance. Tacitus reverts almost to a stock sentence: 'if they resisted the auxiliaries, they were struck down by the sword and *pila* of the legionaries and if they faced up to the legionaries they fell under the long swords and spears of the auxiliaries'.[1] One cannot help but feel that this was written as a fulsome piece of prose suitable for a public reading, rather than having a relevance to the actualities of the battle. It was, he concludes, a brilliant victory (*clara ea victoria fuit*). The wife, daughter and brothers[2] of Caratacus surrendered, but the leader himself had escaped. So too, as will appear later, had a large part of his warriors.

This account by Tacitus of such a crucial battle is very unsatisfactory. It starts well enough, with a brief but realistic appraisal of the position chosen by Caratacus, but once the initial advantage had been gained by the legionaries, there is little to follow. The impression is given that the battle had been decided on the lower slopes and that the rest was merely a cleaning-up operation. Yet there is no mention of heavy British losses and the only notable gain was the capture of the family of the British leader. The Britons had been overcome by the sheer speed and weight of the attack. Tacitus must have read the despatches of Scapula in the archives in Rome, but they contained little he felt able to use. A possible conclusion to be drawn from this is that the British resistance was by a token force, and that Caratacus had planned to hold the Romans at the most difficult part of the slope and inflict heavy casualties there. Once they had broken through, he knew that his men would be cut to pieces; so his plan was for many to escape into the woods for the next stage of the war. But obviously he did not intend his family to be taken. This may have been due to the rapidity with which the Romans had gained the hill-top, so that even a rearguard action by the family bodyguard was of no avail. The suggestion that this was for Rome a hollow victory is based on subsequent events and judgement should be suspended until these are described. Tacitus at least gives us one firm piece of information, in placing the capture of Caratacus in the ninth year from the start of the British war, i.e. 51–52 (see fn 10) with the probability that the closing event was late in 52. Before this, Tacitus deals with the fate of Caratacus (although out of its chronological context) and it seems logical to follow suit.

31

Caratacus and Cartimandua

A commander with the insight and ability of Caratacus would have made detailed plans based on his assessment of the probable results of the battle. Knowing so much about the power and tactical skill of the Romans, he would not have been too sanguine about the outcome. All he could hope to achieve was to cause Scapula as much trouble as possible by inflicting heavy casualties, or holding up his advance, so that the decision-makers in Rome might have serious doubts about advancing so deeply into the hostile mountains. He would never have staked everything on a single defensive battle – although he did his utmost to put the Romans to the maximum disadvantage.

Caratacus now planned the next stage of the resistance movement. This was based on two schemes which could be operated in concert. Firstly, it was essential that his warriors should continue the fight, but in a guerilla-type warfare whilst the Roman army was spread over the frontier preparing their new positions. While the forces of Scapula were to be kept fully occupied by these sudden and unexpected attacks, the greater plan was to be developed. This depended on persuading Cartimandua to change sides and to join him against Rome. A southward sweep of a large force of her tribesmen would trap the main Roman force between the two British pincer armies.

It was a splendid concept, and it would probably have been effective. Caratacus had good reason to believe that he had the sympathy of many of the Brigantes, including the Queen's consort Venutius. Through the agency of the Druids secret contacts must have been established. Caratacus would therefore have set off with hopes of some success. However, he had to be careful for he knew much about the devious and wily nature of this high-born lady. Tacitus gives us two versions of the episode. In the *Annales* (xii. 36) he merely states that he was overcome, fettered and handed over to the victors (*vinctus ac victoribus traditus est*) after he had tried to persuade the queen to join him (*cum fidem Cartimanduae reginae Brigantum petivisset*). But in the *Historiae* (iii. 45) Tacitus tells us that Cartimandua captured the British leader by deceit (*postquam capto per dolum*). This suggests that Caratacus was prepared for difficulties in pursuing his aim, and probably operated through a third party. Cartimandua may have given the appearance of accepting his proposition at first and then, having assuaged his fears, have taken him captive.

We must be careful of imposing our modern attitudes in judgement of the queen. The Britons would never have seen the struggle as between themselves as a single people and the Romans; there was always as much hatred between many of the individual tribes as against Rome. It was in the interests of the Imperial power to keep things that way, by dividing the tribes from each other in separate dealings and treaties. A sense of nationhood did not exist – in fact it hardly developed in Britain until the Tudor monarchy. Cartimandua was a realist and knew that her power and wealth was entirely dependent on Rome. She must have appreciated also that, had she joined Caratacus, he would have been the British leader, with her own status diminished. In fact, she had nothing to gain from such a decision and much to lose The only hope Caratacus ever had was that she would cooperate under pressure from her subjects. But her position at this time was secure and she controlled enough support to keep any trouble in check. So the gamble failed. Caratacus, however, does not disappear from history without a final flourish.

The Scapulan Frontier under Construction

Scapula was awarded the *insignia triumpalia* and he may have wryly reflected on the generosity which Claudius had shown towards the senior officers of the invasion army who had been accorded the same accolade in 43. As Tacitus cryptically comments, the good fortune the governor had so far enjoyed soon became uncertain. He offers two explanations, one that, without Caratacus, it was believed that the war was over, and that efforts slackened; the other, that the undefeated tribesmen now wanted to avenge their leader. Both may be true, but it reads like a set-piece of prose linking the two episodes. From the Roman point of view, Scapula realised that the tribes in the heartlands of Wales would have been by now fully alerted to the threat posed by Rome. The Druids felt especially vulnerable and would have naturally expected the army to advance towards Anglesey. The failure to do so must have mystified them. Doubtless Scapula had urged Claudius to allow him to conquer the whole of Wales and so, in effect, eliminate the western frontier. But in the closing years of his reign Claudius became withdrawn and resisted all attempts to force him to make decisions.

There was now a power struggle developing over the succession, with Agrippina avidly plotting to ensure the success of her son Nero. It was a time when the problems of distant Britain had a low priority. The dazzling display of Caratacus and the spoils of war signified for many the end of any serious trouble in Britain. Whatever may have been the response from Rome, there was clearly no prospect of a further advance. In the circumstances Scapula realised all too well that any independent action of his own could have brought rapid reproof; he may have remembered what happened to Corbulo in Germany.[3] He therefore resigned himself to the problem of establishing a new frontier zone.

There were three possibilities for him to consider: (1) to straighten out his forward alignment and dig in there; (2) to fall back to the River Severn; (3) to fall back to the Plautian frontier. The third idea would have been discarded immediately, since it would have abandoned so much territorial gain and retreated too far from potential hostility, from the north as well as from the west. It must also be assumed that the arrangements made with two client kings in the eastern part of the province must have been effective, and that no serious anti-Roman threats had so far occurred. The second must have been carefully considered, but the river was not a serious enough obstacle in the summer, and it left far too much room for manoeuvre by any hostile elements. Far better, Scapula must have argued, was to pin down the enemy in their mountains by plugging all the outlets from the narrow east-facing valleys. This would also have deprived the tribes of the produce of the great plains of the modern counties of Shropshire and Herefordshire. It was the strategic plan which Agricola was later to adopt in Caledonia, when he stopped up the mouths of the glens to gain control over any movement from the central mountain massif[4] (though the Roman withdrawal came too soon for its defensive capacity to be tested).

Scapula was faced with a most difficult problem since the plan was on such a large scale. From the Dee Estuary to the Bristol Channel was a distance of about 130 Roman miles, and with a fort at every 15-mile interval at least ten would have been needed along the communication route alone. To create the tight network of forts over this newly conquered area of c.4400 square miles would almost certainly have meant the withdrawal of more units from the rear. Formidable as it was, Scapula faced the grim necessity of placing a stranglehold on the undefeated peoples and of being able to use, if necessary, his frontier posts as springboards for attack, rather than concentrating his forces in rearward positions and moving them forward every time danger threatened. This is no mere armchair strategy, since, as will be seen below, the Scapulan frontier zone is now reasonably well supported by archaeology, although there are still many gaps to be filled.

The enormous difficulties and dangers faced by Scapula and his army very soon became apparent. The construction of so many new forts inevitably meant that the army had now to be dispersed over large areas. This applies particularly to the legionaries who provided the construction teams. All this work had to be carried out under the very noses of the unconquered hill-folk whose lands were being invaded and permanently occupied. They also had the great advantage of an intimate knowledge of the terrain.

But threats were not anticipated from the whole of the new frontier zone. The northern part at least would have been reasonably quiet with the savage reduction of the Deceangli and the territory of the Cornovii now wholly occupied by the army — unless, of course, the Ordovices combined with the Silures, but there is no evidence of this at this stage. It was the Silures who took full advantage of the dispersing of the army. Buried in a few terse comments of Tacitus is an unfolding story of a serious frontier war which was to drive Scapula to the point of total frustration and physical collapse. The matter was exacerbated by a singularly incautious remark by the governor that he had determined to exterminate the whole tribe, as once had happened to the Sugambri. This German tribe on the east bank of the Rhine had given the Romans a great deal of trouble from the time of Caesar, until Augustus took the unusual step in 8 BC of seizing their envoys, executing some, dispersing the rest to the Gallic cities[5] and forcibly settled much of the tribe on the west bank of the Rhine.[6] When the news of the threat of annihilation reached the Silures, it provoked them to even greater acts of desperation. They now firmly believed that they faced humiliation and, possibly, immediate death.

So the war continued. The first incident related by Tacitus (xii. 38) is of legionary cohorts being attacked from all sides while engaged in construction work within Silurian territory under the command of a *praefectus castrorum*.[7] A legion was building forts in territory taken from the Silures (though we have no means of knowing where the tribal boundary was situated at the time). This involved the simultaneous construction of a number of forts, so that parties of legionaries would have been spread out, probably over a large area. The whole operation was under the command of the camp prefect, an ex-chief centurion (*primus pilus*) of equestrian status, and third in the command order of the legion. Four or five cohorts must have been involved, since a smaller force or less than half a legion would hardly have required such a senior officer. It is a reasonable assumption that the unit involved was *Legio XX* from Gloucester.

The Silurian strategy was clearly to wait until the army working parties were fully engaged in their projects before their surprise attacks. It would have been the duty of the auxiliary units to protect the legion while at work, either by patrolling in the vicinity of the new forts, or by being encamped on the spot. The wily Silures managed to elude these troops or divert them away from the fort before falling on the construction parties. It was a moment of great danger for the Romans. Despatch riders (*nuntii*) were sent out for help, and it only arrived in time to prevent the total loss of all the men (*occidione obcubuissent*). Even so, the praefectus and eight centurions were killed, in addition to many of the very bravest men (*promptissimus quisque e manipulis cecidere*). It was a serious blow, and had there been five cohorts, eight centurions could have indicated a twenty five per cent loss; but the jubilation of the Silures must have been tempered by their failure to achieve total annihilation and subsequent destruction of the partly built forts. Faced with a pitched battle against a large force, they knew it was prudent to vanish rapidly into the hills and forests.

But this was only the beginning; next a forage party (*pabulantis*) and the cavalry guards (*turmas*) were completely routed. The crops and herds of nearby lands taken from a hostile enemy were always available to the army, and, if the rations were short or needed supplementing, parties were sent out to take what they could find. There was always the additional incentive that some real wealth could be found in goods or captives. There is a splendid scene on Trajan's Column of legionaries cutting the heads from standing crops with small hand sickles, while auxiliary guards stand by (pl 4). This could be especially galling to the hill-folk, since their cereal crops were sparse and could not be easily protected, whereas their animals would have by now been removed from any threat (unless the army penetrated very deeply into their territory, which in these circumstances seems unlikely). Further auxiliary cohorts, probably mounted infantry, were sent to the rescue, but they proved inadequate and legions had to be brought into the operation and this equalised the contest. The battle turned in Rome's favour only at the close of the day and the Silures escaped without serious loss.

This interesting account is unusually detailed for Tacitus and this in itself underlies its significance. It would appear to cover a number of small incidents, but had that been the case it would surely not have been mentioned. It must, therefore, disguise something more serious which Tacitus felt was necessary to his narrative. It can be seen, in effect, as the dramatic build-up to the sudden demise of Scapula. But by careful phrasing Tacitus has adroitly picked his way through the official despatches which he must have read in the archives of Rome. It is possible that Scapula was already showing signs of severe stress and that his despatches reflected this in confused statements or shifts of emphasis, which may have been intended to obscure the truth.

The forage party would have been sent out from one of the forts under construction and would have taken some squadrons of horses with them for protection. When they came under attack more auxiliary forces were sent to drive the British away, but failed. A main legionary force then had to be sent out from the nearest base before their comrades could be rescued, but the enemy withdrew in good order before the Romans could inflict any serious loss. It would appear to have been a running engagement spread over a considerable time if dispatch riders had, on two separate occasions, to be sent for help; but of greater significance is the use of the plural in the deployment of two legions. This implies that a large combined force must have been established at a convenient base, but this may well have been more than a day's march from the original point of attack. These seemingly sporadic events thus begin to appear as a minor campaign involving a large number of legionaries. Once more the Britons achieved a striking success in inflicting damage to Rome without any serious loss to themselves.

The guerilla war was turning into a nightmare for Scapula and his commanders, and it continued with many similar attacks in woods and marshes. The Britons were obviously taking full advantage of the difficult terrain they knew so well. It may have seemed to the Romans that much was due to chance and that there was very little planning in all these attacks. But this view could also have sprung from the sheer exasperation felt by the Roman staff officers, whose attitude to war was conditioned by the basic need for careful preparation and the formulation of tactical schemes before proceeding with any operation. The Britons had no such concept. There wasn't necessarily any overall command, since each group of tribesmen may have worked independently of each other. They all had courage and guile and kept permanent watch on the Roman activities. Their attacks were determined by the opportunities provided by the vagaries of the weather and the possibilities of luring Roman troops into positions which gave the Silures the advantage of surprise and speed. Tacitus gives an excellent example of this kind of action – two auxiliary cohorts, which were foraging and plundering incautiously, were cut off. The word used here – *intercepere*[8] – conveys the meaning of separating and implies that the Britons had been able to cut off the auxiliaries from the main body and then overpower them.

Another factor now enters Tacitus' narrative: the Silures were able to bring to their aid the remainder of the tribes (*ceteras quoque nationes*) by offering them spoils and captives (*spolia* could include armour and weapons).[9] This clearly indicates the growing success of the Silures. The other tribes of Wales, who may have supplied Caratacus with token forces for his last stand, obviously now felt that the Romans were vulnerable and, stirred by the thoughts of great victories and plunder, were eager to join the war. One may see once more the hands of the Druids: their persistent cajoling of the tribes to push the hated enemy back was now having an effect; but the reluctant members needed to be convinced by the example of the Silures that their efforts were to be rewarded.

The Death of Scapula

It is at this point that Scapula died – to the great jubilation of the free Britons. The stress of his exertions and anxieties accelerated the progress of whatever illness or physical disorder he may have suffered. All through his period of office in Britain Scapula had made hasty decisions without full consideration of the long-term consequences. Had his malady been obvious at the time of his appointment, it seems unlikely that he would have been given such responsibility. The indications seem to point to a sudden illness, but as nothing is known of his earlier career, this must remain a matter of conjecture. A fitter, or greater man would never have allowed his army to have been placed in such a difficult situation; on the other hand, we have no knowledge of the instructions, or lack of them, emerging from Rome at a time when there was a lack of direction and decision from the top. It has been assumed by historians that Scapula died in 52, or possibly even 53, the year following the capture of Caratacus (which must have taken place in 51).[10] This allows for a season's campaign and fort-building, which seems reasonable, but it means that Scapula was drawing towards the end of his period of office, if it was a five-year stint. But whoever had been singled out to replace him was not immediately available. It was apparent to those in Rome that some speed was necessary in immediately sending a sound and experienced man to Britain to stop any further losses and to stabilise the frontier.

Caratacus in Rome

By now the fame of Caratacus had spread far and wide; even the Emperor and the people of Rome were anxious to see the celebrated Celtic hero. For Claudius it was the opportunity for staging a great spectacle to celebrate what was then assumed to be the completion of the conquest of Britain. Officials in Rome may possibly have been misled by the euphemistic despatches from Britain. But Scapula must have soon realised that the war was far from completion. For those in Rome, the taking of Caratacus may have appeared as a great crowning achievement, but the governor and his staff officers knew otherwise.

The events in Rome were organised on the large parade-ground on the west side of the Praetorian Fort (*castra praetoria*) which was situated outside the north-east corner of the city walls. The praetorian cohorts were paraded under arms, which was in itself unusual, and had only been seen on rare occasions, such as the funeral of Augustus (*Ann.* iii. 4). There were to be other and quite different circumstances when this was done – as for example, when Nero wished to overawe the Senate during the last days of his tyranny (*Ann.* vi. 27). There were times also in the civil war of 69 when arms were distributed (*Hist.* i. 38 and 80). Claudius sat in state on a tribunal,[11] with Agrippina very conspicuously on another, nearby. Tacitus was quick to point out that it was without precedent for the Imperial Consort to sit in state and receive the homage of the praetorian standards. It clearly shows the degree of power she was now wielding in the final years of Claudius when she was so avidly promoting the advance of her son Nero towards the purple.[12]

Before the Imperial couple and the assembled multitude passed a procession of British captives with all the tribute and plunder taken from the wars, followed by the family of Caratacus. Tacitus contrasts the fearful entreaties of most of the captives with the noble bearing of their leader, who held his head high, in silence.[13] When he arrived before Claudius he made a speech. Maybe Tacitus felt that this was a much better place for a rhetorical set-piece than before the battle. It seems probable that there was a speech by the vanquished Briton, if only to allow Claudius a display of clemency, and also to be balanced by the Senatorial orations which came later. The occasion has all the appearance of careful planning to enhance the image of the Emperor before the Roman public. There was a reminder of the glorious victory of Claudius himself through his legate Plautius and the addition of a province beyond the natural bounds of the Empire.[14]

Caratacus made a considerable impression and a remark is recorded by Dio, among others. Although it is said to have been made when the Briton was walking about the city, it is possible that it was part of his speech before the Emperor. As he looked around at all the magnificent buildings, he asked rhetorically, 'When you have all this, why do you envy us our poor hovels?' The speech Tacitus puts into the mouth of Caratacus is typical of the great historian echoing his constant theme concerning the destiny of Rome and the excesses committed in the name of Imperialism. Was Rome's mission in the world, he asked, for universal peace and prosperity, or for plundering and enslaving her subject peoples? In his first historical work, the biography of Agricola, he put into the mouth of Calgacus, the Caledonian chief, a bitter attack on Roman Imperialism. The florid style of Arthur Murphy in his late eighteenth century translation,[15] although extravagantly free, seems perhaps more suitable than the somewhat prosaic modern variations. The final passage of the speech reads, according to Murphy:

'The Romans are in the heart of our country; no submissions or concessions can satisfy their pride; while the land has anything left, it is a theatre of war; when it can yield no more, they search the seas for hidden riches. Are the natives rich? Roman avarice is their enemy. Are they poor? Roman ambition lords it over them. The east and west have been ransacked and the spoiler is still insatiate. The Romans, by a strange singularity of nature, are the only people who invade, with equal ardour, both the rich and the poor. To rob, to savage, and to plunder in their imposing language are the arts of civil policy. When they have made the world a desolation, they call it peace.'

The sentiments and style are in the tradition of the schools of rhetoric and Tacitus took as his model the writings of the historian Sallust (86–34 BC). There are clear echoes in the speech of Calgacus of the letter of Mithridates to Arsaces, which is one of the few surviving fragments of his *Historiae*.[16]

It is difficult to form a judgement of the basic concept of the Empire held by Tacitus. Some historians have roundly condemned him as a hypocrite, indulging in meaningless rhetorical gestures. But Sir Ronald Syme, our best authority, takes a more sober view. He holds that Tacitus was imbued with the old traditional Roman virtues – courage, dignity and the upholding of the law.[17] Any acts of Romans reflecting the opposite would receive his condemnation; the historian's belief is perhaps epitomised in a passage of the *Annales*: 'The proper function of history, as I conceive it, is to ensure that merits are not passed over, and that base words and deeds will have occasion to fear the judgement of posterity' (iii. 65).[18] In Caratacus, Tacitus saw a man of great integrity and dignity and he used the speech to make an ironic contrast between a noble barbarian chief and the virtues lacking in so many Roman senators. He makes the point with brief and cogent eloquence:

'Had my high birth and rank been accompanied by moderation in my hour of success, I should have entered this city as a friend and not a prisoner. You would not have hesitated to accept me as an ally, a man of splendid ancestry, and bearing rule over many tribes. My present position is degrading to me, but glorious to you. I had horses, warriors and gold; if I was unwilling to lose them, what wonder is that? Does it follow that because you desire universal empire, one must accept universal slavery? Were I one dragged here as one who surrendered without fighting, no fame would have attached to my fate nor to your victory. If you punish me, they will both be forgotten. Spare me, and I shall be an eternal example of your mercy.'

Underlying his words is the Tacitean theme of the virtue of *libertas*. The plea for *clementia* in the final passage found a response in Claudius. The chains were struck from the prisoners and the Britons paid their homage to Caesar and also to Agrippina in the same terms, as Tacitus pointedly indicates. Caratacus and his family were given freedom to live out their lives in Rome.

There is a final event to relate before these historical episodes can be closed. The Senate was convened to deliver to the Emperor a number of long and somewhat tedious orations, full of historical parallels, which include the display of the Numidian prince Syphax by Publius Scipio, and of the Macedonian King Perseus by Aemilius Paullus. These two great triumphs of Republican days were described by Livy (xxx. 13 and xix. 7–8 respectively) and in both cases they were piteous occasions when great and wealthy kings had been reduced to total degradation. Most striking is the case of Perseus, who was put in the common prison in Rome, although he had been assured of clemency by Paullus. He was removed to a more comfortable place by the personal intervention of his victor,[19] but he is said to have starved himself to death later. Syphax, after being sent to Italy, died in prison at Tiber. The contrast offered by the senators, who were well steeped in Republican history, was between the miserable end of these two mighty rulers and the *clementia* by Claudius, thus placing the Emperor in a very favourable position at the side of the heroes of the past – a compliment not lost on such an avid student of the past with a special veneration for Livy.

So, Caratacus passes from history. Although like Cassivellaunus he had little success against Rome, he emerges as an outstanding commander with a grasp of overall strategy and a deep insight into the organisation and tactics of his enemy. His commanding presence won him immediate recognition among the peoples of free Britain, although the influence of the Druids cannot be discounted. By his noble bearing he drew respect from his victors and provided Tacitus with an apt moral on the excesses of Imperialism; his readers would be left to draw their own conclusion that, whatever Rome was able to take from her subject peoples, there was also a responsibility towards their welfare beyond the maintenance of the *pax romana*.

CHAPTER THREE

The Scapulan Frontier: the Legionary Fortresses and the Sea Routes

The different kinds of evidence, their relative degrees of importance and the techniques of study and interpretation have been explained in the first and companion volume on the *Invasion*, and so will not be repeated here. But an exception must be made to acknowledge the outstanding contribution of Professor St Joseph, who has been flying over Wales and its Marches since 1945, and has published his results in regular summaries in *JRS*.[1] The enormous addition to knowledge can be seen on his map of the Marches of 1973[2] on which are plotted 33 concentrations of military sites of forts and campaign camps. Arnold Baker and Professor Barri Jones have also done notable work, the former especially in the Wroxeter area. Without the devoted services of these flyers, the following section could not have been attempted.

The Founding of the Welsh Forts

There are two special problems associated with the early campaigns and forts in Wales. Firstly, there is the idea which has become established that all the Welsh forts were founded by Julius Frontinus, who was governor 73/74–78. This was never the view of Haverfield, who was the first to give careful scholarly attention to the conquest of Wales in a remarkably perceptive paper read to the Honourable Society of Cymmrodorion in 1909.[3] He fully recognised the work of Scapula, which he summed up in the words, 'the attacks on Wales, both north and south, had well begun before AD 50.'[4] After this, however, he considered that the Roman initiative flagged, and 'there followed a long period, full twenty years of inaction (AD 50–70)'.[5] In his final reflections on Roman Britain, he was content merely to state that 'Between 74 and 77/78, Julius Frontinus conquered the Silures. By this time, garrisons had been planted all over Wales and the subjugation of the land was fairly complete.'[6]

It was Wheeler who took a more positive attitude in his excavation report on Brecon Gaer,[7] for, while he was prepared to acknowledge possible earlier Roman penetration up the Usk Valley as far as Y Gaer, he concluded: 'The historical evidence, such as it is, does not demand an earlier date than c. AD 75 for the foundation of the fort' (Report 69). This carefully weighed but magisterial statement was taken by all subsequent archaeologists to be true for the other forts of Wales and, until recent years, this view has never been challenged. The proposition was not so ingenuous as might be supposed, as Tacitus specially stated that Frontinus subdued the strong and warlike Silures by force of arms and, with great efforts, overcame not only a brave enemy, but difficult terrain (*Agricola* 17). This passage is part of a very brief summary of the history of the conquest of Britain, and Tacitus would have wished to honour a great man of his own generation. There is no doubt that Frontinus had much to do in tidying up after the early campaigns begun by Scapula and continued possibly by Didius Gallus, and certainly by Veranius and Paullinus, but ended by the great revolt.[8] By then all tribes had been crushed and it only needed a tight network of forts to be established for effective control against any further hostility. It may be unwise to credit Quintus Veranius with any forts, since he may have died before any were built; but, following his single campaign, units of the army would have been occupying central and south Wales. As they obviously could not remain under canvas, some forts were undoubtedly under construction, either at the time of his death, or soon after, and this work of consolidation would have continued under his successor.

The military aspects of Roman Wales have been well served by the publication of the two editions of *The Roman Frontier in Wales* by V.E. Nash-Williams, the first in 1954 and the second edition, much revised by Professor M. Jarrett, in 1969.[9] Details of all the forts and other military establishments are given and these valuable references must be the starting point of any study. Excavations have taken place on most of the known forts at various times, but not all of them have been published. (Even these usually have very short reports on the pottery and, until quite recently, the chronological significance of the humble coarse wares has not been fully recognised.) The assumption that there were no permanent forts until Frontinus has had a serious effect on dating the artefacts from fort excavations, since any pre-Flavian samian has been considered residual. Large collections of pottery from these early excavations still exist in some of the museums, and it would be worth a student's time and patience to sort through them to see if they contain any pre-Flavian sherds. Fortunately, the samian has been studied by Dr Grace Simpson, although at the time she was concerned mainly with the problems of the second-century occupations of the forts.[10] What is now needed is for a knowledgeable pottery student to do the same for the great mass of coarse wares, especially as so much more is now known of the pre-Flavian wares, thanks to the work of Dr Kevin Greene on the Usk material.[11]

The Campaign Camps

The second problem is the presence of a large number of campaign and practice camps. The latest edition of the Ordnance Survey *Map of Roman Britain* (1978) shows 25 and 39 respectively of these sites, the latter figure including the remarkable assemblage of 18 on Llandrimdod Common. It is not always possible to distinguish between the two types of temporary work and some of the campaign camps could have been constructed by units on summer manoeuvres. They are virtually impossible to date since the troops had only campaign gear with them in the field. There were no pottery vessels to break and therefore no sherds to be scattered around or buried in pits. As a result, while these camps should provide us with valuable evidence of the direction and scale of campaigns, they are in practice of little help. The only possibility is differences in camp sites and recognisable types of entrances, which could group them into different classes and thus into periods. Professor St Joseph has had conspicuous success in applying this method in Scotland,[12] but here the campaign periods were more widely separated, covering a period of over a hundred years. In Wales, however, we are dealing with a very short time span of no more than two decades, which does not allow for development or change in these features. For these reasons, it has been decided not to attempt to use the campaign camps to trace particular campaigns. They

41

do, however, offer useful evidence of the main routes used by the army, for they indicate the key assembly points, which can be attested by the number of sizes of the camps.

The Scheme of Presentation

The same order of presentation adopted in the earlier volume will be used: first the legionary dispositions and then those of the *auxilia* and the military routes they controlled. There are three main frontier organisations and adjustments to be considered, made necessary, as we have seen, by the shifts in potential hostility and imperial policy. These will be dealt with in chronological order:

1 The Scapulan advance and the construction of the Welsh Marches frontier (Chapter 3–4)
2 The advance made by Didius Gallus towards Brigantia and frontier adjustments (Chapter 5)
3 The advance under Quintus Veranius and subsequent consolidation (Chapter 6)

The Scapulan Advance: Movement of the Legions

Legio XX at Gloucester (L5, fig 3)

Three of the four legions were moved forward, but the HQ fortress of *Legio IX* most probably remained at Longthorpe, near Peterborough[13] (although the forts occupied by some of the legionary cohorts may have been subject to change). The legion about which there is the greatest certainty is *Legio XX*, since it was linked by Tacitus with the establishment of the *colonia* at Camulodunum (*Ann.* xii. 32). The most obvious place for its new fortress would have been the lowest bridgehead of the Severn at Gloucester (L5). The layout of the roads and the site of the Wotton cemetery clearly show that the early military nucleus was in the Kingsholm area. Unfortunately, much of this area is now covered by a large housing estate. Gravel extraction, early in the nineteenth century, produced a large quantity of bronzes and ironwork, much of which is recorded by Samuel Lysons the famous Gloucestershire antiquary.[14] Some of the pieces are undoubtedly of military origin, and include two axe-head sheaths for suspending the *dolabra* from the belt (pl xv, 4 and 5), what may be the heads of *pila*, a bird mount for a pendant and a fine bronze mess tin. Lysons also illustrated two rather poor copies of Claudian coins.[15] Finally, a tombstone of a soldier of *Legio XX* was found in 1844 in the Wotton cemetery (fig 3); it consisted only of the lower part and that has since been lost.[16]

Attempts made to find the fortress here were not successful[17] until 1972, when Henry Hurst opened up a small area prior to development in a garden in Dean's Way. In his report Mr Hurst[18] took the opportunity of publishing a gazetteer of finds from the area, which includes fifteen pre-Flavian coins to add to the many earlier finds. The excavation showed the presence of a timber building of military-type construction; it had been deliberately demolished and pits had been cut through the remains, with pottery and coins of the early Neronian period. Associated with this early building were military harness trappings and a decorated bronze cheek-piece. Russell Robinson, who examined and described this item, found that it had never been finished, but it had been intended for a cavalry helmet. This indicates the presence of

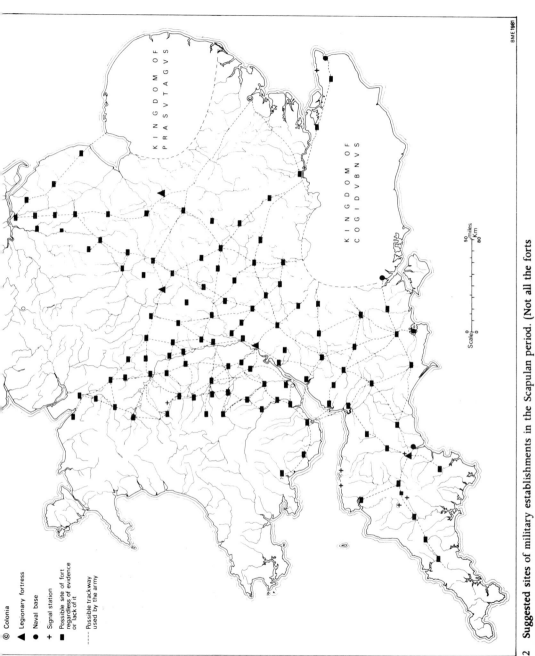

© Colonia

▲ Legionary fortress

● Naval base

+ Signal station

■ Possible site of fort regardless of evidence or lack of it

---- Possible trackway used by the army

KINGDOM OF PRASVTAGVS

KINGDOM OF COGIDVBNVS

Scale

BME 1981

2 **Suggested sites of military establishments in the Scapulan period. (Not all the forts would necessarily have been occupied at the same time)**

43

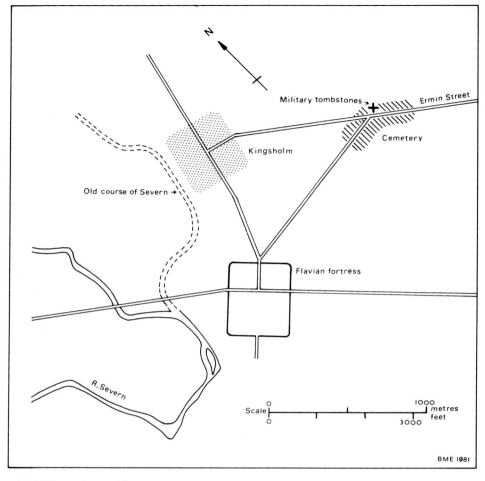

3   Military sites at Gloucester

an auxiliary unit, possibly the Thracian cohort recorded here by a tombstone;[19] it probably pre-dated the legionary fortress and so the bronzes are residual. Slag and metal chippings were also found in the same level, the inference being that it was at one time a workshop. The timber building had two phases and this equipment was in the make-up of the second phase, so it must have belonged to the earlier building. In spite of these interesting finds, there is still no certainty of the presence at Kingsholm of either a legionary fortress or an auxiliary fort; what has been established is that this part of the site was abandoned by the army in the mid-60s.[20]

Legio II Aug.

Legio II Aug. had established its HQ fortress at Silchester in the Plautian phase (see *The Roman Invasion of Britain*, 124-125). Scapula could hardly have afford to keep one of his main units so far in the rear, so he probably moved the legion forward, maybe leaving a cohort behind as a reserve. The only area that he then had left to protect in south-eastern Britain would have been the vital route from Richborough to London, and units could have been distributed along it for this purpose. The main Roman concern in the south-west would have been with the Durotriges and their allies, the southern branch of the Dobunni, both still bitterly hostile. It would seem logical to have stationed part of the IInd in their territory. An obvious site would have been Dorchester, Dorset, near the great tribal stronghold, Maiden Castle, which had been attacked and taken by Vespasian in 43 or 44. Although there is no evidence, as yet, of a fort buried below the later Roman town, pieces of equipment[21] hint of a possible legionary presence. Another possibility is at Lake Farm near Wimborne,[22] where recent excavations have revealed a fort with a pottery dated span c.45−65.[23]

The Exeter Fortress

There had always been the possibility that Exeter (L8) was the site of a legionary fortress since it is thus identified by Ptolemy but it was assumed that there had been confusion over the name Isca which is also that of the legionary fortress at Caerleon.[24] Legionary presence was not proved until 1971, when excavations on the Guildhall site produced barrack-blocks of a suitable size. In the same year the site of the Victorian church, St Mary Major, just outside the west entrance to the Cathedral, became available and this unexpectedly produced the legionary bath-house. The work was continued in 1977, and a fine report was published with remarkable promptitude in 1978.[25] The dating evidence for the founding of the fortress is meagre and only offers a broad span of c.45−65. Exeter has produced as many as 50 sherds of *terra nigra*, but Miss Valery Rigby considers them all to be post-c.55 (*Report*, pp 13 and 189−91). The samian tells much the same story, although three pieces could be placed in the c.50−65 bracket (*Report*, pp 180−4). It is also clear from the excavation that the bath-house was not the first building on the site, so there could have been an earlier phase of the legionary occupation or, of course, there is the possibility that it could represent traces of buildings of an auxiliary fort of the Plautian phase. The possible inference of this is that *Legio II Aug.* did not reach Exeter until c.55.

The legion was transferred to Gloucester in 66 to replace *Legio XX*, then moved to Wroxeter. This does not necessarily mean that the fortress at Exeter was abandoned. There was always a tendency for the army to retain their establishments, if only on a care and maintenance basis, long after it had any further use for them. But in the case of Exeter there was a need for a strong force in the area following the great revolt of 60. *Legio II Aug.* failed to obey the orders of Suetonius Paullinus to join him in the Midlands to face the rebels under Boudica, and its commander at this time, the camp prefect (*praefectus castrorum*), was obliged to commit suicide. A case has been made for a substantial part of the legion, at least the first cohort with his *legatus* and the senior tribune, to have been with Paullinus. With a reduced garrison, Poenius Postumus may have been pinned in the fortress by a great rebel horde of Durotrigian warriors with Dumnonian sympathisers.[26] This would explain why the commander could not obey his orders, but nevertheless could not use it as an excuse. If there is any substance to this idea, it would certainly imply the need for retaining part of the legion at Exeter, which may account for the evidence of the rebuilding of barrack-blocks in the northern corner of the fortress after c.66, and the reduction of the bath-house.[27] There is another interesting but odd fact. Pieces of two antefixes were found in the

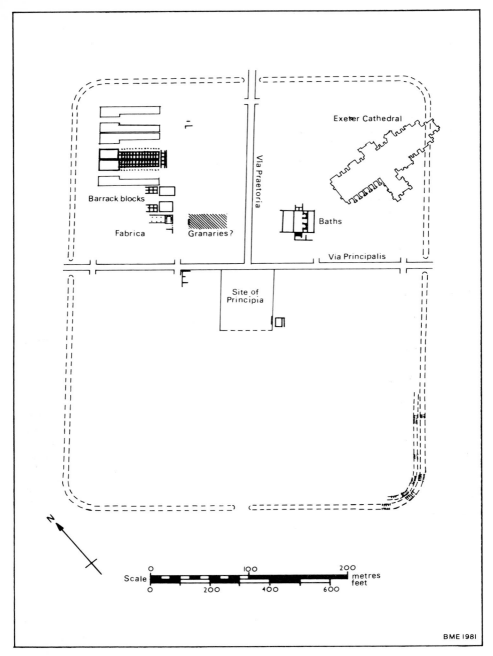

4   Plan of the known buildings in the fortress at Exeter (after Paul Bidwell)

construction deposit of the bath-house. The triangular part at the end of an antefix, which masked the space below the imbrex and presented a 'face' to the viewer from

5   Apron-mount decorated with enamels from Exeter (full size)

below, is decorated in relief with two dolphins with a rosette. An antefix from this same mould has been found at Caerleon.[28] This suggests the possibility that the mould was kept in store at Exeter and transferred direct to Caerleon.

Legio XIV at Mancetter (L9, fig 6)

The fourth legion to consider is *Legio XIV*. It is far from certain where this legion was stationed in the Plautian phase. It was one of the legions Scapula moved forward as part of his drive against Caratacus, and there is now evidence that the site of its base was later established at Mancetter on the main line of advance and communication (to be known much later as Watling Street and the A5).

The pleasant little village, with its church and manor house, lies on the west side of the River Anker on the outskirts of Atherstone, which has developed along Watling Street itself. Fortunately, the village is a conservation area and development has been severely restricted, so there are still open fields and spaces in the area now known to have been occupied by the army. Knowledge has come in bits and pieces, some as casual finds, but the most significant through carefully planned, small-scale excavations by Keith Scott. By a fortunate chance an alignment of military defences was found in 1955[29] along the river edge; this was sectioned again in 1968[30] and has established the line of the east defences (fig 6). In 1978, an improvement to a bend in Quarry Lane led to further investigations. A timber structure found here could have been part of a centurial block; if so, this would indicate that the line of the southern defences can only be a short distance away. The natural ground slope, which increases to the south of this point, supports this. Further work in 1980 produced a ditch system on the western side, consisting of two sets of defences 80 feet apart, and demonstrating an extension or reduction. If this is the same system as the riverside line, the width of such an establishment would be *c*.1000ft – too small for a full-size

47

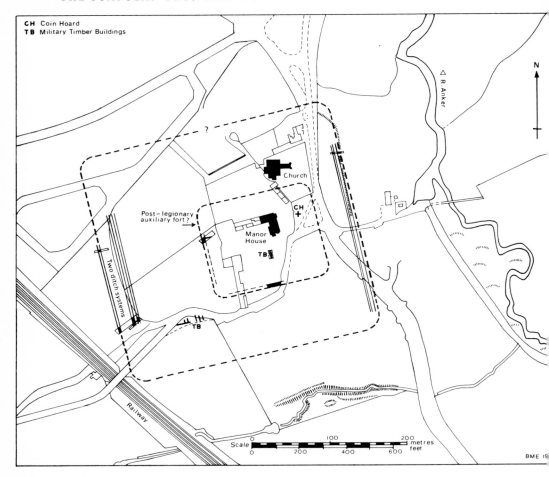

6   Plan of the military features at Mancetter

legionary fortress, but far too large for an auxiliary fort. But the two defence systems need not belong to the same establishment, and there is a strong possibility of an auxiliary unit here in the Plautian phase and another after the transfer of the legion in the mid-fifties.[31]

In two areas small-scale excavations between the two sets of defences have revealed the presence of a sequence of timber buildings of a military type and scraps of equipment which might suggest the presence of legionaries, as well as evidence of deliberate demolition. The first of these discoveries was another lucky chance, when, in 1975, the owner of a house in the centre of the village dug a hole to erect a Victorian lamp-post to illuminate the entrance. The small hole he dug revealed three complete amphorae lying on their sides. He then allowed Keith Scott and his team to extend the hole and excavate part of the front garden. They found the small pits where the amphorae had stood upright and at least three periods of timber buildings, which gave a clear indication of the complications likely to be revealed if it was ever possible to open up a large area. The second of these discoveries was in Quarry Lane, where a building found with a square latrine pit could have been part of a centurion's quarters. The pit had been deliberately filled in, together with its wooden cover and a collection of twelve double-handled flagons, presumably from the centurion's pantry. The vessels are all from the same factory and much the same shape with a flattened ovoid body. These factors do not offer much opportunity of fixing a very precise date, but they can be said to fall between the Claudian and Flavian periods, i.e. c.50–65. The demolition deposit is at present all we have to offer for dating the move of *Legio XIV* from Mancetter to Wroxeter, since there is no dating evidence from the construction levels at the latter. It is, however, too much to expect to be able to state with any certainty that the event took place in say 52 or 54 or 57.

Legio XIV at Wroxeter (L7)

Wroxeter has long been recognised as a nodal point in Roman defensive strategy. From the banks of the Severn it is possible to look westwards towards the foothills of Wales and the valley offers deep entry into its heartlands. To the south-west ran the connecting route to the Wye Valley across the Hereford Plain, while almost due north lies the route across the Cheshire Plain to the Dee Estuary. Evidence of military presence was established in the land clearance in the eighteenth century which produced a number of tombstones. One is of a Thracian trooper of a *cohors equitata* (*RIB* 291), three *milites* of *Legio XIV* (*RIB* 292, 294, 296) and one of a *beneficiarius* of *Legio XX* (*RIB* 293). The absence of the honorific title of *Martia Victrix* for the former legion on two of these is clear evidence that they were erected before AD 60, when the honour was conferred on *Legio XIV* for its part in the victory over Boudica. That great scholar Haverfield also pointed out the absence of a *cognomen* in two of the names, and he suggested that the use of two, instead of the three, names usually employed for a Roman citizen, was evidence of Claudian date.[32] His dictum for such an early foundation to both Wroxeter and Lincoln was followed and widely accepted. However, an American scholar, L.R. Dean, concluded, in his study of the subject in 1916, that this is by no means an inflexible rule.[33] He discovered that in 350 examples of the lack of the *cognomen*, 75 per cent belonged to the period up to the end of the reign of Claudius, but the rest were later, two even as late as Trajan. One is thus not obliged to accept a Claudian date for the establishment of legionary fortresses at Wroxeter and Lincoln and, as we have seen, the historical background suggests dates between c.52 and 56 for Wroxeter but not earlier. It is likely that the first establishment post here in the frontier zone was the Thracian cohort at a fort by the river crossing.

The exact position of the legionary fortress has for many years been a matter of speculation. Two fragments of evidence are difficult to reconcile. The first is the air photograph taken in 1955 by Professor St Joseph, showing a pair of ditches turning a tight but typically military corner, underlying the later city buildings and streets beyond the north-west corner of the forum. The snag about these ditches is that, if their western alignment is extended to the south-west, they would meet the river c.215m from the corner, and it seems evident from a careful study of the behaviour of the river over the last 2000 years[34] that it has not moved by more than a few yards. The second piece of evidence came from the investigation of Kathleen Kenyon into the city defences on the east side in 1936.[35] She found two parallel ditches and a turf rampart below the later civil defences and at a slightly different alignment. The profile of the ditches is odd, being very flat,[36] but they had the typical military shovel slot at the bottom. It was the opinion of the excavator that these defences belonged to a civil circuit of the first century − a view influenced no doubt by Wheeler's work at Verulamium about the same time. There the matter rested until the series of excavations, as part of the annual training schools organised by the extramural department of the University of Birmingham, began in 1955, on the site of the central baths insula. An open area round the ornamental pool (*piscina*) was chosen, since this had received little attention from the nineteenth-century excavators, who had cleared most of the interior of the bath-house. Over the years that followed, it became gradually apparent that a series of timber buildings was present, five to six feet below the present ground level. When enough of the plan (fig 14) had been recovered, they were recognised as military buildings, part of the interior of the long lost legionary fortress. It was also observed that the structures were in the same alignment as the later civil buildings, but the pottery associated with them was Flavian, i.e. dating to c.85, which seems to imply that the army maintained the fortress long after the legion had moved north and also after the founding of Chester by *Legio II Adiutrix*.[37]

The next important discovery was made by Arnold Baker, who observed and photographed a pair of ditches in the northern part of the town, which, when projected, appeared to join those found by Kathleen Kenyon. The possibility of her early defences being legionary now demanded serious consideration. Assuming that she had found the north-east corner of the fortress, it was possible to make a projection of the other two sides. When this was drawn on a plan of the city, it was seen that the western defences would have lain beneath its main north-south street. This at least would explain why this alignment had never been seen from the air, since its ditches were buried deep under several feet of road metalling, and large public buildings. It so happened that by a remarkable chance the annual season's work in the training programme, which coincided with Arnold Baker's discovery, involved the investigation of the *macellum*, a small market at the south-west corner of the baths insula. This square-shaped building consisted of three sides round a portico and central courtyard, and the three sides were divided into small shops or stores. Two of them, in the north-west corner, had been deeply excavated by the Victorians and it was a simple matter to empty their back-fill and so examine the lower levels, without the long and laborious process of a careful excavation necessary for stratified deposits. When the bottom of the western of the two areas was carefully cleaned, to our intense astonishment we found we were standing on the reduced top of a military turf rampart. The projection was proved correct and it was now known for the first time precisely where the legionary fortress was situated. This was a notable advance, but difficult problems remained. It was clear that there were several periods of building and rebuilding. When for example the intervallum road which flanked the rampart tail round the defence circuit was examined, it was found to be eight roads, one above the other, giving a 4ft (1.2m) deposit of consolidation gravel. Below the lowest fortress levels strange factors began to emerge − earlier ditches, small post-holes and an

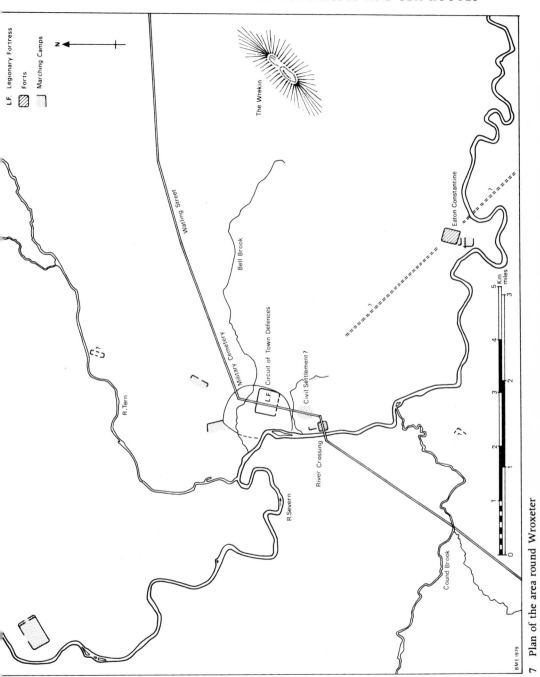

7 Plan of the area round Wroxeter

8   Small bronze belt-mount from Wroxeter (full size)

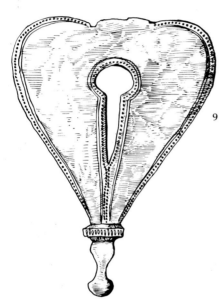

9   Decorated belt-mount from Wroxeter (full size)

10   Bronze pendant of a horse harness from Wroxeter (full size)

11   Two scales of a cuirass from Wroxeter (full size)

oven, which certainly did not belong to a properly organised fortress, but which had
more the appearance of several seasons of wintering quarters (*hiberna*). So it is
evidence that the army had been using the site for some time before the legion was
established in its permanent quarters.

52

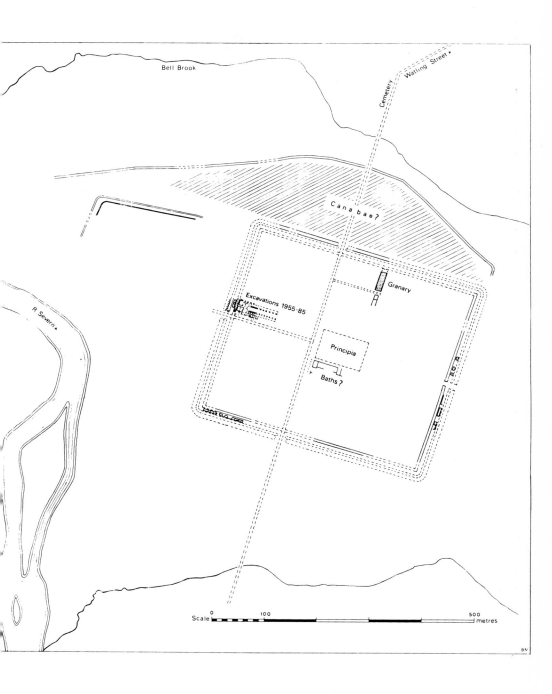

Bell Brook

Cemetery

Watling Street

C a n a b a e ?

R Severn

Granary

Excavations 1955-85

Principia

Baths ?

Scale

0

100

500

metres

Plan of the legionary fortress at Wroxeter

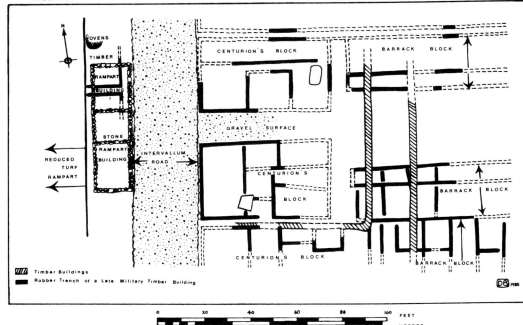

13　A rationalised plan of the military buildings at Wroxeter

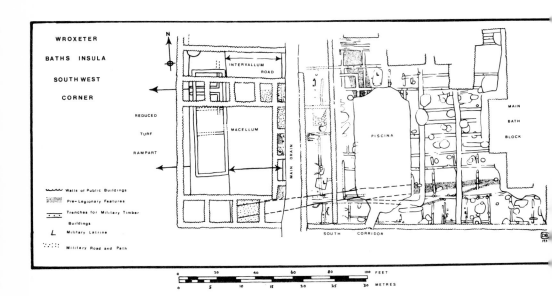

14　A plan of the Hadrianic buildings over military buildings

It may be a long time before the basic layout of the fortress is known, since work is only possible at Wroxeter in limited areas, and the military levels are covered everywhere with several feet of the remains of the later city. The whole area is now under national protection, with the object ultimately of a total excavation, leaving all structures capable of preservation to be seen by the public. While this is a most remarkable project, it places serious inhibitions on a total excavation which would be the only sure way of recovering the whole of the plan of the military buildings, streets and defences. It will only be possible to examine in detail the earlier levels in carefully selected places where there are no later floors and walls to be preserved. It should be possible, however, to discover the southern line of the defences by geophysical means. At present this alignment can only be projected on the basis of comparison with other fortresses, Gloucester in particular. The later city street plan may preserve the line of the principal military cross-street (*via principalis*) since one of the streets is in about the right position and is a continuation of the main roads from the north, and if extended to the south is aimed at the known river crossing. The only other evidence is a fine stone buttressed granary on a N–S axis adjacent to the north defences, which was photographed by Professor St Joseph in 1975. It is a typical military type of building, such as is normally found in this position along the intervallum road and which allows access for carts to unload (as, for instance, at the six granaries at Inchtuthil,[38] situated in the same relative positions on the intervallum road, which allows access for carts and space for unloading).

The Sea Routes

The rapid success of the Plautian campaign in the south-west was largely a result of the control of the sea approaches along the south coast and the establishment of naval bases in the natural harbours from Bosham to the Exe. This gave the Roman army the means of ferrying men and supplies more quickly and efficiently than would have been possible with a land route. Scapula is hardly likely to have neglected this valuable arm, and it was important for him to extend it in his advance into the Devon–Cornwall peninsula and in particular to concentrate units of the fleet in the Bristol Channel, as part of his initial campaign against Caratacus and the Silures.

The main Plautian sea base on the south coast had been at Fishbourne in Bosham Harbour, below the great palace of Cogidubnus. Professor Barry Cunliffe, who excavated this site, concluded that the military buildings had been demolished to make way for workshops of a civil character when the army moved to the west *c.*50.[39] But the dating evidence could never be precise enough to narrow it down to this historical possibility. It would seem logical for Scapula to move the naval store-base nearer to the main fighting area, and the Solent seems to offer the best possibility. A quantity of Claudian pottery has been found in excavations at Clausentum[40] which was later to develop into a Saxon Shore Fort, and a case could be made for a base here by AD 50, if not before. The evidence for the other naval bases along the south coast up to the Exe Estuary is given in *The Roman Invasion of Britain* (140–2).

As soon as Exeter became the fortress of *Legio II Aug.*, the possibility of establishing a naval base on the Exe would have been considered. But whether this was at Topsham (S 3) or nearer the fortress is far from certain. The evidence from Topsham remains rather meagre and only the recovery of fine imported wares of the period offers any support. It would have been quite possible for the army to have cut a deep navigable

channel up to a landing point near the fortress and so avoid dependence on the tides.[41]
The great deep-water inlets at Plymouth and Falmouth were only of interest to the
fleet at this period in providing sheltered anchorage during stormy seasons; the more
important and urgent task was to secure the harbours on the south side of the Bristol
Channel. Since Roman ships would now be passing round Land's End, a system of
signal stations and safe harbours was an essential requirement on this treacherous and
difficult coastline. Certainly one would have needed navigational aids, as one does
today, on such headlands as Star Point, The Lizard, Trevose Head, Hartland Point and
Bull Point. Little is known about any such sites and some may have vanished with
erosion on the cliff faces. A possible site may have been the small earthwork at High
Peak near Sidmouth where first-century pottery was found in an excavation in 1929.[42]

The only Roman sites known along the north Devon coast are at Martinhoe (No 4) and
Old Burrow (No 3, fig 16), which have been carefully excavated.[43] The sites are about
eight miles apart and were built on commanding positions on the cliff top with wide
views over the Channel, extending, in clear conditions as far as the Welsh coastline;
they were not, however, visible from one another. Old Burrow stands on a 1000ft
bluff and excavations revealed the defences of a typical signal-station, with a circular
outer ditch and bank about 250ft (76m) across within its bank and in a central
position, inside an enclosure nearly 100ft square (9.3m²) with a single four-post
entrance which had the function of a watch-tower for observation and signalling.
Other parts of the interior were stripped and the only building found was a cook-
house against the south rampart; the assumption that the garrison lived in tents seems
hardly tenable, unless it had been abandoned very quickly. The only dating evidence
is a *denarius* of Tiberius which is not very helpful; the few pieces of pottery are all of
native type vessels, the form of which persisted for a long time. An excavation in 1911
produced a *dolabra* or pioneer's axe, but this possibly belonged to the construction
party. Martinhoe was found to be a very similar site, in shape and size, but its lower
siting was considered by the excavators to have given it an advantage when hill mists

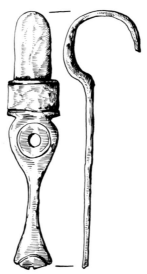

15   Baldric-clip from Sea Mills (full size)

covered the headlands. The other considerable difference is that this site produced the small timber barrack-blocks which would have held about fifty men and two officers. One was clearly senior to the other from the size of his quarters, and there was also much more pottery and two coins of Nero, one a mint issue of AD 64–68. The samian falls into a bracket 55–75, the earliest being a platter of L I C I N V S. The conclusion reached was that Old Burrow was earlier and of a temporary nature, while Martinhoe, on the better placed site, became the permanent establishment and was occupied up to c.75.

The harbour and ferry-points along the south coast would have been under military control during the Plautian phase and there were probably units at the mouth of the Parrett (No 127), at Uphill (No 80) near Weston-super-Mare, at Sea Mills (No 126) and near Berkeley (No 125). They would have been the bases from which Scapula could have launched a seaborne assault against South Wales with the support and protection of the Fleet. There is a number of possible landing places and points of entry along the Welsh coastline,[44] but these must be considered in relationship to the British power centres as reflected in their hill-forts. One of the more interesting was the small site in Lydney Park, famous for its Roman temple, excavated by Mortimer Wheeler in 1928–9.[45] The quality of the later Celtic metalwork suggests wealth and contacts with south-eastern Britain, but it is more interesting to note that, among the bronzes published by Wheeler, are a trumpet mouth-piece of a military type (his No 47)[46] and an officer's belt-mount, finely decorated with coloured enamels (his No 97) of a type fairly common on first-and second-century military sites.[47] Neither of these objects need be first century in date and do not, therefore, necessarily indicate a military presence. Roman material on the river side[48] offers the possibility of a ferry-point connected with Berkeley (No 125).

Of the Wye Valley hill-forts little seems to be known, but the more obvious site for cross-channel contacts must have been Sudbrook near Portskewett (HF3), perched right on the edge of the coast, much of it being lost by erosion. Excavations in the 1930s produced the largest collection of pre-Flavian pottery found in Wales, prior to the large-scale work at Usk.[49] Much of this is Claudian-Neronian samian, and the most significant piece is undoubtedly the ink-pot (Report, 59) which must surely mean that a literate person was here at this time, most probably military personnel. There is also a ballista bolt (Report, 76), and what is described as a 'local copy' of form 24/25 in a coarse grey ware. The copying of samian was characteristic of potters supplying the army at this period, when it was difficult or impossible to find local native wares of suitable quality. The problem thus arises as to how all this material was present in this hill-fort. It has been considered as a trading port but there is no evidence at present of any spread of such imports into the hinterland.[50] It seems more likely that there is a Roman military association with this Iron Age fort.

Forts at the river mouths would have been essential to maintain cross-Channel supplies. The evidence from Chepstow (No 166) on the Wye consists only of a single item of equipment, a fine enamelled harness-mount[51] with a simple Celtic scroll, but the artistic effect is rather spoilt by an inept triangle pattern of alternating red and yellow enamel, which declares its Roman association. The fort must presumably be below the town, or perhaps, with the absence of evidence from this area, the site of the Castle.

The estuary of the Usk was controlled later by the legionary fortress at Caerleon (No 150) and, as noted above, it is probable that an earlier auxiliary fort will eventually be

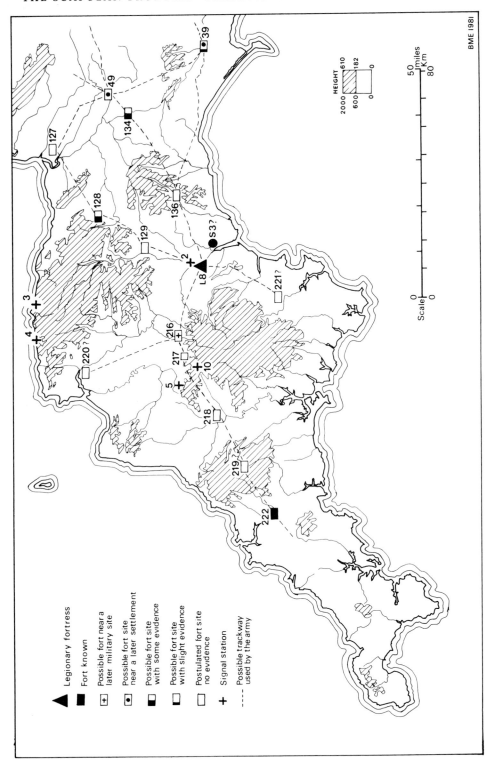

BME 1981

39

49

127

134

128

136

129

S3?

2

L8

221?

3

4

220?

216

217

10

5

218

219?

222

Scale

0
0

50
80

miles
Km

HEIGHT

2000
600

610
182
0

0

Legionary fortress

Fort known

Possible fort near a
later military site

Possible fort site
near a later settlement

Possible fort site
with some evidence

Possible fort site
with slight evidence

Postulated fort site
no evidence

Signal station

Possible trackway
used by the army

found underneath it. There is already slight evidence in the finds of pre-Flavian pottery from recent excavations.[52] The next river mouth to the west is at the junction of the Taff and Ely, where the great city of Cardiff (No 167) now stands. It has been famous for its fourth-century fort, the walls of which were incorporated into the later castle and the remarkable reconstruction by John Ward. An earlier fort has long been suspected from finds made in the interior and in recent years Peter Webster, excavating inside the fort,[53] has found timber buildings at a different alignment to the later fort and associated with Neronian pottery. The site is a very complicated one, with virtual continuity of military occupation, which has caused much damage to the earlier levels.

The next possible harbour is at the mouth of the Ewenni, either at Porthcawl or the little estuary itself. It has been assumed that a settlement, and probably a fort, would have been built at the river crossing to the south of Bridgend (No 178) and it has been further suggested that this was Bomium, the otherwise unplaced name in Iter XII of the Antonine Itinerary.[54] Rivet and Smith,[55] however, considered that this place-name was really Bovium, and link it, from this version of the name, with a Roman settlement at Cowbridge,[56] almost halfway between Bridgend and Cardiff. Unfortunately, this does not help us with our quest for a Scapulan coastal base.

Further west still, the estuary of the Afon Mellte would have provided a useful inlet near the western limit of the territory of the Silures. Here at Neath (Nidum, No 179), a fort is known[57] and has been partly excavated.[58] The earliest occupation with timber buildings was noted but was thought to have been of 'short duration', then demolished to make way for a 'more permanent fort'.[59] This unfortunate early attitude, and the basic assumption that the fort was founded by Frontinus, has inhibited any critical examination of the pottery. One interesting vessel, published from these excavations, is a small carrot amphora[60] normally considered to have been pre-Flavian; but the continued use of amphorae as containers does not make this very reliable for precise dating.[61] 'Early samian pottery' is said to have come from the excavations[62] and a Claudian imitation coin from the early rampart. It is the opinion of Dr Brenda Heywood who examined the N—W defences in 1950,[63] that the foundation date could be pre-Flavian.[64]

16 Map of the military sites of the Scapulan advance in the south-western peninsula

LEGIONARY FORTRESS L8 Exeter

SIGNAL STATIONS 2 Stoke Hill, Exeter 3 Old Burrow 4 Martinhoe 5 Broadbury
10 Sourton Down

NAVAL BASE S3 Topsham
FORTLET 217 Oakhampton

FORTS 39 Dorchester, Dorset 49 Ilchester 127 Mouth of the Parrett
128 Wiveliscombe 129 near Tiverton 134 Ham Hill 136 near Honiton
216 North Tawton 218 near Launceston 219 Upper Fowey 220 near Barnstaple
221 on the River Dart 222 Nanstallon

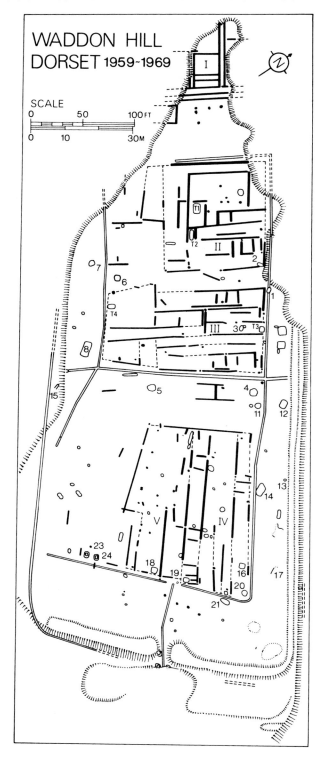

WADDON HILL
DORSET 1959~1969

SCALE
0   50   100 FT
0   10   30 M

The Advance to the South-West

The need to control the Bristol Channel and access to the coast of South Wales forced Scapula to occupy the Devonian Cornish peninsula. This decision may have been upsetting, if not alarming, to the Dumnonii, a tribe which would appear hitherto to have had a friendly relationship with Rome. Whether they resisted and had to be conquered is not known, but these people were now obliged to accept military occupation. This aspect has long been the study of Lady Aileen Fox, who has carried out investigations and excavations over a considerable period, as will be evident from the references to sites below. Recent surveys by Dr Valerie Maxfield in 1979 and 1989.[65] The most striking move was that of *Legio II Aug.* to Exeter. This strongly suggests that either this legion was needed in a more advanced position for the attack on South Wales, or that a serious threat remained in this area, transcending even that presented by the Durotriges. However friendly the Dumnonii may have been towards Plautius, the attitude of the tribe may have changed. Perhaps their fears were aroused by the terror tactics of Scapula, or the influence of the Druids had begun to penetrate; or perhaps Scapula paid scant attention to any earlier Roman fair words and promises, for he was in too much of a hurry to bother with such niceties, and he needed above all the control of the Bristol Channel. It is unlikely that we will ever know what happened unless evidence if found of a violent destruction of a hill-fort associated with military occupation.[66]

Waddon Hill (fig 17, pl 7–10)

One of the new forts associated with the general movement of troops to the south-west is Waddon Hill, near Beaminster, Dorset. This is an interesting fort on a flat-topped hill in difficult terrain. Almost half this fort has been removed by stone quarries but the surviving area has been excavated (fig 17; *Proc. Dorset Nat. Hist. and Arch. Soc.*, 82 (1960), pp. 135–149). The construction trenches for timber buildings are difficult to interpret, but it seems clear that some are barrack-blocks and stables. The finds include both legionary and auxiliary equipment for infantry as well as cavalry. It is possible that this fort replaced Hod Hill and that a legionary detachment was stationed here with part of an auxiliary unit.

17 Plan of the surviving buildings of the fort on Waddon Hill, Dorset

18 Scabbard guard from Waddon Hill (full size)

19 Cuirass-hinge from Waddon Hill (full size)

20 Silver scabbard-mount from Waddon Hill (full size)

21 Belt-hinge from Waddon Hill (full size)

CHAPTER FOUR

The Scapulan Frontier: The Land Routes

The dispositions of the military units will follow the plan which was suggested in the *Invasion* (Chap. 6), i.e. by means of following military routes. The scheme is now extended to the west using the same numbering system. These routes, it should be emphasised, were not roads, but merely cleared ways which were roughly levelled for the use of horses and pack-animals rather than vehicles. The siting of the army units would have depended on the broad strategy considered necessary in each particular circumstance. As the army moved into newly conquered territory, it may have been necessary to have placed units near potentially hostile concentrations, but later the siting of the forts may have been changed to fit into a network designed to control communication. Inevitably, however, the frontier zone would have been subject to change as potential threats shifted from point to point. It is not surprising, in these circumstances, to find that there are occasionally traces of several military establishments within a short distance of each other. This may have been due to the need to move a unit to a better tactical position, or to a change in the unit itself, with a new commander deciding what he considered may have been a better site for his force.

Route 45

Roman military control of this area was maintained by Route 45, virtually bisecting the peninsula. This dominated the watershed between the two river systems flowing north and south, with the exception of the Tamar. The route from Exeter skirted the northern fringes of the bleak granite out-crop of Dartmoor, with the first fort at North Tawton on the River Taw, then swinging south-west to cross the Tamar near Launceston, where a fort must be expected, thence over Bodmin Moor to a fort at Nanstallon on the Camel. The North Tawton fort came to light after a check on a possible Roman road alignment by the Ordnance Survey Archaeology Division. An earthwork, found south of the railway line by the river, was postulated as on the south-east rounded corner of a Roman fort, subsequently some sherds of samian of unrecorded date were found.[1] The Roman military identity was confirmed by Professor St Joseph who recovered the full outline of a fort, the plan of which was 660ft by 425ft (6.4 acres) from rampart crests, with an annexe on the west side.[2] On a later flight he recorded the north side of a campaign camp about 1500ft (450m) long with visible corners at each end, c.2000ft (600m) north of the fort.[3] About 5 miles along the road to the west, a small 2.6 acre fort has been found near Okehampton, guarding the crossing of the River Okement.[4] A section through the defences produced a little pottery, including a sherd of samian f 37 dated to c.70–85 from its provenance at the

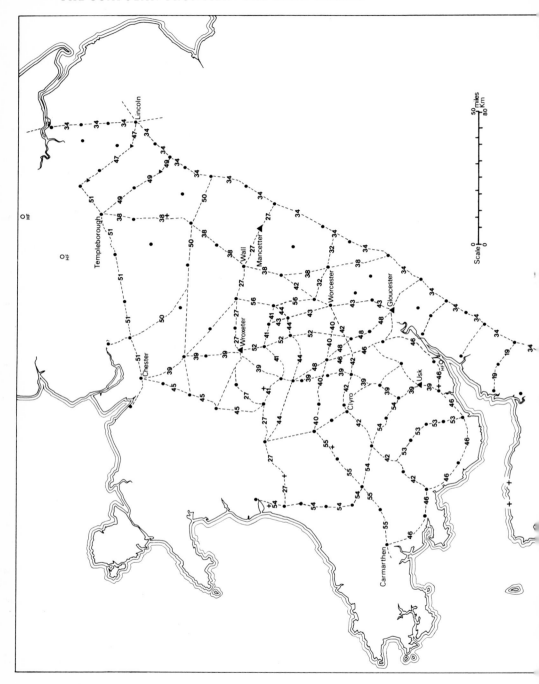

1 Coin of Caratacus: obverse

(Photos: The National Museum of Wales)

2 Coin of Caratacus: reverse

3   The *testudo* as shown on Trajan's Column

4   A forage party, from Trajan's Column

5   Route 39, through the Church Stretton Gap (Photo: Arnold Baker)

6   The auxiliary fort at Wroxeter, at the river crossing south of the Roman legionary and civil site (Photo: Arnold Baker)

PLATE SIX

7 Bust of Mercury from the fort at
Waddon Hill

8 Post-pit for one of the gate
timbers of the fort at Waddon Hill

9   Carnelian intaglio from an iron ring from the Waddon Hill fort, showing Ajax with the body of Achilles (diam. 10mm)

10   Blue glass intaglio from the Waddon Hill fort, with symbols favoured by soldiers; the palm of victory, club of Hercules, corn-ear of Ceres and rudder of Fortune (10 × 11mm)

11 Fort on the high ground overlooking Alcester (Photo; Arnold Baker)
12 Metchley: the north-east post-hold of the corner tower, showing black filling of the
trench into the front of the rampart to remove the post

13   One of the forts at Greensforge (Photo: Arnold Baker)
14   Fort at Pennocrucium, showing also a medieval field with the marks of a swing plough (Photo: the Committee of Aerial Photography, University of Cambridge)

15   Fort at Stretton Grandison (Photo: Arnold Baker)

16   Crop-marks of the military sites at Rhyn Park, Shropshire (No 170)

17   'Vexillation' fort at Newton-on-Trent, Lincolnshire (No 180)

(Photos: The Committee of Aerial Photography, University of Cambridge)

18 'Vexillation' fort at Rossington Bridge, Yorkshire (No 182)
(Photo: The Committee of Aerial Photography, University of Cambridge)

19 Air photograph of Barwick-in-Elmet (HF 3) (Photo: W. Yorks Metropolitan CC)

20 Sketch of motte-and-bailey castle at Barwick-in-Ermet, the trees indicating the outline of the Iron Age hill fort (entrance shown by arrow)

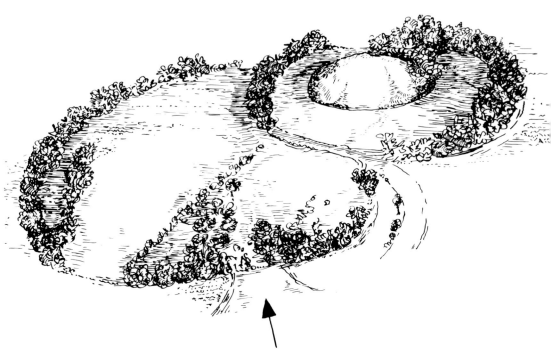

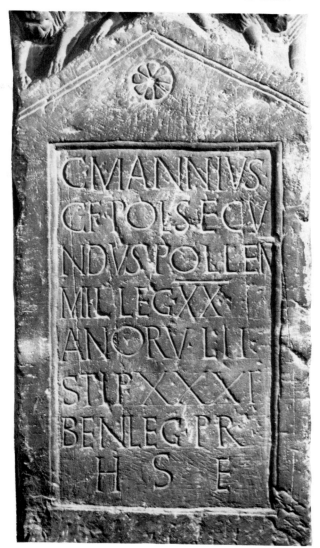

21 Fort at LLwŷn-y-Brain (No 196)

22 Fort at Clyro (No 210)
(Photos: The Committee of Aerial Photography, University of Cambridge)

23–4 Military tombstones from Wroxeter (Nos 1 and 3, p. 136)

25–6   Military tombstones
from Wroxeter Nos 2 and 4, p. 136

back of the rampart, which could have been a demolition layer. The short distance from North Tawton means that this fort was either a later adjustment, or there **may** have been a special need for a small force at this point at the head of the Torridge Valley, which leads to the only large estuary on the north coast of Devon, where Barnstaple and Bideford are now situated. At a point another 4½ miles along the route, a signal station, similar to those on the north Devon coast, has been identified by C.J. Balkwill and R.J. Silvester, among a number of earthworks on Sourton Down.[5] About 5½ miles to the north-west is a fortlet, probably a signal station at Broadbury.[6] The Route crosses the Tamar at Launceston, where the medieval castle and town are on the south side of the River Kensey. Since little has been found in this town,[7] the Roman fort could have been sited on the east side, where it could have been protected from the north by the River Carey. As Professor Rivet has noted, it may be significant that Ptolemy gave the place-name Tamara (No 218), derived from the name of the river in approximately this position, and he has furthermore shown that one of the sources of Ptolemy may have been a Neronian army list.[8] From here to the next known site at Nanstallon is about 24 miles, and one might reasonably expect a fort at the mid-point position, but this would place it at the top of Bodmin Moor at the headwaters of the Fowey. It might fit another name – Voliba from Ptolemy, which he places to the west of Tamara – but the meaning of the name is obscure.[9]

The Nanstallon fort (No 222) (fig 35, p. 86)
The fort at Nanstallon on the River Camel, two miles west of Bodmin, has long been recognised, and sherds of samian f 29 have been published in *VCH*.[10] Excavations were undertaken by Lady Aileen Fox and Professor W. Ravenhill over four seasons from 1965 to 1969.[11] The fort proved to be one of the small 2-acre types and occupied a strategic position on the E–W route, where a unit could control both the Camel Valley and its estuary, and also the Fowey, with its narrow deep estuary.[12] As further investigations have shown, the area was densely occupied in the late Iron Age. The buildings of the eastern half of the fort were thoroughly excavated and proved to comprise a small central *principia*, a *praetorium* and four barrack blocks. While the size of the *principia* had been scaled down, the *praetorium*, commandant's house, is normal, indicating the presence of an auxiliary officer of equestrian status. The small size of the fort can only mean that it held part of an auxiliary unit, perhaps a half. From excavations, the slightly larger width of the northern-most barrack indicated that it was intended for cavalry and that the unit was thus a *cohors equitata*. The few pieces of equipment do not help in this identification. The poor-quality belt, decorated with iron studs with conical heads (Report fig 19, No 13), may not even be military, but if it is, could only have belonged to a low-grade auxiliary. On the other hand, the finely moulded scabbard ring (Report fig 19, No 14) could even be legionary.

Although the foundation date of the fort could not be firmly established since, as usual, most of the coins and pottery came from demolition pits, the conclusion is that it is Neronian. There are, however, timber structures, associated with metal working, predating one of the barrack-blocks (Report p. 83 and pl VA), so the army may have been here under Scapula and the small fort possibly belonged to a later period of reduction and consolidation. The only other evidence for military activity is a small campaign camp found by Professor St Joseph at Alverdiscott,[13] 18 miles north-west of North Tawton on the high ground overlooking the Taw and Torridge valleys. As

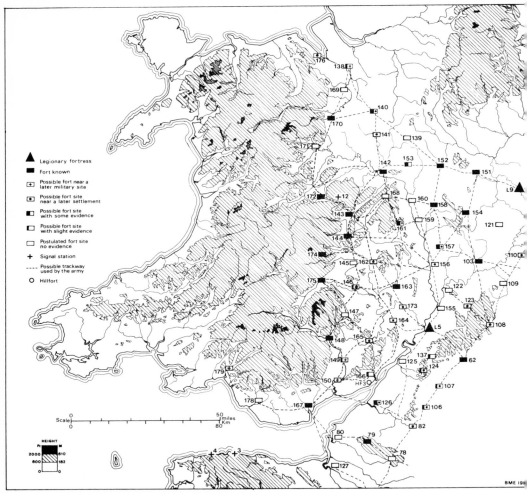

23   Map of the military sites of the advance to the west under Scapula

LEGIONARY FORTRESSES   L5 Gloucester   L9 Mancetter

SIGNAL STATIONS   3 Old Burrow   4 Martinhoe

HILLFORT   HF3 Sudbrook

FORTS   62 Cirencester   78 north of Shepton Mallet   79 Charterhouse   80 Axmouth
(Uphill?)   82 Bath   103 Alcester   106 Nettleton   107 White Walls   108 near Bourton-
on-the-Water   109 near Halford   110 near Chesterton   121 near Temple Balsall   122 near
Eckington   123 near Andoversford   124 Kingscote   125 near Berkeley   126 Sea Mills
127 mouth of the Parrett   137 Rodborough Common   138 Chester   139 Camp Farm   140
Whitchurch   141 Rutinium   142 Wroxeter   143 Stretford Bridge   144 Brandon Camp
145 River Arrow   146 Kenchester   147 Pontrilas   148 Abergavenny   149 Usk   150
Caerleon   151 Wall   152 Pennocrucium   153 Red Hill   154 Metchley   155 Tewkesbury
156 Worcester   157 Droitwich   158 Greensforge   159 Severn Crossing   160 Quatford
161 Wall Town   162 Blackwardine   163 Stretton Grandison   164 Weston-under-
Penyard   165 Monmouth   166 Chepstow   167 Cardiff   168 Corve Valley   169 Holt
170 Rhyn Park   171 Tanat Valley   172 Brompton   173 Dymock   174 Hindwell Farm
175 Clifford   176 Flint   178 Bridgend   179 Neath

Professor St Joseph has pointed out, it is hardly a coincidence that the camp is adjacent to a native fortified enclosure.

When one considers the overall picture now emerging from the discoveries from the air and on the ground, the Roman military control appears to have been rather thin, but this is probably due to the lack of evidence. There is only one full-size fort, that at North Tawton (No 216); the others are half-size or fortlets, or may be signal stations, and there is so far no suggestion of any coastal control. There may be a hint in another place-name given by Ptolemy – Uxella, probably surviving an early army list. It is placed on the north Devon coast, and possibly in the area of Barnstaple and the Taw Estuary (No 226) – appropriately enough since the Uxella means water or river.[14] Assuming units at the larger estuaries, this would have involved only another four units or half units. Other impressions are that, after the initial campaign, the Roman command was not seriously concerned about any further serious resistance or potential hostility. Why then it was necessary to place *Legio II Aug.* at Exeter, is far from clear, unless the potential hostility was overestimated. The Exeter site would enable the legion to look both ways and move rapidly in either direction, should danger threaten.[15] Here we must consider the important link with the nearest port on the Bristol Channel, and it may be significant that the Stoke Hill signal station (S6) to the north of the fortress could have been the first in a chain, passing and sending information up and down the Culm Valley and across to the Parrett where the fleet could have had a base. Looking ahead to the events in the great revolt of 60, one can understand the concern of the army over the uncertain temper of the natives. One explanation for the failure of *Legio II Aug.* to respond to the summons of Suetonius Paullinus to join his forces in the Midlands to face Boudica[16] and her vast horde of rebels, is that the legion was pinned down in its fortress by a large native force. The first cohort was presumably with the governor in Wales, since the man in command at Exeter was the *praefectus castrorum*, and this could only have been possible in the absence of the *legatus* and the senior tribune. Poenius Postumus was placed in a terrible dilemma, and his decision to stay put forced him to commit suicide. The Durotriges may have been able to cajole the Dumnonii to rise with them, significantly there is no evidence of destruction at Nanstallon and the small force would have stood little chance against a determined native attack in any strength. One can only conclude that any help given by the Dumnonii was of a token nature.

Route 38: Bourton-on-the-Water to Wall

This is an extension of the Plautian route from the Fosse Way to the outpost site at Alcester (No 103), thence almost due north to Wall (No 151). A fort at Alcester is known from air photographs (Pl 11) to occupy the escarpment on the south side of the river Alne, overlooking the valley. This would have been an appropriate site for a frontier post, but with the forward advance, the incoming unit may have preferred a position on the lower ground by the river, where the later civil settlement developed. Although there has been a considerable amount of excavation in the past four decades, no sign of any military defences, or structures, has been noticed. Two items of cavalry equipment turned up, however, in one of Steven Taylor's excavations in Bleachfield Street.

Metchley

Midway between Alcester and Wall is the military site at Metchley (No 154), partly covered by the Medical School of Birmingham University. The site was first identified by Professor St Joseph in 1934, when the new Medical School was built. A rescue excavation was carried out, and the outlines of two forts, one within the other, were plotted; the area of the larger one was $14\frac{1}{2}$ acres and the smaller $6\frac{1}{4}$ acres, and it was

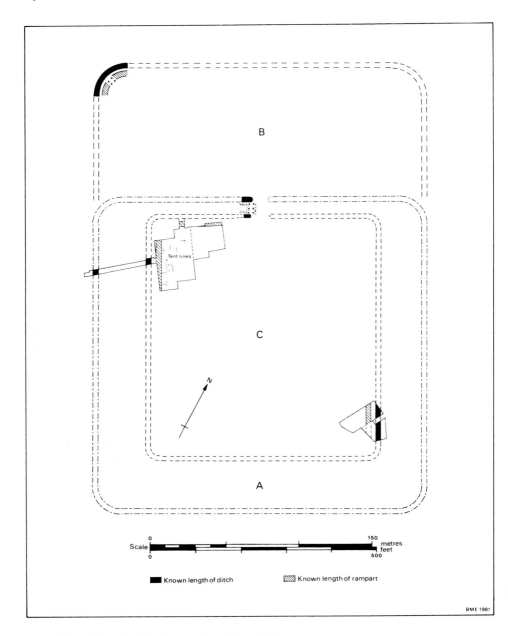

24   Plan of the Metchley forts (after T. Rowley)

evident that the smaller was the later of the two.[17] The scraps of pottery were mainly pre-Flavian, one decorated samian form 29, being identified by Dr Felix Oswald as Neronian (Report No 8). In 1954, small investigations were made at the north-west corner of what was later to be seen as a northern annexe of the larger fort and the plan of the corner tower was revealed.[18] When this fort was demolished, trenches had been dug into the reduced rampart to recover the massive posts. These trenches were then filled with charcoal from the burning of small timbers resulting from the demolition.

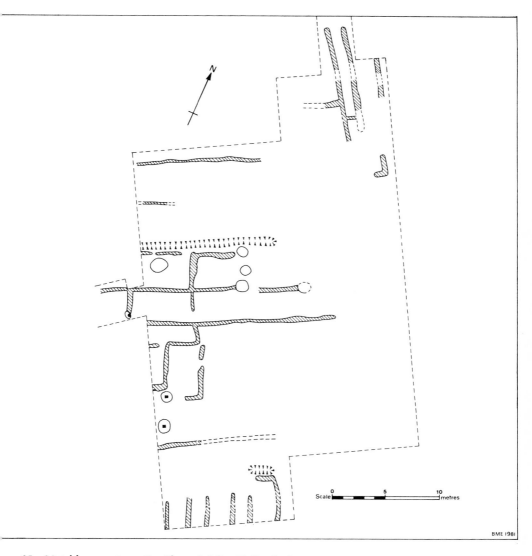

N

Scale 0 5 10 metres

BME 1981

25   Metchley: western site, Phase A (after T. Rowley)

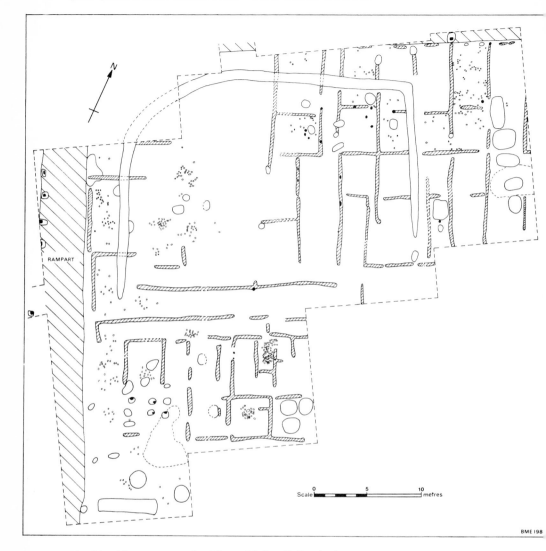

26   Metchley: western site, Phase C (after T. Rowley)

This was clear evidence of the short life of this larger fort; the timbers were presumably used for the smaller one being built at the same time. Through the generosity of the Common Good Trust, a tower was later reconstructed, the same size posts being placed in the four post-holes. This fine public-spirited and educational venture became, however, an obvious playground for local youngsters; no depart-ment of the City Council could be found to take responsibility for protecting the tower and sadly the ruins had eventually to be tidied away. Also in 1954, the west half of the north gate of the smaller fort were stripped and the plan of its six post-pits recovered. Further work was done on 1968–9 in advance of extensions to the hospital. This was

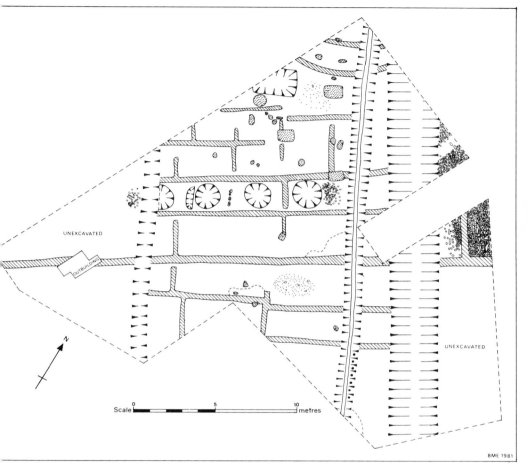

27   Metchley, Camp Cottages site: plan of Phase A buildings (after T. Rowley)

directed by Trevor Rowley and his report is yet to be published although, however, a brief survey has appeared[19] and the excavator's conclusions are that there is evidence of three periods in the following sequence:

1. A 10½-acre campaign camp or *hiberna*, the tent lines of which were found in one area (B on the plan).

2. This was converted into a fort. In the western area there were barrack-blocks on a north-south alignment and to the south a granary. On the Camp Cottage site there was an interesting courtyard building with a row of four rooms, each with a large pit in its centre. To this fort was added a 4-acre annexe on the north side, but this appears to be devoid of buildings (A).[20]

69

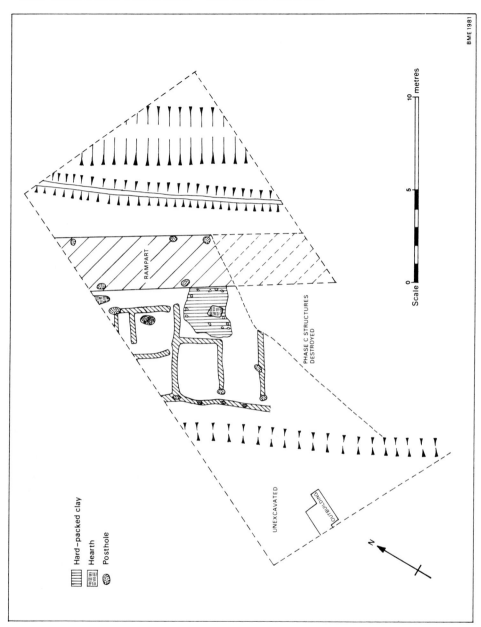

28   Metchley, Camp Cottages site: Plan of surviving Phase C buildings and defences
(after T. Rowley)

3.   The larger fort was later demolished and within it a 6½-acre fort constructed (C). In
the western area there were barrack-blocks on a north-south alignment and to the
south of which was a large courtyard building which in this position may have been a

fabrica. The rampart of this fort had a vertical timber revetment found both on the western side and on the Camp Cottage site.

It is not possible to comment on the chronology of these sequences until the full report is published, but the third phase appears to be late first-century, extending into the second, showing a continual military control of the area as at Wall, Wall Town, etc. Although one would not expect a large fort of over 10 acres to have been fully occupied throughout the previous campaigns, it would fit well into the Scapulan advance.

The Route is joined by Route 42 at Metchley and thence to Wall on Route 27.

The Frontier Route 39 from the Dee to the Usk

The Fort at Chester (No 138)

The most important land route to be considered is the great north to south communication link from the estuary of the Dee to that of the Usk. Starting from the north, while there is no direct evidence of an auxiliary unit at Chester under Scapula, there is enough to support a pre-legionary occupation. The most important discovery, so far, was made in 1848, during the digging for a drain at the rear of a house in Northgate Street, north of the Cathedral.[21] A hole, cut into the rock and covered with a stone slab, contained a flagon full of burnt bones, and two others were later found nearby and a fourth on 'the very edge of the Dean's Field'. The flagon was illustrated by Watkins but it was not appreciated that his drawing was inaccurate until the vessel was found in the Grosvenor Museum; it was subsequently redrawn and published.[22] This flagon shape is difficult to date with any precision, but it has an interesting affinity with the collection of similar vessels from Mancetter (p 49). It would certainly fit a Claudio-Neronian context and this cremation clearly indicates the presence of a military establishment at Chester pre-dating the founding of the legionary fortress. Further adjustments to the frontier may have been made under Didius Gallus, and Suetonius Paullinus probably established a naval base here for his attack on Anglesey. One could thus expect a succession of sites of differing kinds, not all necessarily even in the area of the later fortress. We shall return to this problem when the reorganisation under Gallus is considered in the appropriate sequence below. It should be noted here that the earliest timber phase at Goss Street had been dated from samian and brooches to AD 40–50.[23] If this is a correct assessment, this fragment of building should belong to an auxiliary unit. But the difficulty is that it is the first phase in a sequence of barrack-blocks of the legionary fortress, and the presence of a legion here under Scapula hardly seems likely.

The next site to the south would have been at Whitchurch (No 140) where a military origin has been proved,[24] and a small fragment of a timber fort of the early Flavian period (i.e. 65–75) studied. However, there were earlier features consisting of fragments of timber buildings with wattle and daub, which had been deliberately demolished. Unfortunately, no dating evidence was found.[25] It would need a large-area excavation at Whitchurch to date and identify its earliest military occupation.

Wroxeter (Viroconium, No 142)

The route aligned due south in its next stretch is aimed at Wroxeter. After the Eaton Constantine fort the next establishment in the Scapulan scheme appears to be the auxiliary fort found at the river crossing by Professor St Joseph in 1945, and subsequently trenched by him.[26] It is a 5.66-acre fort, large enough to suggest cavalry and placed to guard the river crossing, which could at this stage have been a pontoon bridge. The dating evidence recovered from the excavation was meagre, and all that the few pottery scraps indicate is a pre-Flavian date (i.e. before 70). The tombstone of a trooper of a Thracian *cohors equitata* (*RIB* 291) was found at Wroxeter 'near the blacksmith shop',[27] but it had probably been moved from its original position, and used as a building stone. An early cremation burial was found by Bushe-Fox in 1912 on the west edge of the later main N–S street of the city. This placed the burial just beyond the outer edge of the legionary defences, which almost certainly means that the two cannot have been contemporary. Thus the cremation must be earlier than the founding of the legionary fortress. The burial is half-a-mile from the auxiliary fort by the river crossing and the possibility of a nearer establishment cannot be entirely discounted. It is not, of course, certain that the burial was that of a soldier, since the only object with the burnt bones was a melon-bead. Although soldiers are known to have decorated their equipment with these glass beads, they were equally used by their camp followers. The 1955–85 excavations at Wroxeter produced much new information (report forthcoming); there is a summary in *Fortress*, pp. 120–136.

Proceeding slightly to the south-west towards the Church Stretton gap, Professor St Joseph has suggested that a site may be found near Leebotwood.[28] The next point at Stretford Bridge (No 143) is just north of Craven Arms, where the unmistakable outline of an auxiliary fort has been recorded by Professor St Joseph[29] in 1969, at the crossing of the Onny. It is $3\frac{3}{4}$ acres in size, but as yet undated. There are two overlapping campaign camps to the south of this fort.[30]

To the south again, the next stop is in the Leintwardine area (No 215) at the junction of the rivers Onny and Clun; this nodal point of routes offers direct access to Central Wales. Its key strategic position is reflected in the large number of military sites, three and possibly four forts and two campaign camps.[31] The three forts have been studied by Dr Stan Stanford, and his excavations[32] have shown that the earliest of them is the Jay Lane 5.6-acre fort, occupying a position commanding the low-lying area north of the Teme. The dating evidence consists of five sherds of samian which Brian Hartley places in the AD 50–70 bracket, which, as Dr Stanford has indicated, would fit reasonably well into the Scapulan advance. However, since then, Professor St Joseph has made a further suggestion, on the basis of traces of Roman military buildings which he has observed inside the small Iron Age fortress at Brandon Camp (No 144) to the south of the river junction and occupying a commanding position. Professor St Joseph, however, has been able to establish by a small-scale excavation that his photographs show a large military granary and a substantial building consisting of a series of rectangular structures, possibly round a courtyard, which is difficult to identify;[33] further excavations by Professor S.S. Frere have produced the plan of a storebase and ample dating evidence. The site now offers a striking parallel to Hod Hill, but the pottery suggests a date which would best fit the advance under Veranius.

Between Leintwardine and the crossing of the Wye near Kenchester, there would have been at least one intermediate post at the crossing of either the Lugg or the Arrow (No 145). These two points are only three miles apart, but much of the land between would have been a marshy flood plain. So the possibilities resolve themselves into either Mortimers Cross, the site of a battle in 1461, or Street Court, about a mile south-west of Kingsland. The position of the outpost fort at Hindwell Farm (No 174) does not help in the choice, but there is also the presence of the large Iron Age fort at Croft

Ambrey, which would favour the northern of the two suggestions, if a large potentially hostile force still occupied the site. The excavations of Croft Ambrey by Dr Stanford in 1960–6[34] produced evidence of the destruction of some of the huts and a reduction of the rampart at the time of the Conquest, although no objects of Roman weapons or military equipment were found.[35]

From this point the route would have been aimed at a crossing of the Wye near Kenchester, the small Roman town, and this may have been at the point where a bridge was later built. The route would have passed by the large Iron Age fort at Credenhill. Dr Stanford carried out a limited programme of excavations in 1963 inside the 50-acre site and concluded that it was the main power centre for the area,[36] probably held by the unknown tribe which occupied much of what is now north Herefordshire and south Shropshire. The evidence from the excavation suggested a quiet and gradual end of this occupation, with no sign of violent destruction. This appears to contrast with the discoveries made 15 miles to the south at Sutton Walls, an hill-fort which commanded the Lugg Valley.[37] Kathleen Kenyon found that in her phase D, 'the ditch at the west entrance was hurriedly recut. Before any silt had accumulated in the recut ditch, a large number of bodies, some decapitated and others with evidence of wounds, were thrown into the ditch and covered with a thin layer of soil.'[38] Later in the Report it is stated (p 7): 'This recutting of the ditch belongs to the last stage in the history of the camp, before a great disaster, and almost certainly to its last stage as a fortified site.' Unfortunately, no artefacts were found with the skeletons, except a single sherd of Roman pottery, but its precise association was not secure (Report, 9). The fact that the defenders were slighted, and the ramparts pushed in over the bodies, was the final evidence that convinced Dr Kenyon that this slaughter was the work of Roman troops. Occupation was, however, allowed to continue on the hill – but whether after an interval of time was not established. It may be significant that in the extensive pottery report there is not a sherd among the Romano-British wares which could be earlier than the mid-second century[39] (Report, 41–57). The only earlier Roman object is a part of a melon bead (fig 25, no 5), a very common object to be found with the army in the first century. There was probably a fort where the route crossed the Wye, but it has not yet been noticed.

Kenchester (Magnis fig 29, No 146)
The Roman town of Kenchester is just over half-a-mile from the river, but it lies to the north-west of the main military route which must have turned sharply towards the known river crossing near Magna Castra Farm (possibly at the crossing of the east-west road, which is the main street of this town). This raises the possibility that the town originated, like so many others, as the civil settlement outside a first-century fort, which on this line of argument should be found to the south-east or east of the town. Even so, military objects have been found in the excavations of 1912–13 and 1924–25 inside the Roman town.[40] They consist of three harness pendants: a fine leaf-shape (1916 Report, pl 50, no 5); a more common type (1926 Report, pl 33, no 15); and a similar one now in the Whiting Collection in the City Museum, Hereford.[41] This suggests the nearby presence of a cavalry unit. No less than five melon beads were also recovered (1916 Report, pl 45, nos 5, 7, 9, 11 and 16), but no coins are recorded earlier than Vespasian. The site of a Roman bridge across the Wye is known from the road alignment on the south bank and also from the discovery of massive timber piles.[42]

29   Leaf-pendant of a horse harness from Kenchester (full size)

This is probably near the early military crossing, although a pontoon bridge may have been used in the campaigning years.

The route is now aimed at the Usk Valley which it joined at Abergavenny. It first crossed to the Dore Valley at a point north of Abbeydore, thence to the junction of the Monnow, turning up this and then down the Gavenny. In this long stretch there must have been a fort at a mid-way position. The terrain between Abbeydore and Ewyas Harald is not suitable, but to the south-west of Pontrilas there is more open country with commanding views along the valleys towards Monmouth and Abergavenny. A suitable site (No 147) would be the projecting spur in a bend in the Monnow almost at the boundary with Wales. This would have been linked with Monmouth, via a route now passing the later castles of Grosmont and Skenfrith. The route then proceeds to Abergavenny which occupies a very commanding position, where the Usk emerges from its narrow valley.

Abergavenny (Gobannium, No 148)
Abergavenny is on the site of the small Roman town of Gobannium, a name associated with iron working.[43] The site is a spur on a steep slope, on the south-west side running down to the river. The southern end narrows sharply and is occupied by the medieval castle. The fort was sited on the small area of level ground and presumably the civil settlement spread out down the slope, in a north-westerly direction along the road towards Brecon. Excavations, in advance of development in the years 1962–9, produced evidence of a military ditch system in Flannel Street and timber buildings in Castle Street.[44] Then in 1972, on the Orchard site,[45] a typical granary was found

behind a turf and timber rampart. The alignment of the building and defences shows that there must have been some erosion on the steep slope on the river side. Most of the datable finds come the 'dump' site at the base of the escarpment; the fact that its lower levels have produced exclusively early Roman material has suggested that this was the military rubbish tip – named by the German and Swiss archaeologists a *schutthügel*.[46] George Boon's report on the Abergavenny finds includes a remarkable coin of Augustus, which had almost worn flat and was counter-stamped to continue its valid life.[47] The samian includes six pieces of form 29 and ten plain vessels, all of south Gaulish manufacture and undoubted Claudian date (Report 178–85); there are other imported early fine wares. All this material would suggest the presence of Roman troops by the early fifties. The bronzes include two buckles from the straps of a baldric and a loop-shanked triskele pendant, showing strong Celtic influence but comparable with similar objects from Claudian military sites in Britain.[48]

Usk (Burrium, No 149)
The route followed the River Usk down to its estuary and the next site is at Usk, where an early legionary base was partially excavated in 1965–76[49] (see p. 108 below). It would seem unlikely that Scapula or Gallus would have placed such an establishment in an advance position, so it probably belonged to the later advance under Veranius. Logically there ought to be an auxiliary fort here as part of the Scapulan frontier. This may well underlie the later site on the highest part of the site where no excavations have yet been undertaken. The pottery from the excavations has been intensively studied, and the conclusion is that occupation belongs to the later rather than the early 50s.[50]

Caerleon (Isca, No 150)
The obvious terminal for the route is at Caerleon on the estuary. This was the site of the legionary fortress of *Legio II Aug.* and the generally accepted date for its foundation is AD 75. Excavations[51] have been limited by the presence of a large modern village and much of the area within the fortress has never been tested. Mr Boon tells me that in his opinion the earliest material seems to be concentrated in the central part of the eastern sector, and it is possible that detailed excavations may yet reveal the presence of an auxiliary fort of the Scapulan period.[52] The small earthwork at Coed-y-Caerau on the hills on the east side of the river, with an excellent view upstream, may have been a signal station,[53] if it belongs to this period. It is unfortunate that one of the earliest fragments of samian in Wales has a doubtful provenance. It is a form 30 assigned to the potter V O L V S (who was working in the period AD 35–55) and is now in the collection of the National Museum of Wales.[54] Sadly it is an old find which has lost its label, and could have come from excavations either at Caerleon or Usk.

Route 27

This became, under Scapula, the main route to the north-west, eventually extending to Chester and the north. It had little significance in the Plautian scheme, the pivot of which was the British capital and main military base at Camulodunum. When the full importance of London was recognised as a nodal point in the army communication network for northern Britain, there was an immediate shift in the pattern: one of the results of which was the development of Route 27. It crossed the Fosse at High Cross (Venonae, No 94), but the only military site so far discovered has been a possible small signal station (*Invasion*, p. 162). Beyond this was the Plautian outpost at Mancetter (Manduessedum, No L9) which, as seen above (p. 47), became the site of the fortress of *Legio XIV* at an early stage of the Scapulan advance, presumably replacing an earlier Plautian auxiliary fort. The next site at Wall, near Lichfield (Letocetum, No 151), was established on the edge of a north-south sandstone ridge, giving extensive views towards the west and the south. This commanding position marked it as a key military site. Much evidence has been found, which clearly shows a succession of permanent establishments of different sizes and dates and a campaign camp half-a-mile to the west.[55] The devoted labours, over many years, of a small excavation team under the direction of Jim Gould, Bert Round and latterly Frank and Nancy Ball, have produced a mass of detailed information which has still to be synthesized. Jim Gould found by excavation a series of forts built on the highest point,[56] beginning in the Claudian period and ending with a small site dated to the early second century – a strong indication of the importance attached to this position by the Roman army. There is evidence of a large, and, probably, legionary base here too, at one time, thought to have been that of *Legio XIV* prior to its move to Wroxeter. However, the pottery associated with it seems to be Neronian rather than Claudian and the discoveries at Mancetter have now discounted this earlier conjecture. Very little military equipment has been found to help in the resolution of these difficulties, but old excavations have produced two inscribed bronze tags bearing the names of centurions (VITALIS and PRO[. . .] MEN. . .). They are now in the site museum and are probably baggage labels, but, as centurions were also officers in the auxiliary units, they are not necessarily legionary.

30   Bronze tags with punched letters of the names of centurions from Wall (full size)

The next site to the west is also a very complicated one around the small posting station and *burgus* of Pennocrucium (No 152). It has been the persistent recording over the years by Professor St Joseph which has produced evidence of military establishments in three different places. In the absence of ground investigations, it is at present impossible to place them in chronological order (fig 32). They are:

1. A 3½-acre auxiliary fort on a small gravel plateau at Stretton Mill (A) on the east side of the River Penk.[57] Arnold Baker has observed that this fort was preceded by a slightly larger one, as one type of auxiliaries replaced another, possibly cavalry followed by infantry. The defences were trenched by Professor St Joseph in 1947, and typical V-shaped ditches lined with clay were sectioned, but no closely datable pottery found.

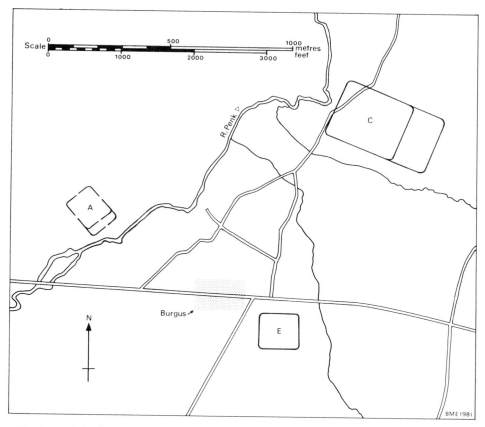

32   Map of the forts at Pennocrucium (after Professor J. K. St Joseph)

2. A 5-acre fort (E) lies immediately to the south-east of the *burgus* and stands on a visible square plateau, which is covered by the sinuous ridge and furrow, typical of the swing plough of a later period. Professor St Joseph, on a surface inspection after ploughing, noted the appearance of 'turfy soil and burnt oven debris' and indications of the metalling of the main north-south street.[58]

3. A 26-acre fort, later reduced to 16 acres, at Kinvaston (C), to the north-east on the east bank of the Penk.[59] This site has been trenched and the few scraps of pottery suggest a Neronian rather than a Claudian date.[60]

There is also a campaign camp or temporary enclosure to the south-west of this fort. It is noteworthy that at this point in the route there is the important branch, in a north-easterly direction towards Chester, which played, no doubt, a significant part in the crucial events of the great revolt of 60. It bears the name of The Longford, and at mid-point there is a place called Camp Farm (No 139) (ST 747249)[61] about a mile east of Sambrook. The farm stands on a small plateau overlooking the small river Meese and would have been a very suitable site for a fort. But no finds have been made here, nor has close ground inspection produced any sign of ditches or banks. There is also a connection from Pennocrucium due south, meeting the Severn at Worcester and then probably continuing north to Trent Vale and the Mersey crossing which was part of a later defensive scheme. Only further and more intensive excavations will ultimately reveal which of the two military sites here belong to the Scapulan period. Proceeding westwards, there are two campaign camps by the route at Burlington.[62]

Red Hill (Uxacona, No 153)

About 12 miles to the west there is another escarpment, similar to that of Wall, with a commanding view of the Shropshire Plain stretching towards the north-west. This is the highest point along the whole length of the route. There is a small settlement and *burgus* here at Red Hill (the Roman name of which seems to mean a 'high place').[63] On the higher ground to the north side of the road the crop-marks of the two forts, one within the other, have been recorded by Professor St Joseph.[64] An apron-mount has been found on the surface[65] and much of the site has been destroyed by the construction of a reservoir, but not before an excavation was carried out by David Browne.[66] The larger site proved to be a single-ditched enclosure with a revetted rampart and was thought to have been a stores depôt. The smaller site had two ditches and appears to have been a small police post or signal station, occupied into the late first century, like a similar one at Wall. The next site is at Wroxeter, which has been considered fully above (p. 49), where the route joins Route 39.

Route 43

This route would have been a crucial communication route along the east bank of the Severn. A road from Gloucester is known as far as Worcester, but there is no evidence that it continued along the river side any further. It seems inconceivable that the army would not have had complete control of this important river and its crossing points. It would in itself have been an important supply route with river craft of the Fleet. In the present state of ignorance one can only make calculated guesses based on possible crossing points connected with known sites and this very tentative forecast is the only one which can be suggested at this stage.

The first post north of Gloucester must have been at the junction of the Severn and the Warwickshire Avon, near Tewkesbury (No 155), the strategic importance of which is demonstrated in its later history. The obvious site for a fort would be the commanding position overlooking the Severn on the spur known as The Mythe (Old English for a river junction). However, although there is a Norman motte (The Myth Tute or Royal Hill) partly lost in a landslip into the river, no evidence of a Roman site is at present known. The later Roman road passed across this area and a section produced material suggesting a nearby Roman settlement.[67] There are two place-names in Ravenna between Gloucester and Droitwich which have not been identified, and this site could have been the first of them – Argistillum, which appears to refer to a hostage.[68] It is perhaps fanciful to imply that the name could have arisen from an incident during which an important Briton was held here by the army at this period. Worcester (No 156) is sited on a river terrace on a crossing of the Severn where it is joined by a small stream, the Frog Brook.[69] This became the site of a Norman motte and bailey castle and the great cathedral church of St Peter, founded in the seventh century. In spite of recent excavations and a careful watch of the recent redevelopment in the central area, no trace of the military presence has yet been found, although there is evidence of a defended Iron Age site[70] and at least seven British coins have turned up in the neighbourhood.[71] This clearly shows the significance of the river crossing in pre-Roman times and why the army would almost certainly have wished to control it.[72]

From Worcester to Wroxeter, following the river, is a distance of about 40 miles, and at least one, more likely two forts would have held key crossing points. The most significant factor in identifying these and the routes to the west is the rugged terrain to the west of the river dominated by the Clee Hills, which rise to about 2000ft, while between the hills and river stretched the Wyre Forest, considerably larger than it is today. The topography would have forced the army to use the Teme Valley to the south and Corve Dale round the north side. The siting of the fort at Wall Town (No 161), near Cleobury Mortimer, implies an E–W route (44) which could have crossed the river at a mid-way point between Worcester and Wroxeter in the Alveley-Highley area (No 159). There are elements of a trackway from Greensforge to Alveley on the one-inch map, but it is very difficult country to traverse, with its rocky hills and, what, at that period, was probably dense forest. The northern of the two possible routes would have meant a crossing at or near Bridgnorth where it joins Route 41. There are two significant place-names nearby; one is Oldbury on the west bank of the Severn, the other Quatford (No 160) lower down on the east bank, the site of a Norman motte. The name of Cwatbrycg[73] (i.e. Cwatt's bridge) for this place is given in the Anglo-Saxon Chronicle as the wintering place of the Danish army in 890. A bridge at this date could only have been of Roman origin, which seems to be clear evidence of a road crossing at this point. This further implies a route (41) from Greensforge (No 158), but the only possible surviving element is a track over Gags Hill and, at the south-eastern end, a short stretch of parish boundary from Greensforge. From the Quatford crossing point of the Severn to Wroxeter, there would have been the problem of establishing a route through the Iron Bridge gap. It may have been better for the army to have used the more open country on the west bank and cut off the river bend, following, more or less, the line of the modern A58 from Morville to Cressage, which according to Ogilby,[74] was the road from London to Shrewsbury in the late seventeenth century. It may be significant that the large Eaton Constantine fort appears to be guarding a N–S crossing of the river somewhere near the present bridge at Cressage.

There is another possible route linking Greensforge with Wroxeter, which can be followed in small lanes and tracks in a north-westerly direction, making for a crossing of the River Worfe near Roughton or Wyken. Part of this route was Ogilby's highway to London, and along it one finds names such as Highgate Common, White Cross and The Cross; but, more relevant to our purpose, is the significant name of Winchester, a small hamlet less than a mile south of Claverley. However, the place is only 4½ miles from Greensforge and could hardly have been a staging point. Beyond the Worfe this route would have run into serious difficulties in the broken country north of Coalbrook-dale. It is always better to work from the known, rather than to launch into speculation. We should therefore note that there is a short length of road from Greensforge (Route 56) pointing towards Red Hill on Watling Street (Route 27). This distance of 18 miles would not have needed a fort midway, except perhaps to keep an eye on the occupants of the large univallate hill-fort at Chesterton Walls – a name derived no doubt from the Iron Age defences, rather than from a nearby Roman Fort.

Route 42

This is the route from the Wye Valley crossing the Severn at Worcester (No 156) and then on to Metchley (No 154) where it joins the north-south Route 38. The only known fort along the stretch north-east from Worcester is at Droitwich (Salinae, No 157), a place of considerable economic importance due to the presence of the brine springs which produces some of the purest salt in north-west Europe.[75] Excavations have produced evidence of the Iron Age and Roman industry.[76] This site is also the centre of a web of salt-ways which can be traced to the coast. While most of these are medieval routes, many probably have a prehistoric origin. As Droitwich is only six miles from Worcester, the placing of a fort here suggests some protection for this valuable natural commodity which was probably under Imperial control, like the silver works. The fort is on the hill-top at Dodderhill overlooking the River Salwarpe, but, in spite of recent investigations, very little is known about it. The site was first excavated by Professor St Joseph and H.R. Hodgkinson in 1938–39, after pottery had been found in digging a trench for a sewer. Trenches were cut across two parallel ditches, the outer one having an almost vertical outer face, typical of the military Punic ditch. The profiles of this ditch and the plan of the enclosure prompted the conclusions that this site was an early Roman fort, although only two sides could be found. The defended area seemed to be at least ten acres. Two Claudian coins were found and a quantity of samian sherds of Claudian-Neronian date, although some pieces were somewhat later.[77] A further investigation in 1961–62 by David Whitehouse located the western side of the defences and traces of internal timber buildings showing at least two periods[78] c.47–70 and c.120–150; but whether the second period was military was not established. Further work was carried out by David Freezer in advance of an extension of the burial area round the church. He found elements of timber structures and two large rectangular pits which may have been tanks filled with rubbish on demolition. More remarkable is his coin series which includes 12 Claudian imitations and an *as* of Nero. There were also six interesting early brooches and his few pieces of equipment seem to be of harness, which suggests cavalry.

Proceeding in the other direction from Worcester to the Wye Valley, the Severn crossing has always been an important one[79] and the route across the flood plain was probably carried by a log causeway laid down by the army. On the west bank the route may have divided, since there is a hint of a Saxon name of a road skirting off to the north-west towards Blackwardine,[80] or possibly Leintwardine. In the latter case, it would have passed by a fort postulated at Tedstone Wafer. This is a site found by Professor St Joseph and has every appearance of being a Roman fortlet, an acre in size. A section was cut across the south side in 1954[81] and this showed military type ditches (one a V-shaped profile and the other a Punic type) and the base of an 18ft wide rampart. The difficulty in accepting the site as of Scapulan date was the discovery of fragments of a vessel in the inner ditch fill of a type of wide-mouth bowl which is normally dated to the second century. The main route heads for Stretton Grandison (No 163), then crosses Route 46, thence to Kenchester (No 146) where it seems to by-pass the town to the south (which may in itself indicate an earlier nucleus (i.e. a fort, see p. 73 above), then westwards to the outpost fort at Clifford (No 175). Further work has been carried out by the Central Unit and a report is forthcoming.

Route 44: Greensforge to Leintwardine

As indicated above, this route would have been through very difficult country and nothing is known of it; even the site of the Severn crossing had to be guessed. But at Wall Town[82] (No 161), about two miles to the north-east of Cleobury Mortimer, is a sequence of forts. The site is listed in *VCH. Shrops* (i, 1908, 378–80) among the 'simple defensive inclosures' and road widening in 1929 produced roof and hypocaust tiles and fragments of Roman pottery.[83] It was Professor St Joseph's observations from the air that identified the earthwork as military.[84] The defences were examined in 1960 and 1961 by Ian Walker and the Kidderminster Archaeological Society. The visible rampart was found to have been built on an existing site represented by a clay floor covered by demolition material, suggesting the presence of an earlier fort, but no associated dating evidence was found. The earliest pottery consisted of two sherds of Neronian-early-Flavian samian, but the defences belong to a Flavian fort to which was added a stone wall in the second century. There is evidence of an earlier enclosure on the north side and it seems likely that this is on the side buried below the later occupation, a Neronian fort, and further work is clearly needed. The route presumably followed the Rea Valley to the Teme, then turned towards the Ludlow gap and Leintwardine.

Route 46

The southern part of this route is linked with the Bristol Channel. The sea passage across this stretch must have been highly significant in the early phases of Scapula's campaigns, and has been considered separately (see p. 53). The land route connected the coastal sites from Cardiff and possibly others to the west at the Usk crossing. It may have passed through Caerwent, which was to become Venta Silurum, the tribal capital of the Silures. The question of its origins has often been asked, and one answer could have been the presence here of a first-century auxiliary fort.[85] It is doubtful if the early excavations of the town[86] would have been deep enough to have recovered evidence, or even to have recognised any timber structures.

Route 48: Gloucester to Stretford Bridge

This was an important route across the Herefordshire Plain and the shortest line of communication between the Gloucester base and the upper Severn Valley. The first possible site would be Dymock (No 173), where there is evidence of a late Iron Age and Romano-British settlement. Small-scale excavations in and around the village by the Malvern Research Group failed to locate a military presence except for a coin of the Republic, *denarii* of Tiberius and Nerva and an *as* of Nero.[87] The next site to the south of Stretton Grandison (No 163), a known Roman settlement,[88] is more certain since Arnold Baker has recorded from the air a definite fort on the south bank of the River Frome (pl 15);[89] but no site investigation has yet been carried out. It is 4.8 acres in size and could have held a cavalry unit, but no dating evidence has yet been obtained. The Roman road passes about 1300ft to the west of the fort on its way to the river crossing and a point where there was presumably a bridge. North of the river the route keeps to the fairly level terrain and crosses the road between Kenchester and Worcester, then joins Route 46, at or near Blackwardine, where an extensive Roman settlement is known (No 162).[90] Surface finds and small-scale excavations by local enthusiasts seem to suggest that the settlement was to the east of the accepted line of the Roman road, which makes this particular alignment suspect. Across the northern part of the site is a deep railway cutting, of the old Leominster to Worcester line, which suffered the axe, became disused and had the tracks removed. In 1980, the Leominster District Council decided to fill the cutting with refuse, thus reclaiming useful land. A short length of the north side cutting was removed by machinery and this exposed several pits and possibly timber structural features. One of the pits produced a small collection of decorated samian of Flavian date;[91] but among the earlier finds coins of both Augustus and Claudius are mentioned as having been discovered, which may possibly indicate a military presence somewhere in the vicinity.

Route 52

Tedstone Wafer, precisely half-way between Stretton Grandison and Wall Town, lies on an ancient route called High Lane. This could well have connected Gloucester, via Route 48 from Stretton Grandison, to Wall Town, thence up the Rea Valley to join Route 41.

Route 56: Greensforge (No 158)

The route to Greensforge is well known and has been examined near Chaddesley Corbett.[92] The military establishment at Greensforge was first investigated in 1928 by the boys from Wolverhampton Grammar School, who cut a section through an earthwork known as 'Wolverhampton Old Churchyard', and identified it as a Roman fort of the first century.[93] Since then aerial reconnaissance by Professor St Joseph and Arnold Baker have indicated the importance of this site with the discovery of another fort adjacent to the known one to which is attached an annexe or campaign camp, and four more examples of the latter in the vicinity.[94] Excavations by the Kidderminster Archaeological Society on the fort more recently discovered have not added a great deal, except to place it firmly in the Claudian-Neronian period.[95] Among the pottery found is a group of distinctive ware which is unusual on non-military sites. The military equipment includes cavalry items such as harness trappings and a barnacle-bit.[96] Local field groups have plotted the spread of later civil occupation on the west side of Smestow Brook − presumably along a road in this direction making for Wall Town. Greensforge, which occupies a key position in the centre of a larger area bounded by the Severn, Watling Street and the Worcester-Wall route, could well repay closer study.

The Outpost Forts

The main objective in the placing of forward units was to control the points of exit from north and central Wales from which hostile bands could emerge. In the northern section, the tribe concerned was the Deceangli, which had suffered badly from the sudden and savage reconnaissance at the start of the Scapulan campaign. The Romans may have considered these people as having been beaten into submission but nevertheless requiring careful watching. For this purpose, a fort in advance of Chester along the Dee Estuary may have been Flint (No 176), where later Roman remains have been associated with lead smelting.[97] There may well have been a route south from Chester on the west side of the Dee, and a possible site would have been at a crossing of the river at Farndon or near Holt (No 169), which was later to become the works depôt

33   Baldric-mount with eyelet from Greensforge (full size)

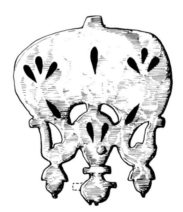

34   Bronze pendant, decorated with niello inlay, of a horse harness from Greensforge (full size)

of *Legio XX*.[98] From this point southwards, the course of the Dee swings towards the west into the Llangollen Pass. The river has two sharp bends, first to the south, then to the east in an inverted S pattern. The point at which it finally emerges into the Cheshire plain had been that chosen as a base for the strong reconnaissance thrust at the beginning of Scapula's campaign (see p. 22 above) and this continued to be held.

Rhyn Park (No 170, pl 16)

The Rhyn Park site is on the River Ceiriog, blocking its exit. The site is a flat plateau, well protected by the deep cutting of the Ceiriog on the north side, and the little Morlas Brook to the east, at a point almost a mile south of the actual junction with the Dee. It was first noticed by Professor St Joseph[99] and later studied from the air, and excavated by Professor Barri Jones of the University of Manchester[100] and proved to be extremely complicated. There are two quite distinct establishments. The first is a legionary-size enclosure of about $48\frac{1}{2}$ acres (10.57 hectares), including the defences while the second is a fort of about 11 acres. The former began, however, as a campaign camp with associated ovens, and this, presumably, belongs to the initial raiding force. After a brief interval it was strengthened with additional defences. The rows of field ovens, paucity of pottery and absence of timber buildings, clearly indicates the presence of troops under canvas during a campaign. The smaller fort has not yet been investigated, but it is possible that this was of a more permanent nature, with a strong force stationed here as an outpost fort to prevent the Ordovices from using the Dee route for sending raiding parties into the Cheshire Plain.

Brompton (No 172)

The blocking of the Upper Severn Valley presents a difficulty. The obvious site would appear to be that of the later fort at Forden Gaer, which occupied a commanding position in a bend of the river, but there is no evidence here of pre-Flavian occupation. There is, moreover, 4 miles to the south-east, a fort and three campaign camps identified by Professor St Joseph, at Brompton near Church Stoke, on the little river Caebitra.[85] It was sited on a river terrace, which commands extensive views to the north towards the Severn and to the south-east up the Camlad Valley. The presence of the campaign camps, which are quite large, strongly suggests that it was a key position in the Scapulan campaigns, as Professor St Joseph has suggested. He has also found a campaign camp at Glanmihell, about six miles west of Brompton in the small valley of the Mule.[102] This may give us the clue to the siting of the Brompton fort, since it was on a main east-west trackway to the Upper Severn, part of it being the Kerry Hill Ridgeway.[103] The narrow Severn valley below Newtown was probably subject to serious flooding and it would have been difficult to have established a passable route along the marshy valley bottom until extensive drainage had been carried out. Another important factor may have been the need for strong Roman control of this area due to the menacing presence of the two large hill-forts of Ffridd Faldwyn and The Breiddin, guarding the entrance into the Upper Severn Valley. Excavations have shown not only much of their long and interesting histories[104] but also that in the late Iron Age there was a considerable occupation with substantial timber buildings, mainly four-post structures thought to be granaries. It must be presumed that, had this tribe been hostile, both forts would have been stormed and taken, and their warriors killed or enslaved; but this would have left a large number of natives, over whom a watchful eye was necessary. There is a hint of a communication system in the presence of a small signal station on Linley Hill (No 112).[105] One of its sight lines could have been towards Leintwardine, and another to the hills to the south of Brompton fort, but one needs more of these sites for a satisfactory pattern to emerge.

The next valley to consider is that of the River Clun. Thanks to the extensive field work of Tom Hamar, who founded the Clun Museum, and Miss L.F. Chitty, there is no doubt about the importance of this valley as a route in the early prehistoric periods,[106] but there is, as yet, no evidence of a Roman fort.[107] Considering the obvious importance of the Leintwardine area, it may be thought more likely that the Tame offered a greater threat, in which case a fort could be expected in the Knighton area. The identification of a small fort at Discoed in the Upper Lugg Valley, just west of Presteigne, has been disproved by a trial excavation.[108]

Hindwell Farm, Walton (No 174)

The next site to the south is Hindwell Farm, Walton, where an early fort has been investigated. The site was first noticed and trenched in 1956 by Frank Noble, who was the first to suggest the possibility of it being a fort.[109] This view was supported by Professor St Joseph who also observed four campaign camps in the vicinity.[110] Further material, recovered from ploughing in 1969 and published by Mr W.R. Pye,[111] included fragments of samian form 24/35 and form 15/16 and a butt-beaker with fine rouletting. In 1975 excavations from a new silo in the farmyard revealed two ditches, one cutting into the other;[112] the earlier is a V-shaped profile 17ft (5.2m) wide and 8½ft (2.6m) deep and the second, of Punic type (i.e. with a vertical outer side) 21.3ft (6.5m) wide and 7.7ft (2.35m) deep. These ditches appear to be the west side of the fort; 26.3ft (8m) from the inner edge of the ditch inside the fort, was found a sequence of ovens, presumably built into the back of the rampart, which, from the description of the material in the earlier ditch fill, was built of turf. The samian and objects were described in the same report by George Boon. These consist of four Claudian imitation coins and the head of a ballista-bolt with a square section similar to those from Hod Hill. The pieces of samian are all pre-Flavian, including a bowl of Passienus (c.55–65) and, among the coarse wares, a carrot amphora and, what could be, from its description, a 'Pompeian' red-slip dish (No 23).

Proceeding southwards, the next valley is the Wye, which gives access into the Black Mountains and Brecon Beacons and the difficult hill terrain of Mynydd Eppynt. There are two military sites, one at Clyro (No 210) and the other at Clifford (No 175). Clyro has been shown by Professor St Joseph to be a large well-defended site of 26 acres[113] and a limited excavation in 1964 produced evidence of two periods.[114] The earliest piece of samian has been dated to c.60. Professor St Joseph has also found a large campaign camp nearby.[115] Clifford is only 2½ miles east of Clyro, so it could hardly have co-existed with it. This fort found by Professor St Joseph[116] lies in a bend of the Wye and has been cut through diagonally by a railway line, which became disused in 1960.[117] Professor St Joseph makes the point that, although the site is above the normal flood level, it could, in exceptional seasons, have been inundated, which may be the reason for supposing it is the earlier of the two sites, i.e. that it was given up for a site on higher ground. The internal area of 16 acres marks it as a site held in strength, which is hardly surprising since this was the main point of egress for the Silures from their mountain fortress. Excavations may eventually show that it had a legionary complement, but may have been occupied for only a short time in favour of Clyro – which is the general prevailing opinion.[118]

To the south, the outpost forts appear to be on a main N–S communication, Route 39, already described – at Abergavenny (No 148), Usk (No 149) and Caerleon (No 150). This leaves the problem of the important Usk Valley above Abergavenny and whether it may have been felt necessary to have an advance post in it. Abergavenny is well sited to block the valley exit and this may have been considered sufficient, providing the force established there was strong enough. There is a fort midway between Abergavenny and Brecon at Pen-y-Gaer (No 209), a 3.7-acre site[119] suitable for a *cohors equitata*. An excavation in 1966[120] produced only one coin, a *denarius* of Nero (AD 67) and very little pottery, but it did include the rim of a platter in 'Pompeian red' ware[121] (Report No 44) and sherds of a tripod bowl.[122] Although these vessels appear in early Flavian contexts, they are more frequent on Claudian-Neronian sites. Unless there is another establishment below the known fort, it would appear that the foundation date for this establishment must be in the 60s or 70s.[123]

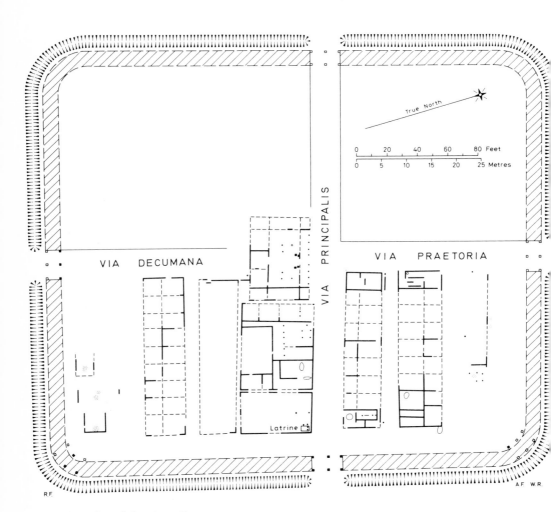

35 Plan of the Nanstallon Fort

CHAPTER FIVE

Aulus Didius Gallus[1] and the Northern Advance

The choice of governor fell on a most experienced and distinguished senator, Aulus Didius Gallus, who had been *cos suff.* in 39, and there is evidence that he actually asked for the appointment. This information comes from Quintilian (AD 35–95), a famous teacher of rhetoric, in his book *Institutio Oratoria* which has as its theme the education of the orator. As an example of irony, he quoted comments by Domitius Afer (vi. 3. 68) on the complaints of Gallus when he was appointed to a province for which he had canvassed. The confirmation that this was Britain is the statement on the tombstone of Quintus Veranius, his successor as governor (see p. 104 below), which tells us that he was appointed to Britain – *cum non petierit* ('without having sought it') – which seems to be a tart comment on Didius Gallus. But how this came about is not immediately obvious. He could have asked to succeed Scapula before the guerilla campaign became serious. Then having been given the post on the governor's unexpected death, he found on his arrival that conditions on the western frontier had seriously deteriorated. By then Gallus had led a very full career, although his *cursus honorum* is only known from a fragment of an inscription erected in his honour from Olympia.[2]

The family of the Didii originated from Histonium on the east coast of Italy,[3] the same town from which sprang the Hosidii; one of them, C. Hosidius Geta, commanded one of the invasion legions of 43. These two families may have helped each other in their rise through the ranks of the aristocracy. There is evidence to suggest that he was a quaestor in AD 19 under Tiberius;[4] from this, according to Professor Anthony Birley, the date of his birth was probably *c.*8–7 BC. His first senior post was as legate to the Governor of Asia, but the date is uncertain. He then became governor of Sicily, still presumably under Tiberius; according to Frontinus, he became *curator aquarum*, i.e. in charge of the aqueducts and water supply to Rome, from late 38 until 49.[5] He was succeeded in this post by the famous orator, Domitius Afer[6] with whom he had shared the consulship in 39.[7] Gallus may have been one of the *comites* who accompanied Claudius to Britain in 43, when the Emperor needed military expertise. The invasion of Britain has been associated by some scholars with an appointment which is difficult to place; that of *praefectus equitatus* which came early in Gallus' career. It was a most unusual command, apparently connected with campaigns when a large cavalry group operated as a special detached corps.[8] As he probably received his command as an ex-praetor, it may have been between 20 and 30, during one of the wars under Tiberius. The most likely of these is the campaign against Tacfarinas, in Africa, where cavalry played an important role.

Soon after the invasion of Britain, Gallus was involved in the creation and large-scale reorganisation of the province of Moesia, Macedonia and Achaia. During this period, he carried out a special mission to the Crimea to establish the young prince Cotys on the throne.[9] It may have been for this, or another action at this time, that he was awarded the *ornamenta triumphalia*. The name of his next province is not known, but the spacing of the letters on the Olympia inscription (*ILS* 970) suggests the rich lands of Asia. This appointment would have been *c*.49–51. He was evidently highly regarded by Claudius and a special relationship may have developed when Gallus was *curator aquarum*, since the Emperor had a strong personal interest in the water supply of Rome. His high standing at court is reflected in his appointment as one of the *XV Viri* to organise the Secular Games in 47.

The question for which it is not easy to find an answer is just why Didius Gallus should want another province after such a full and interesting career, when, already in his early sixties, he was at the point when most senior senators would want to retire to their estates and less strenuous duties. Perhaps he still had ambitions to fulfil, or was he needing more wealth and imagined that rich pickings could be gained in Britain, still in a state of war? Whether Gallus succumbed to a craving for more money, or whether he had suffered serious financial misfortune, it is impossible to say. Gallus may have calculated that Britain would have produced plunder in precious metals, slaves and cattle. If so, he must have been bitterly disappointed, as it soon became apparent that any prospects of glorious victories and glittering prizes were remote. One senses a testy and disappointed elderly man chasing phantoms of success and glory. Tacitus is significantly dismissive in his curt comment – *senectute gravis et multa copia honorum* ('heavy in years and honours', *Ann.* xii. 40). It has been assumed that this verdict was the result of the failure of Didius to secure great victories in Britain, but Tacitus must have appreciated that he was engaged in a holding operation. It is more probable that it was a judgement based on the earlier career of Gallus related in the lost books. In addition he may even have collected some of the odium felt for his adopted son, the infamous Fabricius Veiento.[10]

The War Continues and Worsens

Between the death of Scapula and the arrival of Didius Gallus, an interval of three or four months must have elapsed. Although Gallus made a rapid journey, there would have been preparations to be made, and during this time the Roman hold on their western frontier deteriorated seriously. A legion commanded by G. Manlius Valens had been defeated, although which legion this was is not recorded; it may have been the XIVth or XXth. This unfortunate disgrace for Manlius Valens affected his career in a remarkable way, as he was still a *legatus legionis* in 69, when he commanded *Legio I Italica* on the Rhine[11] (which did him little good, as he favoured Vitellius). This appears to make him the oldest known legionary commander, since he appears to have survived to become consul in 96 at the extraordinary age of 89, dying in office.[12] It is interesting to reflect that this disgruntled old man must have known Tacitus, and may even have provided him with a prejudiced view of Didius Gallus.

The defeat of a legion in the field was certainly a serious blow for the Romans, and demonstrated the growing strength and confidence of the Britons – who naturally made much of it, spreading the news throughout the province (doubtless with the aid of the Druids). This was not designed to scare the new governor, as Tacitus would have it, but to bring new hope to the conquered tribes still smarting under the crass tactics of Scapula and the brutal ways of the colonists. Tacitus also allows himself a scathing comment on Gallus, who, he alleged, exaggerated the losses to gain more credit for himself when he gained control of the affected zone. This sounds like a case of personal spite, perhaps passed on by Manlius Valens. Didius Gallus must be given some credit for his long years of experience and for the fact that he was no longer anxious to promote his own career since it was unlikely that he would receive any further provincial appointments.

It is difficult to judge the result of the actions of Gallus in the absence of any reliable information. Tacitus remains silent, merely telling us that he met and repelled the Britons (*donec adcursu Didii pellerentur*); the verb used here (*pello*) was used in a military sense by Caesar to mean 'overcoming' (*B.G.* 1. 7) so it may be stronger than most translations allow. One has to accept the fact that no further trouble is mentioned on the west frontier in Britain, and the only reasonable conclusion to be reached is that Gallus was successful in establishing the zone. How did he accomplish this? One possibility is that the Britons had so gained in confidence that they were tempted to face the Romans in open combat, rather than continue their quick forays. If so, they would inevitably have been defeated. Moreover Gallus would then be able to complete the building of forts and communications routes in the frontier zone, and so prevent any serious losses. But it remained a difficult frontier and a decision was needed from Rome. Gallus could not have reached Britain before the campaign season of 52 was well advanced and probably only two further seasons were possible before news came from Rome of the death of Claudius on 13 October 54. This would have meant a halt in all military operations until further instructions were received from the new Emperor.[13]

Nero's Early Years as Emperor

In the early years of the reign of Nero, major policy decisions were taken by two elderly advisers, Seneca and Burrus. Cautious by nature, they needed time to consider the future of Britain, and were content, for the moment, to allow Gallus to strengthen his grip and so prevent the hostile Britons from springing their surprise attacks and narrowing down their areas for grouping and deployment. But Gallus was soon to be faced with another problem on his other frontier to the north.

Cartimandua Breaks with her Consort, Venutius

There are two varying accounts by Tacitus of the break between Cartimandua and her consort Venutius. In the *Annals* he merely mentions the divorce and the subsequent war which was waged during the governorship of Gallus (xiv. 40). In the *Historiae* however, his earlier work, he gives more details (iii. 45). Cartimandua had been well rewarded for her capture of Caratacus, and her wealth and close relationships with Rome tempted her into what may seem as an untypically rash action. She turned away from Venutius to the greater attraction of his young squire, Vellocatus. Had she treated this as a casual leisure pursuit, the affair might have been contained within the court circle, but she was wilful enough to want him to share the throne. This unfortunate lapse on her part scandalised and enraged many of her people, most of whom would have shown their sympathy to Venutius. Had Vellocatus been of noble birth, as some have assumed, the reaction might not have been so great, but it has been pointed out that he was probably, according to Celtic custom, of servile status.[14] Tacitus may not have been overstating the case in his words *concussa statim flagitio domus* ('the royal house was immediately shaken by this disgraceful act').

Clearly the queen for once had lost her political acumen. The mantle of Caratacus had fallen on the shoulders of Venutius, and the loyalty of many of the Brigantian tribesmen had passed to him. But far more than this, the hopes of all free Britons were suddenly raised. While Cartimandua had a firm grip on her large territories there was little hope of the Druids and their agents collecting much support from any of her subjects. Now, by her rash act, the real possibility of a new frontier war was apparent. If a concerted plan could be agreed between the Welsh tribes and the peoples of the north, the Roman army would be faced with a very serious problem. But Cartimandua had not entirely lost her reason. By an astute move, she seized Venutius' brother and other members of his family. With these hostages, the British chief was placed in a difficult position. Nevertheless, he invaded Brigantia with a hand-picked force.

Venutius, who must have retired to his former kingdom which may have been in the north, was surely reluctant to start an all-out war. But if Tacitus is using phrases from official dispatches in his few curt comments on this episode, the move could be interpreted as a carefully planned raid by a band of selected young warriors in an attempt to release the hostages, and so remove the impression of a large-scale invasion. Cartimandua had foreseen this probability and had asked Gallus for his help in guarding her prisoners. Didius Gallus must have been appalled at the prospect of a war on his northern frontier while the western frontier was only being held by constant vigilance. It was, however, in Roman interests to maintain Cartimandua on her throne as long as possible. Although by then Gallus and his advisers probably regarded her as an unstable female who could cause them great trouble, he would have had no moral scruples over her matrimonial troubles. The force sent to prevent any seizure of the hostages consisted of several auxiliary cohorts. There was a sharp engagement without any result, but a legion was brought into action under Caesius Nasica,[15] before the threat was removed. The legion involved would almost certainly have been *Legio IX*, the HQ fortress for which was still at Longthorpe near Peterborough.

This brief account appears to relate to two phases. Firstly there was the main operation to keep Cartimandua on her throne; and secondly an attempt to prevent the hostages from being taken by Venutius. Tacitus states definitely that Venutius directed his hostilities against Rome – *etiam adversus nos hostilia induerat*. This would suggest that a battle was fought between the hostile Britons and *Legio IX*. As in the case of the *auxilia*, the outcome was at first in doubt before victory could be claimed. This vague description of the events cannot be interpreted with any confidence, but it does now appear that the northern frontier suddenly changed from being a zone of proven security to one of grave uncertainty. The immediate effect would undoubtedly have been rapid adjustments to the old Plautian frontier based on the Trent. It then became necessary to move troops to posts much nearer to the stronghold of the Brigantian queen. There is, however, the problem of identifying this place.

The Site of Cartimandua's Stronghold

There are remarkably few hill-forts in Brigantia on the Wessex–north Wales patterns, and it must always remain a possibility that the Queen's royal palace was on a settlement not protected by massive earthworks. One might expect the site of the cantonal capital Isurium Brigantum to be an obvious choice but there is little indication of any pre-Roman occupation. The Romanised town occupies a commanding position in the rich Vale of York and it seems unthinkable that this area was not under large-scale cultivation in the late Iron Age.[16] Others have appreciated the importance of the fertile Ouse Valley; Brian Hartley has suggested that the seat of Cartimandua may have been near York, but this is based on the pre-Roman name of York,[17] while Hermann Ramm prefers Barwick-in-Elmet[18] (pl 19, 20).

There is a place-name which offers a good pointer and that is Rigodunum, listed by Ptolemy as a *polis* of the Brigantes. As this means the 'royal fort' it could lead us to a Brigantian power-centre. It has been identified with the Roman fort at Castleshaw, which is on the great Pennine cross-route from Manchester to York.[19] The next fort at Slack, ten miles to the north-east, has been linked with Camulodunum. But in both cases these are names which could well have been transferred from native sites, and one of these is Castle Hill at Almondbury (HF1), an impressive hill-fort, although only eight acres in extent.[20] There are two discoveries from this fort which may have some significance. One is the finding of a sherd of 'Arretine' ware during the excavations of W.J. Varley, the other that the fort was destroyed by fire to such an extent that the *murus gallicus* (the stone rampart laced with large cross-timbers) had become vitrified. If the identification of the pottery is correct, it suggests a trade contact with Rome at a time just before the Conquest, and that the destruction could be connected with the later Roman advance in 71. This was the view of Ian Richmond[21] and Wheeler,[22] but their opinion was probably influenced by a coin hoard allegedly found on the hill, and which was supposed to include British gold and two hundred Roman Republican coins.[23] This provenance has, however, been satisfactorily dismissed by Derek Allen as an invention to disguise the disposal of the Lightcliffe hoard discovered *c.*1829.[24] But the most devastating discovery which has put Almondbury completely out of court is the Carbon 14 computations on the charcoal from oak timbers of the rampart, which places its destruction to the fifth and sixth centuries BC. This accords with the accepted date for this type of rampart construction with horizontal and vertical timbers laced into stone rubble, which was later described in favour of dump construction with a stone facing.[25]

The removal of this evidence has led to a search for other possible sites for the seat of Cartimandua. Barwick-in-Elmet (HF2), the site favoured by Hermann Ramm, is a 15-acre hill-fort at the east end of the Aire Gap.[26] Larger than Almondbury, it had the great advantage of commanding not only the great east-west cross-Pennine trackway but also the north-south route from the Trent, continuing up the west side of the Ouse Valley. This, from the military and economic aspects, gives it a distinct advantage over Almondbury. Unfortunately, much of the Iron Age work is obscured by the later construction of a motte and bailey castle by the de Lacy family, who also converted Almondbury into one of their strongholds. Although little excavation has been carried out, Roman coins have been found, both of the late Republic and of Claudius.

If Barwick was the stronghold of Cartimandua, one has still to explain the Celtic place-names associated with Almondbury and its vicinity. The name Rigodunum appears only in Ptolemy's Geography. Although it is difficult to pin-point places from Ptolemy's figures of longitude and latitude, this site seems to be along the Pennine trackway. Although it has been linked with Castleshaw[28] it must be a name transferred from a nearby native hill-fort. But the only one near here is the tiny univallate at Buckton Castle, on the Tame, about five miles to the south-west. The

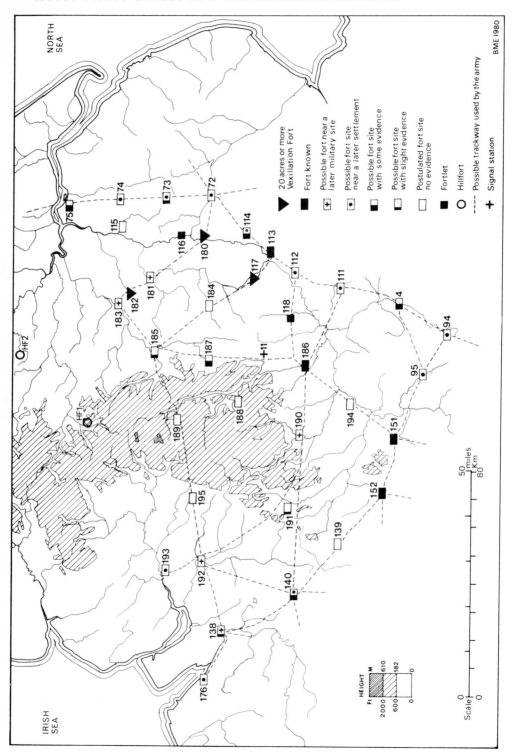

NORTH SEA

IRISH SEA

BME 1980

20 acres or more Vexillation Fort

Fort known

Possible fort near a later military site

Possible fort site near a later settlement

Possible fort site with some evidence

Possible fort site with slight evidence

Postulated fort site no evidence

Fortlet

Hillfort

Possible trackway used by the army

Signal station

HEIGHT
Ft   M
2000   610
600   182
0   0

Scale
0
0   50 miles
         80 Km

75
74
73
72
115
114
113
116
180
117
112
111
181
182
184
118
4
183
185
187
11
186
94
HF2
95
188
189
190
194
151
195
152
193
191
139
192
140
138
176
HF1

name Camulodunum occurs in Ptolemy and Ravenna (No 106) and appears to be much nearer Almondbury, the name having been transferred to the Roman fort at Slack.[29] The presence of two hill-forts, one with royal associations and the other named from Camulos, God of War, clearly shows important Celtic influence along this route and may have belonged to a primary settlement of migrants seeking control of this area of the southern Pennines.

Important as this cross-route was, a centre here could hardly have controlled Brigantia, whereas Barwick is a much better possibility since its inhabitants were in close contact with the vital Ouse Valley and the Humber. Perhaps one could make a closer approach to the truth by assuming that Barwick is the site we are seeking, and then relating it to what we know of the Roman military strategy. There are two approaches to the Lower Ouse Valley. One is from the ferry-point across the Humber at Brough (Petuaria); the other from the Trent crossing at Littleborough (Segelocum), via Doncaster and Castleford. The latter passes within four miles of Barwick and then swings abruptly away towards York. But it must originally have followed the early prehistoric route which continues towards Aldborough (Isurium) and Catterick (Cataractonium). This is obviously the route which the Roman forces used for the rescue of Cartimandua, and, furthermore, it would have been very necessary to control it.

The Frontier Changes Made by Gallus (fig 36)

Gallus was forced to take stock of the existing northern frontier which was still basically that laid down by Plautius on the Humber–Trent line. The nearest legion was the *IX Hispana* at Longthorpe, about 120 miles away, at least four days' hard marching. *Legion XX* at Wroxeter, was even further away, about 150 miles distant. There was also a vast tract of country west of the Trent and up to the Scapulan frontier, over which the army had very little, if any, control. What steps Scapula may have taken to remedy this serious anomaly is difficult to judge. Up to the time of his death he was fully occupied with the turbulent tribes to the west. As far as he was

36 Map of the military sites of the advance to the north under Gallus

VEXILLATION FORTS   117 Osmanthorpe   180 Newton-on-Trent   182 Rossington Bridge

HILLFORTS   HF1 Almondbury   HF2 Barwick-in-Elmet

SIGNAL STATION   11 Pentrich

FORTLETS   116 Marton   118 Broxtowe

FORTS   4 Leicester   72 Lincoln   73 Owmby   74 Hibaldstow   75 Old Winteringham   94 High Cross   95 Mancetter   111 Willoughby-on-the-Wolds   112 Margidunum   113 Thorpe-by-Newark   114 Brough   115 Owston on the Trent   138 Chester   139 Camp Farm   140 Whitchurch   151 Wall   152 Pennocrucium   176 Flint   181 Scraftworth   183 Doncaster   184 Crossing of the Poulter   185 Templeborough   186 Littlechester   187 Chesterfield   188 Mid-point Rocester/Brough-on-Noe   189 Brough-on-Noe   190 Rocester   191 Trent Vale   192 Northwich   193 Wilderspool   194 Mid-point Wall/Littlechester   195 Mid-point Northwich/Brough-on-Noe aware, the protection afforded by the client kingdom of Brigantia was still unquestioned. Now Gallus was faced with military problems of some complexity – quite apart from the scale of operations and the distances involved. He may well have had time to deal firmly with the Silures and their allies, and stabilise that frontier, before distress signals emanated from the north.

Having dealt with the immediate problem of recovering Cartimandua and driving Venutius back to the north, still smarting in his humiliation and enraged by Rome's interference, it was immediately clear to Gallus that the northern frontier of the province required immediate adjustment. All this would doubtless have been relayed to Rome and approval given for the necessary forward movement. This is reflected in Tacitus' grudging admission that he pushed forward with a few forts – *paucis admodum castellis in ulteriora promotis* (*Agricola* 14) – but Tacitus then ruins the effect by adding that Didius did this only so that it could be known that he had extended his official area of responsibility. In the *Annals* he merely recorded that Didius acted through his agents and was content to keep the enemy at a distance. Thus Tacitus castigates the governor for being punctilious in obeying his instructions to stabilise the frontier, in order to give time for a careful appraisal of Britain.

Viewed from Rome, the province of Britannia had indeed become a serious problem. The long dangerous frontier against the undefeated tribes of Wales had already cost the army dear, and further large-scale hostilities could be expected, since, in the face of the implacable hatred inspired by the Druids, diplomacy had no chance of success. Didius Gallus at least prevented any further serious trouble by putting the Scapulan frontier plan into operation and successfully stopping the exits from the hills. It would have required a major effort by the Britons to attack and overwhelm enough forts for a major breakthrough. The intercommunication network which could move out into the field to crush any invading force, was organised to give warning to the legions in their rear. Nevertheless the army had to be on constant alert against any sudden attack. Thus, although the frontier had been effectively sealed, the state of war remained. The northern frontier, hitherto safe, then needed similar treatment, but here the threat was greater, since it involved the tribes from the large territories in the north. What measures could Didius take to ensure the security of this frontier? Clearly the old Plautian zone was totally inadequate, as it was too far to the south. The obvious move would have been to advance in order to bring those areas nearer to the Brigantian frontier under surveillance and control.

Brigantia was formed by an amalgam of many tribes or septs.[30] The Parisi, which were the most wealthy and sophisticated, occupied the territory stretching as far north as Scarborough and the River Derwent, and including the hills and the eastern border of the Vale of York. The tribe had a distinctive culture known from the type site at Arras,[31] and the remarkable square barrows and La Tène culture associated with them. Whether the Parisi were friendly to Rome or not, it would have been desirable for the army to control the Humber crossing. It would seem from the evidence of a considerable Iron Age settlement at North Ferriby[32] that this was the normal terminal of a pre-Roman crossing of the Humber. But the possible fort at Old Winteringham (No 75) was opposite the later Roman fort and town of Brough (Petuaria). This suggests that the crossing was moved to the west of Reads Island in Roman times.[33] It also raises the possibility of a military pontoon bridge to give rapid access to the area north of the estuary, especially for cavalry. But there are no finds to date, which may indicate the presence of a pre-Flavian establishment at Brough. The north-west route from the

Humber controlled the eastern side of the Ouse Valley, but this may not have been crucial to Rome until the advance by Cerealis against Venutius in 71. The other route into the Ouse Valley was more circuitous as it had to avoid the low-lying marshes between the Trent and the Don. The route followed the higher ground from Lincoln through to Doncaster, Castleford and Tadcaster, thence to the north to York. This later became a major road with permanent forts at the places mentioned. There are also indications of earlier military establishments at Newton-on-Trent (No 180) and Rossington Bridge (No 102), which could belong to the period of Didius Gallus (see p. 99 below). Another route to the south would have crossed the Trent at Ad Pontem, (No 113) thence to Templeborough (No 185) and away to the north-west; but so far there is no indication of this on the ground, although there is early Neronian pottery from Templeborough (see p. 101 below). On the west side an obvious advance would have been to the cross-route from Littlechester (Derventio, No 186) through Rocester (No 190), Chesterton, Staffs, Middlewich to Northwich (Condate, No 192) and possibly Wilderspool (No 193). The only evidence of this at present comes from Littlechester and Trent Vale (No 191) (see p. 100–1 below).

On the slender evidence as yet available, one could postulate a patrol zone based on out-post forts at Brough-on-Humber, Doncaster or Rossington Bridge (No 182), Templeborough, Brough-on-Noe (Navio, No 189), a site half-way to Northwich or Wilderspool. There is a definite fort south of the Humber at Kirmington. This would have added about 1300 square miles to the province, a fairly substantial increase to the responsibility of Gallus. The most unfortunate aspect for Rome would have been the deployment of at least ten more auxiliary units into these outlying districts, and they could only have come from the rearward areas, diluting the hold of the army there even more. Difficult decisions would have been needed by Gallus and his staff officers, and much would have depended on their assessment of the programme of pacification in the case of each tribe. It would not necessarily have meant the abandonment of forts but the removal of odd cohorts and squadrons, here and there, to supply the required numbers which would replace the mounted units needed to maintain a constant vigilance on the southern borders of Brigantia. It is probable that by then, with or without the permission of the Queen, Roman troops were inside the tribal area. But Gallus had to place a tight collar round the southern and western boundaries, whether to be ready for sudden trouble, or to mount another rescue operation. The governor must have cursed the day he made obsequious overtures for Britannia. Nor was he likely to fail to make much of the frail condition of the province in his dispatches to Rome.

Argument in Rome

The first five years of Nero's reign, known as the *quinquennium Neronis* (if indeed it belongs to this period), are seen as a brief spell of sanity when the Emperor was taking sound advice. There had been strong hostility towards the freedmen who had gained power and wealth under Claudius. Although they ran the Departments of State with efficiency almost amounting to professionalism, the senators were still looking back to what they considered as the glories of Republican Rome and bitterly resented the power wielded by the Greek ex-slaves. Under Nero the balance seemed to have been restored. The eminent and distinguished philosopher, Seneca[34] and the pragmatic man of action, the equestrian Praetorian Prefect, Burrus,[35] were in control and the result seemed fair enough;[36] Nero was yet to show his irrationality and cruelty. The tactic of the two senior advisers was to divert the youthful Emperor from state matters, towards physical pleasures in which he was allowed licence to indulge. The only restraining hand was that of his mother Agrippina, and this is why Nero employed so much time and thought to her removal – which he finally accomplished in 59. The state of Britain and its frontier were now on the agenda of the meetings of the imperial *consilium* (the private council advising the Emperor) and remained under discussion for three years before a decision was reached. The argument, one must assume, revolved round the advisability of retaining the new province or giving it up altogether.

Britain's Assets

The balance sheet of *Britannia* must have been carefully studied. Silver there was in plenty, but the ores had a very low silver content – an average of about .01%[37] or 3.26 troy oz per ton, whereas the Spanish ores, although they varied greatly, contained as much as 6% or 200 troy oz per ton.[38] This means that about sixty times as much was needed from the Mendips to produce the same amount of silver as was gained from the best of the Spanish ores. But at least the British ores could be extracted by open-cast mining, whereas the great depths of the shafts and the consequent water infiltration and flooding were causing serious difficulties in some of the Spanish mines. Britain also offered the use of prisoners from the wars to carry out the heavy digging and crushing. Thus, so long as refined silver was on stream, this important metal could be considered as a distinct, although hard-won, benefit. There was, however, little indication of any gold and the chief copper deposits were beyond the frontier zone.

The only abundant and widespread mineral was iron. The ores were being exploited by the army on the Weald of Kent – as were, in all probability, the richer ores of the Coriotauvi.[39] There was timber in plenty, stone for building and clay for tile and pottery factories. The wars produced an annual batch of slaves, but they were the cheaper sort, only suitable for rough work in the mines and farming. Against all this, there had to be weighed the serious costs to Rome. To make the province safe for economic development, another large campaign was needed against the Welsh tribes, and it was clearly only a matter of time before Cartimandua lost her grip on the Brigantes. This could result in an even more troublesome and costly war, involving peoples as yet unknown in the far north (although, by now, Roman intelligence would have provided an estimate of the wildness of the country and the people in their distant territories). A governor as experienced as Gallus could also have reported on the mood of the tribes within the province and have drawn attention to their restless and uncertain temper – especially that of the Trinovantes, now suffering under the behaviour of the colonists at Camulodunum and the still smouldering resistance in the south-west. The far-reaching power of the Druids would also have been appreciated, and thus the need to eliminate this hostile threat, before any real and lasting peace could be achieved. It is not surprising that the arguments continued in the *consilium* and that the cautious advisers were even suggesting that the cost was too great; Britain had to be considered against other potential threats, especially in the west and on the Danube. A case could, and was being, made for calling a halt to the Claudian adventure; Rome could possibly gain all she wanted by trade. This, after all, had been the view of Augustus and Tiberius.

Seneca's Loans

Evidence of these comes from Dio (xxi. 2), who in reciting the causes of the great revolt of 60/61 lists the recovery by the procurator of sums of money loaned by Claudius to the leaders of the Britons, and also the loans Seneca had made, amounting to 40 million *sestertii* at a high rate of interest. There is an additional passage, which has become corrupt with much copying but could have the meaning that the natives neither sought or wanted this money in the first place (Appendix 1). It is possible that the British had very little understanding of the operation of financial loans and may have regarded the money as gifts.[40] If this assumption is correct, the bitter feelings of the Britons can be understood. This has been a point of controversy between historians since loans and their recall are not recorded by Tacitus. The wealth of Seneca was well known, and was in 58 the subject of a vicious attack by Publius Suillius Rufus, during his trial for extortion and embezzlement. On the grounds, presumably, that attack was the best means of defence, he asked by what philosophical principles Seneca had, within four years of Imperial favour, acquired 300 million *sestertii* (*Ann.* xiii. 42). Furthermore, he was roundly accused for his widespread usury ('Italy and the provinces had been drained dry by his boundless usury')[41] and Suillius had many supporters for his charges. While Tacitus was prepared to report the accusations of Suillius, he remained silent over Seneca's dealings in Britain. There is a great difference between the rhetoric of a trial by a man who in this case was found guilty and banished, and the sober fact behind the revolt. Tacitus may have been prejudiced in favour of Seneca and ignored the report as too exaggerated for inclusion,[42] or (as some have argued) he was using for his account of events in Britain the lost work of Fabius Rusticus[43] who owed much to his friendship with Seneca (*Ann.* xiii. 20). Dio, on the other hand, had little time for philosophers and would have seized on the more unsavoury aspects of Seneca with some relish, using, it has been suggested, the lost history of the elder Pliny. But there was probably a third work which dealt with the revolt and the factors which led to it – the memoirs of Suetonius Paullinus, the governor of Britain at the time, who had good reason for writing his justification of his savage reprisals against the Britons. It is possible that both Pliny and Fabius Rusticus used this work,[44] but that the latter chose deliberately to ignore anything hurtful to the memory of his patron Seneca.

There would be little point in considering the pros and cons of the matter, but for another piece of evidence recorded by Suetonius Tranquillus in his biography of Nero. In this he stated that the Emperor had no ambitions to extend his empire, and even considered withdrawing from Britain, but rejected the idea since it might have reflected adversely on the glories won by Claudius (*Nero* 18, Appendix 1). This incident has been placed by some modern writers at the time of the revolt, but it seems hardly likely that this would have been contemplated after such a great victory; in any case, by then Nero had ceased to have feelings of piety towards Claudius. The discussions about Britain, although considered by some to be related to the period of the revolt, could be fitted with greater logic into the years of Gallus, when a decision about the future of Britannia was being delayed. The ferment on the Brigantian frontier, fully reported by Gallus, could well have caused a serious argument being advanced for a complete withdrawal. But it was not to be. Whether Nero himself did regard it as a slight against the Julio-Claudian line or other factors turned the balance we shall never know. The youthful emperor may have relished the thought of military glory and wished to emulate the triumphs of Claudius, and so overruled Seneca and Burrus. All we know is that, in 57, it was decided to move forward and take over the whole of Wales – and a much relieved Didius Gallus was recalled.

The Route Network

As indicated above, the main line of advance to the north would have been along Route 47 from Lincoln via the Trent, crossing at Marton (No 116), to Doncaster (Danum, No 183). A parallel Route 50 from another Trent crossing at Ad Pontem (No 113) could have proceeded towards Chesterfield (No 187) or direct to Templeborough (No 185). Further routes could have branched from the main supply Route 27 to Viroconium (No 142). There would also have been an extension of Route 40 from Wall (Letocetum, No 151) to Littlechester (Derventio, No 186), thence northwards to Chesterfield and Templeborough, and possibly other routes from Pennocrucium (No 152) and Whitchurch (No 140) aimed at the head waters of the Trent. One of the other main routes would have been a communication link extending, perhaps, as far as the Mersey crossing near Wilderspool (No 193) via Northwich, Trent Vale, Rocester and Littlechester, joining the Fosse Way, near Willoughby-on-the-Wolds (Vernementum, No 111). Finally, there was the frontier itself which could have linked Northwich (Condate, No 192), Brough-on-Noe (Navio, No 189) and Templeborough through to Doncaster. These will now be considered in the light of evidence so far available.

Route 47

The potential importance of this line of advance was probably recognised at an earlier stage, since Roman officials and traders would have been using it as the main access to the kingdom of Cartimandua. It has the appearance of an early trackway following the firm ground round the marshes at the junction of the Ouse and Trent with the Humber. The Route starts at Lincoln with a 4-mile stretch along the straight road aimed due north at the Humber crossing, and branching off along what has since become known as Till Bridge Lane (named from a bridge over the little River Till). The Trent crossing was protected by a small 2-acre fort at Marton[45] (No 116, see *Invasion*, 165); the river was probably bridged by the army, although there is evidence of a well-paved ford 18ft wide held by timber piles, but this could have been medieval.[46] About 4 miles to the south of Newton-on-Trent, an interesting military site has been recorded by Professor St Joseph (No 180).[47] It consists of a large double-ditched enclosure, 1135ft (346m) by 1025ft (313m) and at least 26.5 acres in area, although the location of the west side is not known. On the north and east sides are several lengths of single ditches overlapping at openings, which Professor St Joseph has identified as a large earlier temporary camp; but these ditches could have been additional protection for the fort, or an annexe. What is more certain is that part of the outline of a campaign camp has been located 700ft (213m) south of the fort; neither site has been investigated on the ground and dated. Newton-on-Trent, from its size, has prompted Professor Frere to include it among his 'vexillation' fortresses, housing a composite force. He has further linked this site with the problems of Gallus in dealing with Cartimandua.[48] A carefully selected striking force at this point would have been well placed to move forward rapidly in an emergency. But it would have been based on the old Plautian frontier and this would only apply to an early stage of the operations; once Gallus had advanced his front line, a task force could occupy a more forward position and this may account for the site at Rossington Bridge, near Doncaster (No 182). The distance of Newton from the well-established crossing does provoke the thought that there may have been an earlier crossing point of the Trent hereabouts, and that Till Bridge Lane was a later adjustment. In this case, the approach from Lincoln must have been on the south side of the stream the Romans were later to canalise into the Foss Dyke.

The distance from the Trent crossing to Doncaster is about 22 miles, a good day's march. If any mid-point was selected it could have been the crossing of the Idle. It is here at Scraftworth (No 181), half-a-mile east of Bawtry, that Professor St Joseph found a small fort of half-an-acre. The defences were trenched in 1952 and the ditches found to have a V-profile. Fourth-century pottery was found in the upper filling, but this could have come from later occupation.[49] Air photography shows traces of a ditch system extending beyond the small fort, and which was considered by the excavators as an annexe but the ditches appear to have been cut off and it seems more likely that they may indicate the presence of an earlier and larger fort. It seems impossible that small forts such as this one and Marton would belong to the period of potential hostility under Gallus; they would fit better into a later context under Cerealis, when this route would have been a main link with the south.

The next site of significance is Rossington Bridge (No 182, pl 18), a large 23-acre fort on the south side of the River Torne, found by Professor St Joseph in 1968.[50] A large task force could have been well positioned here for a dash north to support Cartimandua, and could have belonged either to Gallus or his successor Bolanus, who finally had to rescue her by force in 69 or 70.[51] The site of the permanent fort was at the crossing of the River Don, on the south bank, where the later town of Danum developed, eventually to become Doncaster (No 183). The military site is known and excavations have shown that, below an Antonine fort, there are two periods of timber forts starting in the Flavian period. Not enough details are at present known, but it has been suggested that the early forts were quite large, c. $6\frac{1}{2}$ acres.[52] The road, aimed at Doncaster from the south, turns sharply to the east at Rossington Bridge. There is also evidence of another road continuing in the alignment from the south towards a crossing of the Don to the east of Doncaster.[53] This raises the possibility of an early fort at this point.

Route 49

This route is speculative, but is based on the known crossing of the Trent at Ad Pontem (No 113).[54] It was suggested in the *Invasion* (p. 165) that the spacing would have required an advance unit in the Bilsthorpe-Eakring area (No 117). There is good evidence from the observations of Dr Derrick Riley that this was a probable line of advance. He found at Osmanthorpe (No 117) about six miles from the Trent, in a north-west direction up the Valley of the River Greet, the site of a 20-acre fort, with the hint of an internal street.[55] In conjunction with the similar fort at Newton-on-Trent, the combined units would have been a useful task force for Gallus, poised to strike into southern Brigantia along the two main eastern routes. There are also two campaign camps, one at Farnsfield[56] and the other near Worksop on the River Meden.[57] The latter seems to indicate that the direction of the route was towards Templeborough rather than Chesterfield, and a mid-point fort could be expected, perhaps at the crossing of the River Poulter, about five miles south-east of Worksop.

Route 40

Littlechester (Derventio, No 186)

This is a continuation of a route from Metchley (No 154) to Wall (Letocetum, No 151), striking down the Trent to the Derwent Valley to a well established fort at Strutt's Park on the high ground on the west side of the river. Coins and pottery found over the years have clearly indicated the presence of an early fort. The evidence was gathered together by Maurice Brassington, who also carried out a small-scale excavation in 1970.[58] Unfortunately, the whole site was buried below a modern housing estate before any large-scale investigation could be made, so the chances of obtaining any further information about the fort are now remote. The 1970 investigation produced two parallel buildings slots which could have been part of a barrack block, and they give an indication of a N–S alignment. From the filling of the slots, it seems that the vertical timbers were removed when the fort was dismantled. Part of the same, or another, barrack block was investigated by Miss Dool in 1974.[59] The coins and pottery finds seem to show that occupation may have continued into the early Flavian period, perhaps up to the advance under Petillius Cerealis in AD 71. The four published pieces of equipment are not helpful in identifying the type of unit in occupation, but it is interesting to note that some of the fragments had been gilded, whereas silvering was the more common practice. The later fort and civil settlement, which became the village of Littlechester, and the pottery works on the Race Course site all occupy the lower ground on the other side of the Derwent.[60]

The route continues up the Derwent Valley and 11 miles from Littlechester Professor St Joseph has sited a small (c.150ft square) earthwork within a larger enclosure at Pentrich (No 11), sited on a commanding position.[61] This is probably a signal station similar to those on the north Devon coast. The next site across the watershed is at Chesterfield (No 187) where another Neronian fort was found in rescue excavations, 1975–79, below a Flavian fort on a different alignment.[62] The evidence suggests that the early fort was demolished and replaced by another (thought to be smaller) under Agricola. The route continued to the River Don which was most probably the limit of the advance under Gallus.

Templeborough (No 185)

The fort here at Templeborough, a mile-and-a-half west of Rotherham, was built on an elevated plateau with steep sides dropping towards the river, while, to the east, marshy ground would have afforded further protection. The site was clearly chosen for its natural advantages, which made it a position of strength, designed to meet the potential threat from the north. Because of its ancient remains, the site became known as Castle Garth, a typical field name given by local folk whose knowledge of the past did not often stretch beyond the Middle Ages. In 1916, the area was bought by a steel firm needing to expand to meet the rapid increase in demand for munitions during the Great War. In spite of the urgency, one of the earliest rescue excavations was mounted, thanks largely to the public spirited Corporation of Rotherham, through which expenses were met, an appeal launched and a publication, excellent for its period, produced.[63] Thomas May, who directed the work, was a very competent excavator, but lacked skills in interpretation. His real interest was in pottery, but, although he included 13 plates of drawings in his report, a vast collection remains unsorted and waiting further study in the Rotherham Museum.[64] May recognised the presence of three forts, the first of which was about 6.5 acres in total. Considering that he had only eight months for excavation during a difficult winter and had problems finding labourers, it is remarkable that he recovered so much. He recognised the rows of vertical posts of timber barrack blocks, but they appear to be of only one period and may not necessarily have belonged to the earliest fort. He had an appreciation of the historical background and fully understood that the first fort could have been erected under Gallus. This now has been accepted by later writers.[65] The pottery has been subject to further study by Dr Grace Simpson, who has dated the earliest pieces of samian to the early Neronian period.[66] Eight sherds were published in 1964, with a fuller commentary in 1973. Dr Simpson also saw the coarse pottery, but made a brief study only of the second-century wares. One would expect rather more small finds from the excavation than the four published by May. Though not stratified, they have a definite cavalry bias,[67] and could well belong to a later period.

Route 50

At this period there may have been a link route terminating at the Mersey crossing, a road which was later to become the shortest way from the north-west into the Midlands, most probably through Leicester (Ratae, No L4) by a route up the Soar Valley. In this initial period, however, the route may have stemmed from the Fosse Way at Willoughby-on-the-Wolds (Vernemetum, No 111), crossing the Trent near Radcliffe, the first known post being at Littleborough where a fort has been found. From here it proceeded due west to Rocester (No 190) where a Flavian fort and settlement have been found,[68] but nothing so far of an earlier period.

Trent Vale (No 191)

The next site would have been in the Trent Valley area. Although no fort of this period has been located, a small pottery work has been investigated at Trent Vale, which produced military type wares[69] of the Neronian period. This clearly indicates that a fort cannot be far away and it was probably on the higher ground where five coins have been recorded, including three Claudian imitations, a Claudian *as*, too corroded for precise identification, and an *as* of M. Agrippa. Unfortunately, this area has long since been quarried away. The military association with the pottery works is strongly suggested by the discovery of a set of five rosette studs with niello decoration (Report, pl VII), similar to others found on military sites of this period. The kiln is of a sophisticated type and the pottery made there has a distinctly military flavour. The samian sherds are Claudio-Neronian, although some may be a little later. There is one extraordinary vessel which may have come from this site, or that of the fort. It is the base of a samian crater[70] which found its way into the Stoke-on-Trent Museum, but its provenance is totally lost. It appears to have been made at Tindari, a well-known factory in Sicily, working in the mid-first century. Exotic pottery from far off places has occasionally been found on early military sites in Britain and the most astonishing is perhaps the plain black colour-coated bowl, with a central finial, from the post-Boudican fort at the Lunt, for which there are only two known parallels, one in Gaul and the other in Spain.[71] It is not, therefore, impossible that the fragment of a Sicilian crater should have been found on the Trent Vale fort during nineteenth-century quarrying.[72] The conclusions reached by those who excavated and studied the Trent Vale finds is that there was probably a fort on this hill overlooking a ford across the Trent at Hanford. This would fit reasonably into the suggested frontier network of Gallus.

There is a Flavian fort at Chesterton-under-Lyme,[73] four miles to the north-west, suggesting an adjustment to the disposition of military posts. The route continues to curve away towards the north, and the next known fort is at Northwich (Condate, No 192) at the crossing of the Weaver. This site was investigated prior to a redevelopment programme in 1970 by Professor Barri Jones.[74] A two-period fort was found, the earlier one being of Flavian date, although insufficient dating evidence was recovered to be more precise than c.65–80. A find of some interest was of an almost complete iron cavalry helmet, but in a very bad state of corrosion (Report 45–48). It is possible that an earlier fort lies elsewhere.

It seems logical that Gallus would have wanted to control the Mersey crossing and a fort here would also have been able to watch the south-eastern exit of the trans-Pennine trackway. An obvious place would be Wilderspool, where a great number of finds have been made on either side of the river, both in the past and in recent excavations. The discoveries so far have been of industry, including metal working and pottery making, from the late first century.[75] The area covered by all this development is very large. The recent excavation, for example, was c.3000ft (900m) to the north-east of the late nineteenth-century discoveries. It is, therefore, perhaps not surprising that no indication of a military presence has, as yet, been found. The Mersey crossing would have been of crucial strategic importance, and it seems most unlikely that a fort would not have been placed here during the conquest of the north. Although Manchester (Mamucium) would appear to be a nodal point of the military network of South Lancashire and the south-west Pennines,[76] the Mersey crossing, at or near Wilderspool, would have offered a quicker route to the north for the legion at Chester, from Wales and the West Midlands. This route would have continued towards the Ribble crossing at Walton-le-Dale and would probably have had an earlier origin from the late Flavian period.[77] But whether Gallus advanced as far as the Mersey, it is impossible to be certain without evidence, and a fort may not have been established here until 71.

Route 51

This is the frontier link road which connects Chester (Deva, No 138) with Doncaster (Danum, No 183). After the first stretch to Northwich (No 192) the route would have proceeded almost due east through Macclesfield Forest to Brough-on-Noe (Navio, No 189). An alternative suggestion would be to have included Buxton in the network. This place is on the site of a medicinal spring which was developed by the Romans and known as Aquae Arnemetiae. This name includes the Celtic word *nemeton* which means a 'sacred grove' and indicates that the spring was in use for religious purposes in pre-Roman times. Unfortunately, little is known about the origins and development of the site. The earliest pottery reported is some Flavian samian from the Silverlands area.[78] The only reasons for the army to be interested in the site would have been either the presence of a large native community or the development of the healing spring for the benefit of the troops. The distance of 32 miles clearly indicates the need for a mid-way position which could be at the crossing of the River Bollin, near Macclesfield (No 195).

Brough-on-Noe (No 189)

Although the fort at Brough-on-Noe has been excavated several times[79] (the most recent work being that of Professor G.B.D. Jones and Dr John Peter Wild)[80] only brief interim reports have so far been published. There is a small two-acre fort of the second century, but there is an earlier and larger one below it, which had been broadly dated to the Flavian period. The pottery and other artefacts have not yet been studied, so it is impossible to know just how early the foundation date could be.

It will now be appreciated that the evidence for the advance by Gallus is very uneven. When the sites for which there is no certain evidence are placed on a map (fig. 92), the only certain route is that of Wall to Templeborough. If this was continued northwards, it could be seen as directed towards Barwick-in-Elmet, via Castleford (Lagentium). Only the forts at Trent Vale and the 'vexillation' forts at Newton-on-Trent and Rossington Bridge hint at any other possible forward movement at this period. It seems rather unlikely that Gallus would have thrust a single fortified route forward unsupported by a wider area control, but the question must remain open and the suggestion made above should only be considered as a guide or model for further work.

CHAPTER SIX

The Advance under Quintus Veranius

The new governor was Quintus Veranius and the full significance of his appointment, in association with a change in the Imperial policy for Britain, was first recognised by Professor Eric Birley as long ago as 1952.[1] There is much useful information about Veranius, his father, of the same name, who was with Germanicus in Asia, became the first governor of Cappadocia (*Ann*. ii. 56), was after the death of Germanicus involved in the accusations against Piso (*Ann*. iii. 10, 13) and was afterwards rewarded by Tiberius with a priesthood (*Ann*. iii. 19) (though he never gained the consulship). His son would thus have had an excellent start, and on the basis of an inscription from Cyran in Lycia,[2] which gives details of his earlier career, Eric Birley has shown how the backing of the Emperor ensured a rapid advance.[3] The assessment of Tiberius on the potential of the young Veranius was not lost on Claudius,[4] who had good reasons for showing gratitude towards Veranius, since he played a significant role in negotiating the new Emperor's acceptance by the Senate. The members of that body had overlooked the existence of Claudius immediately after the death of Caligula, and, in fact, had started to annul the Imperial decrees in an attempt to restore the Republic.

Further details of the career of Veranius are given in an inscription now in the garden of the Museo Nazionale Romano in Rome. This inscribed marble fragment was found in 1926 at Pratolungo about ten kilometres north of Rome, where extensive ruins of a villa had been recorded. The inscription was recognised by A.E. Gordon in 1948 as from a mausoleum of the Veranii, and he subsequently made it the subject of a detailed study.[5] Q. Veranius was appointed by Claudius as the first governor of Lycia and Pamphylia and stayed there for his full *quinquennium* (five-year period), c.43–37. It would have been a difficult assignment requiring diplomatic skill since there were several adjacent client rulers and unruly mountain tribes. The Rome inscription records fighting in hill country against a tribe which cannot be positively identified. Nor is it possible to be sure whether it occupied part of the new province or was an adjacent area, and if so, may have been in a client kingdom. The surviving wording of the inscription is tantalising, possibly meaning that hill-folk had invaded the province and destroyed the walls of a town. Veranius defeated and drove them back into the hills and later restored the town defences. All this would have given Veranius useful experience in mountain warfare. His charm and diplomacy was also effective, as local inscriptions testify.[6] He became *consul ordinarius* in 49 and also an augur and a patrician. Nothing is known of any posts he may have held between 49 and 57, except as curator of sacred buildings and he was also in charge of some games.[7] At some stage in his career a treatise on military science, *On Generalship*, was dedicated to him by the Greek writer Onasander, and there could have been a personal connection dating to his period as governor of Lycia.

The Campaign of Veranius

The governor for Britain, selected to implement the newly formed policy, can be seen as a judicious choice. Veranius combined the talents of a soldier with those of a diplomat, and both were badly needed in Britain. It is sad to record that all we know of his period of governor is that he died within a year of taking up his post; the phrase used by Tacitus *intra annum* (*Agricola*, 14) could mean either the calendar year, or year of office. Had he came to Britain in the winter of 57/58, the latter interpretation would be the better, since it would have allowed him at least one season's campaign, although this was cursorily dismissed by Tacitus.[8] We know this is more likely since his successor, Suetonius Paullinus began operations against the Ordovices with no mention of the Silures. The presumption is that Veranius conducted a vigorous and successful campaign against the tribe which had been the bane of Scapula's existence, as they are heard of no more as a hostile force. But Veranius had no time to exercise his diplomatic skills against the anti-Roman forces, who now had a list of serious grievances, including the loans they had been forced to pay back to Seneca. Tacitus adds a further piece of information, that in his will Veranius stated that with two more years he would have taken the province. But this could mean no more than the conviction that it needed only two further campaigns to complete the task for which he was selected, and that does not seem an unjustifiable hope. Tacitus, however, took exception to the flattery of Nero which also appeared in his will – though this may have been necessary to ensure the continued well-being of his family. It would seem from this that Veranius did not die without warning, but had time to prepare his will. Whether this was occasioned by illness or injury, is not recorded.

The springboard for the advance under Veranius was the Scapulan fortified zone, strengthened by Gallus. One must presume that the plan would have been to isolate the southern tribes from the Ordovices, as Scapula may have tried to do. This meant control of the Upper Severn Valley, while the main drive was up to the Wye into the head-waters of the Usk and down the Tywi to Carmarthen Bay to make contact with the Fleet. It seems possible, in the light of later developments, that the Demetae of the south-west offered no resistance. At present there is very little evidence to do more than suggest the network of forts constructed to put a stranglehold on the Silures. The most important move was the establishment of a legionary supply base at Usk (L6), presumably by *Legio XX* (see Introduction).

The Advance Westwards

It must be assumed that the objective of the one season's campaign of Veranius was the reduction of the Silures. The main route of the striking force must surely have been the Wye, across the watershed with the Usk to Brecon (Cicutio, No 208), while another could have struck northwards from the coastal base at Neath (No 179) to join it. This would have ensured a rapid encirclement of the Silures, whose territory could then have been divided by thrusts from the coastal bases at Isca (No 150) and Cardiff (No 167). The occupation of these coastal bases would have been essential at this stage, but it seems possible that they were already in Roman hands. Veranius may have had cause to be concerned with the possible reaction of the other tribes, especially those in central Wales, and it may have been necessary to secure the Tywi Valley, as well as the key strategic points in Central Wales in the Llandrindod and Castell Collen area.

105

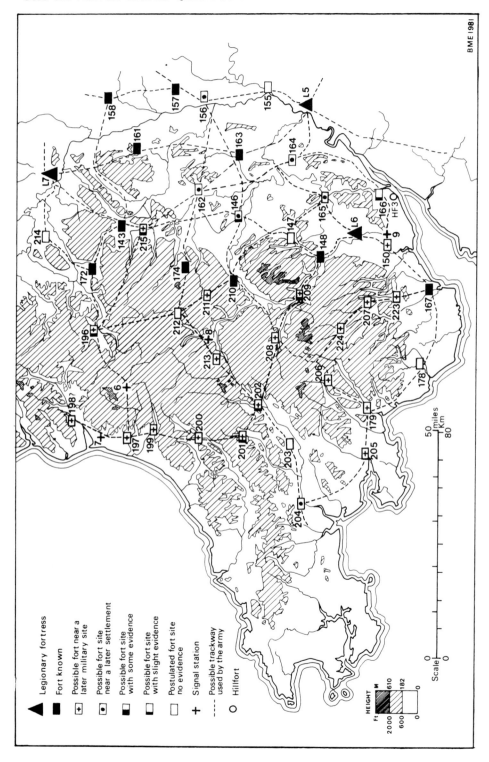

BME 1981

The Ordovices could have been an even greater threat, and an advance up the Severn, at least to Caersws, may have been felt necessary. It must be assumed that Veranius would have been given extra auxiliary troops for the advance and for the occupation of the dozen or more new forts needed to establish firm military control over these areas. Unfortunately, the archaeological evidence is very tenuous; the most important fact to emerge over the last decade has been the presence of a large legionary base at Usk. This would have been a useful place from which the campaigning army could have been supplied and controlled. A major base of this kind here could hardly fit into any other period, before or after Veranius.

Ptolemy's List of Place-names for Wales

Ptolemy only gives five place-names for Wales and the list is a curious one. Bullaeum in the territory of the Silures is clearly Burrium, i.e. Usk; the absence of the cantonal capital Venta Silurum merely means that the list predates its foundation. Maridunum = Moridunum, the capital of the Demetae at modern Carmarthen; but there could well have been a fort here under Veranius. The other three are more difficult to identify. Two of them, Mediolanum and Brannogenium, are placed by Ptolemy in the territory of the Ordovices. The former is a commonplace name indicating a central position in relation to a community or territory. It has been assumed that this was Whitchurch, halfway between Wroxeter and Chester; but, if so, Ptolemy was wrong in ascribing it to the Ordovices and his longitude and latitude figures are patently incorrect. A possible solution to this difficulty comes from the Ravenna Cosmography[9] where a place, listed as Mediomano (No 181), is grouped with places in north Wales where Ptolemy's figures would place his Mediolanum. Thus there could be two places with the same or similar name and a suitable situation would undoubtedly be Caersws,[10] where there is a sequence of military sites occupying a key position in the Upper Severn Valley. It could be argued that Veranius would have been wise to have placed a unit here to protect his right flank from interference from the Ordovices, while undertaking his campaign against the Silures. The other name in north Wales is Brannogenium, which Ptolemy has placed to the south-west of

37   Map of the military sites of the advance into Wales under Veranius

LEGIONARY FORTRESSES   L5 Gloucester   L6 Usk   L7 Wroxeter

SIGNAL STATIONS   6 Cae Gaer   7 Erglodd   8 Pen-min-Cae   9 Coed-y-Caerau

FORTS   143 Stretford Bridge   146 Kenchester   147 Pontrilas   148 Abergavenny   150 Caerleon   155 Tewkesbury   156 Worcester   157 Droitwich   158 Greensforge   161 Wall Town   162 Blackwardine   163 Stretton Grandison   164 Weston-under-Penyard   165 Monmouth   166 Chepstow   167 Cardiff   172 Brompton   173 Dymock   174 Hindwell Farm   178 Bridgend   179 Neath   196 Caersws   197 Pen-Llwyn   198 Pennal   199 Trawscoed   200 Llanio   201 Pumpsaint   202 Llandovery   203 Llandeilo   204 Carmarthen   205 Loughor   206 Coelbren   207 Gellygaer   208 Brecon Gaer   209 Pen-y-Gaer   210 Clyro   211 Colwyn Castle   212 Castell Collen area   213 Caerau (Beulah)   214 Westbury   215 Leintwardine (Jay Lane)   223 Caerphilly   224 Pen-y-darren   HILLFORT   HF3 Sudbrook

Mediolanum. It has been identified with Bravonio in the Antonine Itinerary at Leintwardine, and Brannogenium in Ravenna, a key military area in the Tame Valley. The fifth place is Luentinum in the territory of the Demetae to the north of Moridumum. On the grounds that the word could have been derived from a Celtic word meaning 'to wash', Rivet and Smith have accepted the suggestion of George Boon in identifying this place-name with the gold mine at Dolaucothi. There is some evidence, although slight, which suggests pre-Roman gold workings (see below) and, of course, it is possible that, like the legionary bases, this is an addition from a later source.

The Legionary Base at Usk
(No L6, figs 39, 40)

The excavations which, prior to development, revealed this site, were undertaken in the years 1967–76, under the direction of Dr W. Manning. However, of the 48 acres of the fortress area, only about $4^{1}/_{2}$ acres were excavated.[11] Of the reports published, Dr Kevin Greene's study has a considerable significance for the student of the military dispositions in Britain in the Claudian-Neronian period. Dr Greene includes a distribution map of the wares imported from Lyons in Central Gaul (fig 38). This is remarkable, covering not only the area occupied by the army up to this time, but also that of the 42 find spots, of which 35 are known or postulated mid-first-century fort sites. Of the other seven sites, Bagendon and Salmonbury are hill-forts of the friendly Dobunni, where early imports could be expected, and South Cadbury is another hill-fort of a hostile tribe, the Durotriges, but with definite army connections (*Invasion* 108). Eccles and Faversham are on the main route from Richborough to London and early imports need have no military association. Likewise, Wilkswood is on the south coast near the port of entry at Hamworthy in Poole Harbour, a possible Roman naval base. This only leaves York as the oddity, especially as seven different vessels are recorded (report p. 42). Dr Greene has shown that the production of these wares ceased at Lyons abruptly in 69 during the troubles of the Civil War. So it is rather surprising that so many vessels appear at York which was occupied from 71,[12] although it is possible that the site could have been held by the army a little earlier under Vettius Bolanus.[13] Although Dr Greene makes no attempt to date the founding of Usk, his study clearly underlines its Neronian origin.

The position of three sides of the fortress are known for certain, and the fourth on the west and river side can be postulated with fair certainty (although an excavation in 1975 failed to locate the presumed alignment).[14] This gives a dimension of c.400m by 470m (c.1310ft by 1540ft), about 48 acres, and the total area so far investigated thoroughly is less than 10 per cent. However, since the two excavated sites are in a central position (fig.39), it is possible to formulate ideas about the fortress. The sites are along the *via principalis*, one in the *retentura* and the other the *praetentura*, but the buildings fronting this main road of the fortress are not normally found in this position. In the eastern area, with its elaborate drainage system, are three granaries in a row supported on sleeper walls with a metalled area for loading bays. To the west there is a blank area filled with pits, associated with iron working,[18] and to the south a narrow street parallel to the *via principalis*, fronted by five pairs of granaries which are all supported on vertical post-piles driven into the ground. The difference between

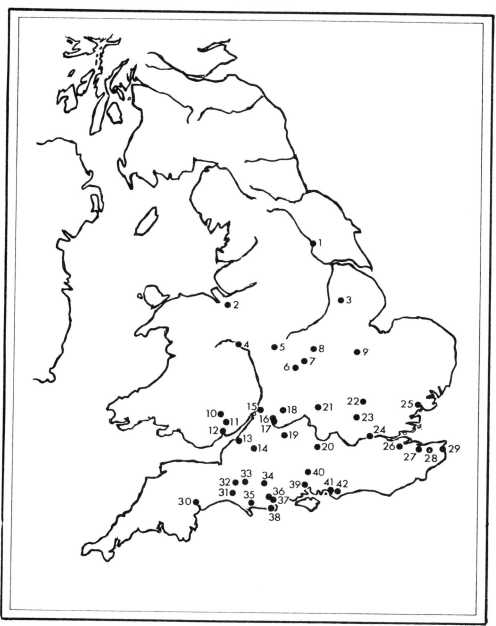

38   Lyon ware: distribution in Britain   1 York   2 Chester   3 Lincoln   4 Wroxeter   5
Wall   6 The Lunt   7 High Cross   8 Leicester   9 Longthorpe   10 Abergavenny   11
Usk   12 Caerleon   13 Sea Mills   14 Bath   15 Gloucester/Kingsholm   16 Bagendon   17
Cirencester   18 Salmonsbury   19 Wanborough   20 Silchester   21 Alchester   22
Baldock   23 Verulamium   24 London   25 Colchester   26 Eccles   27 Faversham   28
Canterbury   29 Richborough   30 Exeter   31 Waddon Hill   32 Ham Hill   33 South
Cadbury   34 Hod Hill   35 Dorchester   36 Corfe Mullen   37 Hamworthy   38
Wilkswood   39 Bitterne   40 Winchester   41 Fishbourne   42 Chichester

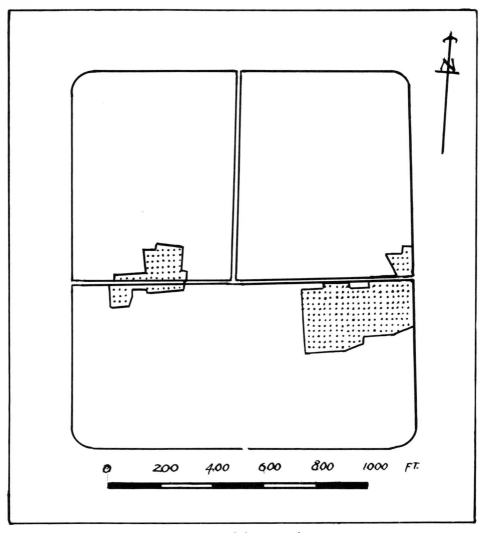

35 Plan of the Usk fortress, showing stippled excavated areas

the two methods of construction is most striking, but the reason for it is not known, unless possibly there were two different types of material stored in them, for example, one for grain, the other for other kinds of food such as meat etc. There are no other buildings in this area except for traces of one on the western edge of the site. In the other area towards the western end of the main street, where it was flanked by a double colonnade, the remains present a problem in identification. On the north side there are two side streets between which are fenced enclosures which Dr Manning has identified as stores compounds. On the eastern edge of the excavated area there was part of a courtyard building which may have been workshops or offices. On the other side of the main street, only in one small area was it possible to extend the excavation

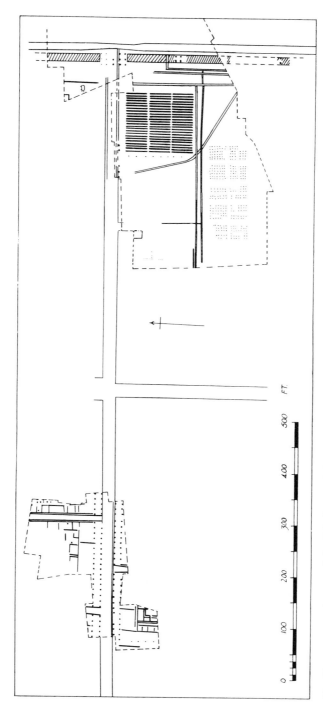

39 Two excavated areas of the Usk fortress (after Dr W. Manning)

to the south, and the corner of a building was revealed which could be part of a tribune's house. The last of these is the only building normal to the *via principalis*.

In spite of the highly irregular plan, Professor Manning accepts Usk as a legionary fortress. It would follow that he must regard it as the permanent base of the *Leg. XX*, having moved there from the Kingsholm fortress. But the evidence produced by Henry Hurst in his excavations of this site was that it was not demolished until the mid-sixties when presumably the legion moved to Wroxeter. It would seem unlikely that the legion would have kept two fortresses in occupation for ten years. The datable artifacts from Usk incline Professor Manning to Didius Gallus for this forward move. But Gallus was sent to stabilise the frontier as a holding operation until a decision could be reached on the future of Britain. Nero refused to give the province up and in consequence it was necessary to advance and conquer the hostile Silures. Q. Veranius was sent to do this. Logically, it follows that Usk would have been his forward base, *c*.56. Any earlier pottery could have come from an auxiliary outpost of Gallus below the legionary base. The legion had its permanent fortress at Gloucester and would presumably winter there.[16] Enough troops would be needed to be established at Usk to protect the base, but this could have been no more than a few cohorts and does not appear to have included the first. Usk would have occupied a rearward position once the advance army had penetrated deep into Silurian territory. There must, therefore, be more forts in south and central Wales which have a Neronian origin, but the evidence to date is sadly lacking. One might, however, seek some consolation in the map of early Flavian sites occupied *c*.74–8 published by Dr Jeffrey Davies.[17] This shows strings of forts and fortlets filling the valleys, but leaving the Demetae severely alone. Although this tribe may have been an ally, the fleet would have needed a harbour here, and probably harbours to the west, for their patrols and operations on the Irish Sea Coast. So a fort at Carmarthen (Moridunum, No 204) would not occasion surprise.[18] The other possibility in this territory would be a fort at the gold mines at Pumpsaint (No 201) which would help to support the Neronian origin of Ptolemy's list. Much depends on whether the presence of gold was known to the Britons. In his detailed survey of the whole area of the mines,[19] Professor Barri Jones has drawn attention to his Area VIII which lies beyond the Roman workings. An excavation produced a group of circular huts with daub-built walls, apparently connected with small-scale mining on an exposed rock face. Unfortunately, no dating evidence was forthcoming, and it is known that circular huts continued to be built in rural and highland areas throughout the Roman period. However, it seems rather surprising that the Roman procurator of the mines would have allowed any native exploitation when full control of the area had been established; on this argument alone, one might postulate pre-Roman workings. A clause in any treaty with the Demetae would have allowed Roman state monopoly to operate; that is part of the price the tribe would have paid to avoid worse exploitation. Excavations on the site of the fort at Pumpsaint have not produced a fort as early as Veranius.[20] Early Flavian samian has, however, been recovered from the eroded river bank in the village.[21] The only fort in the west for which pre-Flavian pottery has actually been claimed is Llandovey (No 202), which was trenched by Dr Jarrett in 1961 and 1962.[22] A water-main trench was observed in 1969,[23] and Dr Jarrett has made it quite clear that he considers that the sherds were residual.[24]

For the other possible sites founded by Veranius, one must use 'intelligent guesswork'. One cannot, however, include the sites of civil settlement, as it is often possible to in the lowland zone (see *Invasion*, p. 122), since there is very little civil development, except along the south coast. But much of Wales remained under military control, at least until well into the second century, and it is reasonable to assume that some of the permanent sites were founded as early as Veranius.

The Routes of the Veranian Campaign
Route 27 extended

As indicated at the beginning of this section, one of the routes Veranius may have established is that of the Upper Severn, extending to the coast. The object of this would have been to prevent any interference with his operations against the Silures from the Ordovices. This route could be considered as an extension of Route 27 via Brompton, and there are three possible sites for units at this period – Westbury (No 214), Caersws (No 196) and Pen-Llwyn (No 197). The distance between Wroxeter and Brompton is about 25 miles and one might reasonably expect a fort in a mid-way position. When this road was fully established, it was directed to Forden Gaer. It has been surveyed by W.G. Putman, and Professor Barri Jones, in an appendix, has suggested a fort at Westbury where there is slight evidence of Roman occupation.[25]

Caersws (Mediolanum, No 196)

Caersws occupies a key position where the Severn Valley broadens at the junction of two streams; one of these, the Afon Garno, provides an important valley route[26] over the watershed into the Dyfi Valley, and the other, the Afon Trannon, continues the known route over the difficult hill country to link with the coast. There are two military sites at Caersws, about three-quarters of a mile apart, which have become known as I and II.[27] Caersws II is the westerly of the two, at the junction of the Garno, where the modern village has developed. It was excavated by Bosanquet early in the century,[28] and its defences and vicus have more recently been studied by Charles Daniels and Barri Jones in 1966 and 1967, and their interim results published.[29] It is clear from this work that Caersws II was the permanent fort which was held in strength up to the end of the second century. The important factors, from our point of view, are firstly the discovery of pre-Flavian pottery, which suggested to the excavators of the 1966 section that the fort rampart 'antedates the work of Frontinus'.[30] The other factor is the discovery by Professor St Joseph of Caersws I (Llwŷn-y-brain). This was first thought to have been a campaign camp,[31] but subsequent flying showed that it was a large 9.3-acre fort, with additional defences on two sides at least.[32] There is no known fort site to the west of this route until the coast is reached. It would have had to cross the barrier of the Plynlimon mountains, and the sole route would have been that out by the Wye and the tributaries of the Rheidol. The only indication of any Roman presence is the signal station at Cae Gaer (No 6), now buried in a conifer plantation.[33]

The next site, 4.5 miles from the mouth of the Theidol at Pen-Llwyn (No 197), was found by Professor St Joseph in 1976.[34] It is a large seven-acre fort and, as its finder suggests, was probably occupied by a cavalry *ala*. Excavations by Dr Jeffrey Davies on the defences produced a small quantity of pottery thought to be provisionally Flavian–Hadrianic.[35] Further work is clearly needed to obtain more definite information about the fort's foundation date.

The two large forts Pen-Llwyn and Llwŷn-y-brain would have fitted quite well into a protective screen established by Veranius, blocking any movement to the south while engaged on his campaigns. The route at this point joints the coastal route which was soon to be extended to the north, but Veranius would have needed the southern route connecting his forces with the Tywi Valley. It is difficult to know what the coastline of Cardigan Bay was like in early Roman times, since much erosion and submergence has taken place,[36] but it could have been that the tidal Dovey Estuary provided better harbourage than the Rheidol, where Aberystwyth now stands, with its steep cliffs and shifting shingle beaches. Possibly Veranius would have held the Dyfi. Hopes have been raised by the discovery at Pennal (No 198) of two central Gaulish lead-glazed bottles with relief decoration (Déch. forms 60 and 62) in a burnt deposit with other pottery, including a mortarium similar to examples from Usk.[37] However, Dr Greene has shown in his report on the Usk pottery that the manufacture of lead-glazed vessels continued in the Allier region until c.70.[38] His map shows examples from Carlisle, Malton and York, implying continuity after 70. Another sherd has been found on the Caer Gai fort at the south-west end of Bala Lake.[39] Between Pennal and Pen-Llwyn, is a signal station at Erglodd[40] (No 7) with an extensive view of the Dyfi Estuary, which gives a little support to the use of this by the Fleet.

Continuing the route to the south from Pen-Llwyn, the next known fort is at Trawscoed (No 199) on the north bank of the Ystwyth, found in fieldwork by Professor St Joseph in 1959.[41] It is a five-acre fort and a small-scale excavation has produced a few sherds of pottery, suggesting a Flavian–Trajanic span. A section through the defences produced evidence of two periods,[42] evidence which is obviously inadequate to support a Veranian origin. The next fort to the south is Llanio (Bremia, No 200), but little is known about it. The bath-house was found in 1887, but the precise site of the fort was not known until 1969,[43] when Dr J.L. Davies trenched the southern defences. But the pottery he recovered appeared to fit the traditional date of c.75.

Ten miles to the south is the gold-mining area of Dolaucothi and its protective fort at Pumpsaint (No 201), the evidence for which has already been considered above. The special value of this site may well have attracted Roman interest as early as Veranius. The next fort on the route at Llandovery (No 202) where it joins Route 40. This site has also been discussed above and is one of the few from which pre-Flavian pottery has been claimed, but not, as yet, substantiated. We continue the route by means of the Usk Valley round the north hills of the Brecon Beacon[44] to its junction with the Scapulan frontier Route 39 at Abergavenny.

Y Gaer (Cicutium, No 208)
There are two known forts on this route, the first is the well-placed Y Gaer. This was the site of an extensive excavation by Mortimer Wheeler[45] and it is hardly surprising to find that he produced the traditional date of c.75 for the foundation (Report 69). While he admits that, during the thirty years of intermittent warfare, 'Roman troops may have found their way up to the arterial valley of the Usk to the point when the remains of the Brecon fort now stands,' his excavation produced a large amount of material and his report includes as many as 80 coarse pottery vessels. This gives one an opportunity of searching for pre-Flavian items. Among the coins are seven of Republican date, but all are much worn and could have been lost any time in the first century, especially the two galley types of Mark Antony. The samian report was written by T. Davies Pryce, and it includes only one sherd which could be considered

pre-Flavian (Report S155), but there are several early in the Flavian period.[46] The coarse pottery was published in stratified groups, but only one appears to be an earlier one. This was from a pit 'dug during the earliest occupation of the fort' and includes five vessels (c.52–56) which are all early mid-first century in date, but any proposed bracket would have to include the early Flavian period and much the same could be said for Nos C18 and 19. More hopeful are the pieces of millefiore glass from three different vessels. This kind of polychrome glass is extremely rare in Britain on any site later than the Claudian-Neronian period.[47] Such vessels would have been treasured and had a high survival value but nevertheless the vessels offer a hint at least of a pre-Flavian occupation at Brecon. More recent excavations by John Casey have concentrated on the defences,[48] and do not help with the dating problem.

The fort halfway between Brecon and Abergavenny is Pen-y-Gaer (No 209)[49] which has already been considered as an outpost in the Scapulan frontier system; but the evidence is not adequate to support a foundation date of the Veranian period.

Route 40

This route, which starts at Worcester, has already been traced through Blackwardine (No 162) to the crossing of the Scapulan frontier Route 39 at a possible fort on the River Lugg, thence to the outpost fort at Hindwell Farm (No 174). From here it presumably connects with the key site in the centre of Wales, Castell Collen[50] (No 212). This is a fort with a long history of excavation, starting in 1911, but the most important work was done by Leslie Alcock in 1954–6.[51] There are two main periods, the earlier was a timber fort of five acres and given the traditional foundation date of c.75. The samian pottery from the excavations does not prove to be very helpful. The earliest pieces dated by Dr Simpson are a form 15/17, c.55–80 (S1) and two sherds of form 18, c.60–80 (S2 and 3). If there is an earlier fort in this area, as one can reasonably expect, it would be in a different part of the valley, possibly in the Crossgates – Penybont area.

Route 42

This is an extension of the Route up the Wye Valley to Clyro (No 210) which probably replaced Clifford (No 175), then crossed over the watershed into the Usk Valley to Brecon Gaer (No 208), thence over the hills of Forest Fawr, into the Mellte Valley to join the coast at Neath (Nidum, No 179). The only known fort on this long stretch between the last two forts is at Coelbren (No 206) where the valley opens out. This 5-acre fort situated slightly above a marshy area was excavated in 1904.[52] The samian has been examined by Dr Simpson, who found the earliest sherd to be forms 29 and 15/17, which indicates a Flavian occupation.[53] There is probably an earlier site elsewhere, but there are few suitable places. Coelbren is halfway between the Neath and Swansea valleys, and, to control the narrow valley where Aberdare and Mountain Ash are now situated, it may have been necessary during the conquest period to have established a fort in the Rhigos area. The accepted Roman road, known as Sarn Helen, uses the high ground of the Hirfyndd ridge, north-east of Neath,[54] but turns sharply towards Coelbren. Its original course would have been aimed at the junction of the Neath with Afon Mellte, thence up the River Hepsie, to cross the Brecon Beacons via Glen Tarell, the accepted route to Brecon Gaer.

Route 46

Weston-under-Penyard (Ariconium, No 164)

The route continued along the Bristol Channel through Chepstow (No 166), a site which has been considered under the coastal route, then turned north into the difficult terrain of the Forest of Dean to Weston-under-Penyard. There appears to have been a settlement here associated with extensive iron workings, but little is at present known about it.[55] The only excavations, both on a small scale, have been those of G.H. Jack in 1922[56] and by N.P. Bridgewater in 1963.[57] The site, has, however, produced no less than 27 British coins, according to Derek Allen's list,[58] and the supplementary one of Colin Haselgrove.[59] All but three are Dobunnic types[60] and this evidence points towards the existence of a pre-Roman settlement,[61] possibly connected with iron workings. This suggestion is strengthened by another find from this site,[62] for among the brooches is an interesting proto-rosette type,[63] rare for Britain and dating to *c*.20 BC–AD 30. The only hint of a military presence are the two Claudian imitation coins, and two fragments of samian form 24/25, of Claudian Neronian date.[64] The deposits of iron ore would certainly have been of interest to the Roman army. Indications of the site of a fort have been found to the north of the settlement.

The Route skirted the large bend on the Wye by How Caple, crossed the River Frome at the junction of the Lugg, then would have intersected Route 42 between Stretton Grandison and Kenchester. There is a straight length of modern road which is also a parish boundary from Longworth to Withington; the actual crossing of the river is just south of Withington Station, and a fort might be expected hereabouts. The next site to the north is Blackwardine (No 162) where it joins Route 48.

The Extension of Route 46

The coastal route has already been described above since, it is argued, it may have been established by Scapula, or the Fleet may have held the harbours. Whatever may have been the earlier arrangement, Veranius would have controlled the coastal area in his plan to surround the Silures, and it seems reasonable to assume that this would have been extended to the west to Carmarthen. A fort long suspected[65] was eventually located at Loughor (Leucarum, No 205) in 1969, and subsequently excavated by Dr Roger Ling.[66] The fort was found to be buried under the village, with the church in the centre and an early medieval castle in its south-east corner (Second Report, fig A). It occupied a commanding position at the lowest crossing point of the river, but where it was still accessible from the sea. It was a rescue excavation in 1968, near the castle, that first revealed the fort defences; further work was naturally restricted by the presence of the later ancient monument and the built-up area. There was very little found in the rather limited excavation to suggest a pre-Flavian date.[67]

The evidence of early occupation at Carmarthen (Moridunum, No 204) is slightly more positive, with a pre-Flavian sherd of form 29, published by Dr Simpson.[68] Although no fort has been found as yet, it would be surprising if one is not eventually found, since the Fleet would have found the estuary and its extensive harbourage of considerable strategic importance.

Route 53

This important link route ran from the coastal fort at Cardiff, over the high ground between the Rivers Rhymney and Taff, to join Route 42. The route may well have played a significant role in the initial conquest of the Silures, since it effectively cuts their territory in half and the old Roman adage *divide et vince* was always applied where and whenever possible. There are three known fort sites on this route at Caerphilly (No 223), Gellygaer (No 207) and Pen-y-darren (No 224).

The first of them at Caerphilly[69] was, like so many others, disguised by the proximity of a castle in the Middle Ages, although in this case it was recognised as a separate earthwork and thought correctly, as was later discovered, to belong to the Civil War. In 1963, this theory was tested by a trench and the defences of a Roman fort unexpectedly encountered.[70] It was only possible to carry out a limited investigation, but the site has remained an open one, even though there are a few later buildings and the construction of a Civil War gun-platform has caused some disturbance. Little dating evidence was recovered but it is interesting to note that at least three sherds were found in the turf rampart, which suggests that it may not be primary. A coarse ware bowl was considered as probably early Flavian (Report, fig 7, no 1) on the grounds that it had 'Belgic' characteristics. But these tended to fade out very slowly and this particular vessel need not be much earlier than the late first century; nor were the tiny scraps of samian any earlier. One would thus have to wait for larger-scale investigations to give more precise evidence of the foundation date.

Gellygaer (No 207)

The next fort, at Gellygaer, has been made famous by the excavations of John Ward who in 1900 took over the investigation started earlier by the Cardiff Naturalists Society. He continued the following year and came back to the site in 1908 and 1913.[71] John Ward was an excavator well in advance of his day and his excellent photographs clearly show the tidiness of his work.[72] He acknowledged, in the Preface, his debt to Haverfield. This shows in the discussion on the period of the fort, since he recognised the possibility of a Scapulan foundation (Report 96), but dismissed it for lack of evidence. Apart from two Republican *denarii*, the earliest coin was Vespasian. However, Professor Jarrett has since demonstrated that an adjacent site, previously thought to be a campaign camp or labour camp, is an earlier Flavian fort and that Ward's stone fort was built under Trajan. Dr Simpson has noted South Gaulish samian, but none of it appears to be pre-Flavian.[73]

The third fort, at Pen-y-Darren, near Merthyr Tydfil (No 224),[74] has a history of sporadic excavations, without much firm evidence, and the position of the defences is only partly known.[75] A substantial portion of the southern part of the fort was damaged or destroyed in the levelling of a football ground in 1905. A large collection of pottery survives from the early excavations, but Dr Simpson has not been able to detect any pre- or early Flavian sherds. The junction of the route with Route 42 is uncertain, as noted above. While it would seem necessary for any serious attempt to crush the Silures to have controlled this route, the evidence of any pre-Flavian occupation does not, as yet, exist along it. Nevertheless, one feels that permanent military control would have been established long before the advent of Frontinus.

Route 55

From Carmarthen there is an important link route with Caersws which would have offered control of the Twyi Valley and the central Welsh hill country. A possible military site halfway between Carmarthen and Llandovery has been found from the air by Terrence James near Llandeilo (No 203),[76] but its size (c.9 acres) makes it too large for a fort, so it may be a campaign camp. The next site at Llandovery (No 202) has already been considered. Beyond this is Caerau (No 213), also known as Beulah,[77] a fort of at least two periods, the earlier being 4.2 acres. The only excavation has been a few trenches in 1965[78] and the pottery was in poor condition due to the acid subsoil; a Frontinan foundation was assumed. Crop-marks recorded by Professor St Joseph suggest other military activity, including a possible signal station.[79] About six miles further along the route is the fortlet, or signal station, of Pen-min-Cae (No 8), only a third of an acre, standing on high ground on the north bank of the Wye. It was found in 1971 by Professor St Joseph, who visited the site and found some first century samian, including a fragment of form 15/17.[80] He also noticed indications in the form of field boundaries of the ridgeway route which if continued crosses Llandrindod Common, where there is a very interesting collection of Roman practice field works.[81] The site of the fort which preceded Castell Collen has been considered above, the route would have followed the Ithon Valley over the high ground on its west bank and the distance to Caersws of over 20 miles would have needed a fort midway along it, but at present there is an unfortunate blank on the map.

Route 57

A link route would have connected Castell Collen or its predecessor with Clyro (No 210) and a mid-point fort has been found below Colwyn Castle (No 211) which effectively disguised the earlier work.[82] No artefacts have yet been recovered to make the date of origin of the site certain.

Rome had been particularly unlucky with her British governors – two of the first dying suddenly in office, both at crucial times. It was important for Rome to maintain the pressure of her attack against the Welsh tribes and complete the subjugation of their lands. There was no time for any long period of discussion, and in any case it would have been unusual had a man of the diverse talents of Veranius been available. What was now required was an able soldier with experience in mountain warfare. Suetonius Paullinus was ordered to Britain immediately to finish off the war. He was not the man to help the aggrieved Britons, now under great pressure from the Druids, who realised far too well that their first line of defence had been removed with the defeat of the Silures, and that their sacred groves were now under real threat. The scene was set for the awesome events of the great revolt, which was to be so traumatic for Britain and Rome alike. But that is another story, which is covered in my volume on *Boudica* (1978).

Translation of Relevant Texts from Tacitus, Dio and Suetonius

BY MARY BEARD AND CHLOE CHARD

Tacitus, *Annals* xii. 31–40

31   In Britain the governor, P. Ostorius, faced a confused state of affairs. The enemy had invaded allied territory with particular violence, since they thought that a new general, hampered by an unfamiliar army and the approach of winter, would not be able to confront them. Ostorius was aware that it was his first moves that would produce either fear or confidence in the enemy, and therefore hurried on his hastily mobilised cohorts. He killed those Britons that had resisted, pursued those that were scattered; fearing that they might muster again and that a peace fraught with hostility and suspicion would create a situation in which neither general nor soldiers could enjoy any respite, he prepared to disarm those he thought suspect and control the whole area south of the rivers Trent and Severn. The first rebellion came from the Iceni, a tough people who had never been crushed in war because they had entered alliance with us willingly. The surrounding tribes followed their lead and chose a site for a battle enclosed by a rough earthwork and with an entrance narrow enough to prevent the cavalry getting in. The Roman general set himself to break through these defences even though he was commanding allied troops without legionary strength. He deployed his infantry in their cohorts and made use of the cavalry in addition by assigning them the duty of fighting on foot. Then he gave the signal and his soldiers stormed the earthwork and threw the enemy into disorder, for they were obstructed by their own defences. Aware that they were rebels and with their escape routes blocked, they fought with prodigious bravery: in this battle the governor's son, M. Ostorius, won the award for saving the life of a citizen.

32   Those who were hesitating between war and peace were reduced to docility by the defeat of the Iceni. The army was then led against the Decangi. Their territory was ravaged and booty was seized far and wide. The enemy did not dare to engage in open warfare and, if they attempted to plant ambushes harassing the army on the march, such subterfuge was punished. The Romans were now not far from the coast facing Ireland, when rebellion breaking out amongst the Brigantes forced the general back, for he was firm in his resolve that he should undertake no new ventures until his earlier achievements had been consolidated. The Brigantes in fact returned to calm once those who had resorted to arms had been killed and the others had been pardoned. Since neither violence nor clemency moved the Silures to abandon hostilities, they had to be kept down by legionary camps. In order to implement this strategy more speedily, a colony was established on captured territory at Camulodunum – with a strong presence of veteran troops – to act as a stronghold against rebellion and as a means of instilling in the native allies a sense of legal responsibility.

33. The Romans now moved against the Silures, whose natural spirit was reinforced by their faith in the prowess of Caratacus, whose many battles against the Romans – some of uncertain outcome and some clear victories – had raised him to a position of pre-eminence amongst the other British chieftains. Since his strength lay not in military superiority but in the tactical advantages to be gained from knowing difficult terrain, he transferred the scene of the conflict to the territory of the Ordovices. He recruited from those who dreaded the establishment of the Roman peace and staked his fate on one last confrontation. He chose a place for the battle where the entrances and exits were to our disadvantage but favourable to his own troops. On one side there was a precipitously steep gradient, and where there were gentler approach routes he piled up stones to form a kind of embankment. There was also a river of uncertain depth flowing past and here bands of fighters were stationed to provide defences.

34. Moreover the tribal leaders went round giving encouragement and stiffening the spirit of their troops, calming their fears, raising their hopes and offering other incitements to battle. Caratacus in particular was rushing from place to place, invoking that very day and that very battle as either the rebirth of liberty or the beginning of eternal servitude. He called upon his ancestors by name, those who had driven out Julius Caesar, the dictator. The valour of these men had preserved their descendants from the power of Roman officials and the imposition of tribute and had kept the bodies of their wives and children from defilement. His words were greeted by voices of assent, as each man bound himself by the oath of his tribe that he would not yield before any weapons or any wounds.

35. These energetic efforts amazed the Roman general. At the same time he was alarmed by the barrier formed by the river, by the rampart that had been built up, by the threatening mountains, by the whole grim prospect and the crowds of defenders at every point. But the Roman soldiers demanded battle, shouting out that bravery could overcome all opposition. The Prefects and the Tribunes put forward similar arguments and so increased the enthusiasm of the army. Then, after a survey to discover which points in the defences might or might not be penetrated, Ostorius led out his troops, eager for battle, and crossed the river without difficulty. When they reached the rampart, while the fighting was still conducted with missile weapons, it was our troops who suffered more wounds and more casualties; but afterwards, once they had formed a defensive cover with their shields, they managed to tear down the Britons' rough and irregular wall of rocks and battle was engaged on fairer terms at close quarters. The barbarians were then forced to retreat into the mountains. But here also our soldiers followed up their assault. They were both light-armed and heavy-armed; the former attacked the enemy with javelins, the latter pressed on in close order breaking up the ranks of the Britons as they met them, since these did not have the protection of breast plates or helmets. In fact, if they resisted the auxiliary troops, they were massacred by the swords and spears of the legionaries, and if they turned against these, they met the same fate at the hands of the auxiliaries with their broadswords and lances. It was a renowned victory: the wife and daughter of Caratacus were captured and his brothers were taken in surrender.

36. As adversity invites further troubles, Caratacus himself was put in chains and handed over to the victors, although he had sought refuge with Cartimandua, the queen of the Brigantes. It was the ninth year after the war in Britain had begun. As a result of his resistance, however, his fame spread beyond his own island and was acclaimed as it filtered through not only the neighbouring provinces, but also Italy.

People longed to see who it was who had defied our power for so many years. Not even in Rome itself was the name of Caratacus lacking in honour, and the Emperor's attempts to enhance his own glory increased the renown of his vanquished enemy. The people were summoned as though to a splendid spectacle. The cohorts of the Praetorian Guard were marshalled under arms on the parade ground in front of their barracks. Then the clients of the king were led past and the torques, military trappings and spoils of his foreign wars were likewise displayed. Next his brothers, his wife and his daughter were put on show, and finally Caratacus himself. The others, in their fear, made degrading entreaties, but not so Caratacus. He avoided a downcast gaze and appeals for mercy, but stood on the tribunal and spoke as follows:

37.   'If I had been blessed with only a moderate measure of prosperity to accompany my noble birth and high rank, I would have entered this city as a friend rather than as a captive, and you would not have thought it beneath your dignity to receive into formal alliance a man sprung from illustrious ancestors, holding sway over many tribes. My present fate confers as much glory on you as shame on me. I possessed horses, men, arms and wealth. Is it surprising if I have been unwilling to give these up? For if it is your desire to rule over the whole world, does it follow that all men should readily accept servitude? If I had been dragged here after instant surrender, neither my ill-fortune nor your glorious success would have won such renown. If you were to put me to death, I should be forgotten. But if you preserve my life, I shall be an everlasting witness to your clemency.' In response to this speech Caesar granted pardon to the king himself and to his wife and his brothers. After they had been released from their chains, they paid homage to Agrippina in much the same terms of gratitude and praise as to the Emperor, for she was sitting in a prominent position on another dais close by. It was certainly a new and unprecedented development, not in keeping with the traditions of our forebears, that a woman should sit before the Roman standards. She behaved as a partner in the Empire that had been won by her ancestors.

38.   The Senate was then assembled and many resounding speeches were made about the capture of Caratacus. It was represented as no less glorious than P. Scipio's capture of Syphax, L. Paulus's capture of Perseus or any other example of a foreign king being exhibited as a captive to the Roman people. The insignia of a triumph were awarded to Ostorius; his fortune had been good up to that point, but did not continue unmixed. This was either because our military operations became slacker once Caratacus had been removed, on the assumption that the war was completely finished, or because the enemy's desire for vengeance grew fiercer out of pity for such a great king. They surrounded the legionary cohorts who had been left behind under a senior officer to build defences in Silurian territory. So if help had not been sent from the neighbouring forts to the besieged men, immediately on receipt of the news, they would have been utterly slaughtered. As it was, the officer, eight centurions and all the bravest of the ranks lost their lives. Not long after this setback the enemy put to flight a foraging party of ours and the squadrons of cavalry sent out to its rescue.

39.   Ostorius then sent his light-armed cohorts against the attackers, but even by this strategy he would not have stopped the rout if the legions had not joined in the battle. Their strength put the fight on more equal terms, and finally our men came off the better. The enemy fled but because light was failing they sustained few losses. There were now a series of skirmishes, generally fought with guerilla tactics over the wooded or swampy land. The result depended either on the luck or on the courage of the individual soldiers; sometimes the fight was entered on impulse, sometimes with great forethought; the motive might be revenge or booty, and the operation might be conducted at the order of their leaders or sometimes completely without their knowledge. Particular stubbornness was shown by the Silures, who were angered by a reported remark of the Roman general, to the effect that the very name of their tribe should be completely erased, just as in Germany the Sugambri had once been exterminated or deported into the Gallic provinces. They therefore made a surprise attack on two auxiliary cohorts who were plundering without due caution because of the greed of their officers. They were tempting other tribes to revolt as well, by generous distributions of spoils and captives, when, worn out by the burden of his responsibilities, Ostorius died. This was much to the enemy's delight, as they felt that a general of considerable stature had been carried off, if not by pitched battle then at least by the pressures of the war they were conducting.

40.   As soon as the Emperor heard of the death of the governor, he appointed Aulus Didius in his place, so that the province should not be without a ruling hand. This new appointee travelled quickly to the province but did not find a satisfactory situation there, for in the meantime a legion under Manlius Valens had suffered a reverse. Reports of this event were greatly exaggerated, especially by the enemy, so that they might instil panic in the new governor as he arrived. He also exaggerated what he heard, so that he might win greater glory if he settled the province, or might, at least, be more justly forgiven if the rebels held out. The Silures were responsible for this damage as well and they ranged over a wide field of plunder until they were forced back by the advance of Didius. But, in fact, after the capture of Caratacus, Venutius was the most outstanding of the Britons for his military skill. He was, as I have said, from the tribe of the Brigantes. While married to Queen Cartimandua he had long been a loyal ally and had been protected by Roman military strength. But afterwards, when their divorce was followed by immediate war, he directed his hostilities towards us also. At first, however, fighting was confined to the Britons concerned. By a cunning plot Cartimandua trapped the brother of Venutius and his other relations. But her enemies, angered by this, smarting under the shame of being subjected to a woman's rule, invaded her kingdom with a strong military force. Our officials had foreseen this and sent cohorts to support her. A fierce battle ensued; the early stages were indecisive but the final result was in our favour. Similar success followed a battle fought by a legion under the command of Caesius Nasica, for Didius himself, weighed down by his advanced years and laden with honours, thought it sufficient to act through his juniors and merely keep the enemy at bay.

Although these events took place under two governors, over several years, I have related them as a single narrative for fear that they might become unduly difficult to remember if divided up year by year. I now return to the strict order of events.

Tacitus, *Agricola*, 14

The first consular governor in command of the province was Aulus Plautius; he was succeeded by Ostorius Scapula. Both these men were renowned for their military prowess. Gradually the southernmost part of Britain was formally constituted as a province, and a colony of veteran troops was also planted there. Certain districts were granted to King Cogidumnus – remembered up to our own day as a faithful ally – on the ancient and long-accepted principle of the Roman people that they should use even kings as instruments of control. After this Didius Gallus held onto the land won by his predecessors. He also advanced further into native territory, building just a few forts so that he might win the glory of having increased the area under his control. Veranius took over from Didius, but he died within a year. Suetonius Paullinus then enjoyed great success for two years, conquering tribes and strengthening our garrisons. Confident in these achievements, he advanced on Anglesey as this island was supplying the rebels. By such tactics, however, he exposed his rear to attack.

Suetonius, *Nero*, xviii

He was never driven by any desire or hope of increasing and extending the size of the empire, and he even considered withdrawing the army from Britain. He only gave up this plan out of fear that he might thus appear to detract from the glorious achievements of his forebear.

Dio, *Histories*, lxii. 2. 1

An excuse for the war lay in the reclaiming of the money which Claudius had given to the leaders of the Britons. According to Decianus Catus, the procurator of the island, that sum had to be paid back. It was for this reason that they rebelled – and because Seneca had lent them several million sesterces, even though they had not requested it, in the hope of making a large amount of interest, and had then recalled all the capital at once, exacting it with considerable harshness.

Tiberius Claudius Cogidubnus and the Claudian Conquest

BY PROFESSOR ANTONY BARRETT

In Britain, as elsewhere in the Empire, an important aspect of Roman expansion was the use of local rulers who exercised a nominal authority over their people but were in reality obligated to maintain Rome's, rather than their own, interests. This practice can be traced back to the third century BC. At the outset, the monarch in question was bound to the Roman people by formal treaties, which helped to create the illusion of equality between the two states, but by the late Republic this notion of equality was barely maintained even in theory, and in the Imperial period had disappeared completely. 'Client kings', as they are aptly known,[1] were appointed or dismissed at the whim of the current emperor. The institution provides a good illustration of Rome's traditional readiness to adapt to circumstances. Usually the king's task was to form a buffer between Roman territory and potential enemies; within the borders of the imperium, however, he might be appointed to rule areas whose terrain made them difficult to police, as in Cilicia in Asia Minor, where a mountainous area known as Rough Cilicia seems to have been administered by client-kings through most of the Julio-Claudian period.[2] Judaea forms a category of its own – a country without particular military importance but with special social and religious sensitivities, where direct Roman rule invariably led to problems.

The most familiar of the British client-kings is Tiberius Claudius Cogidubnus. He is known to us from two sources. Tacitus, in his brief summary of events in Britain before Agricola (*Agricola* 14), picks out two noteworthy features of the pacification of southern England before the arrival of Didius Gallus in AD 52, the establishment of the *colonia* at Colchester and the granting of a kingdom to Cogidubnus: *quaedam civitates Cogidumno regi donatae (is ad nostram usque memoriam fidissimus mansit), vetere ac iam pridem recepta populi Romani consuetudine, ut haberet instrumenta servitutis et reges* ('certain *civitates* were granted to Cogidubnus – he remained most loyal right down to our own days – in accordance with an ancient and long-established practice of the Roman people of using kings also as instruments for domination'). The second reference comes in the famous dedicatory inscription on a slab of Purbeck marble, from a temple of Neptune and Minerva, found in Chichester by workmen in 1723 (RIB 91). This inscription has been the subject of much discussion, since until recently it was believed that it contained a description of Cogidubnus as *rex* and *legatus Augusti*, a combination of offices unparalleled in the Roman empire.[3] Professor J.E. Bogaers, however, has recently shown this assumption to be incorrect, and in place of the key letters R LEGAT AVGN proposes to read REG MAGN.[4] The inscription, as revised by Bogaers, now reads in its full form: *Neptuno et Minervae templum pro salute domus divinae ex auctoritate Tiberi Claudi Cogidubni regis magni Britanniae* (or *Britannorum*) *collegium fabrorum et qui in eo sunt de suo dederunt donante aream*[. .]*ente Pudentini filio* ('the guild of artisans and its members provide this temple to Neptune and Minerva at their own expense, for the protection of the divine house, on the authority of Tiberius Claudius Cogidubnus, great king of Britain [or the Britons]. The land was donated by -ens, son of Pudentinus'). That the two references, in Tacitus and in the inscription, are to one and the same person, seems a fairly safe assumption: the Latin spelling *mn* is a natural assimilation from *bn*.[5]

The singling out of Cogidubnus for mention by Tacitus in his brief summary can leave little doubt that the king played a significant role in the early phase of the conquest. Apart from that, however, he is also of great interest to the student of Roman history in general, since he seems at first sight something of an anomaly, not fitting readily into any of the familiar categories of client king. For most, if not all, of his reign, Cogidubnus' kingdom lay not on the line of forward military activity, but well within the *provincia*. Yet it was located in a geographical area that does not pose any special problems of terrain, nor was the population inherently averse to Romanization.[6] Another curious feature of Cogidubnus' reign is that he does not seem to have minted coins, the one ancient privilege jealously maintained by client kings elsewhere.

There is little direct evidence that might shed light on this apparently anomalous arrangement and on the special status that Cogidubnus seems to have enjoyed as a Roman client king. We should logically start with his origins and family background, but can do little more than speculate. Chichester was located in the territory of the Atrebates, who had remained loyal to Rome until subdued by the Catuvellauni from the north in the years before Claudius' invasion. Verica of the Atrebates had been forced by *stasis* to seek refuge with Claudius (Dio, lx. 19) and it has long been assumed that Cogidubnus succeeded him. This might have happened immediately, and Cogidubnus could have been king before the Claudian invasion,[7] but in view of Verica's allegiance to Rome it seems unlikely that the head of the opposing party that ousted him was also pro-Roman. The general view is that Cogidubnus was installed by Claudius, and there is even a possibility that he was brought originally to Rome by Tincommius, another Atrebatic ruler, whose flight to the city some time before AD 7 is mentioned in Augustus' *Res Gestae*.[8] The tradition of rulers sending their successors to Rome as children was an old established one, much encouraged by Augustus, who, according to Suetonius (*Augustus* 48), *plurimorum liberos et educavit simul cum suis et instituit* ('brought up and educated the children of a large number of men together with his own'). The Atrebatic kings sought refuge for political and dynastic reasons, and it is not unreasonable that they should have brought their families for safekeeping. A good example of how useful such personal contacts in Rome could be to a young prince is provided by the sons of Cotys I of Thrace. They were taken to the capital and brought up with Caligula, who on his accession rewarded each of them with a kingdom, in Thrace, Armenia Minor and Pontus. There is, of course, no way of proving that Cogidubnus belonged to the Atrebatic ruling family, or even to that particular tribe, but it seems a safe assumption. The Romans had been known to establish new dynasties in areas where the previous rulers had proved unsatisfactory: the establishment of Amyntas and Polemo by Marc Antony in kingdoms in Asia Minor, for instance.[9] But tribal loyalties in the east were not nearly as strong as in Britain, and Claudius would doubtless have wished to avoid needlessly antagonizing local feeling. We can be somewhat more certain about the grant of Roman citizenship, whose possession is indicated by his Romanised name. It was the practice for newly enfranchised provincials to adopt the *nomen*, or family name, of the emperor under whom the grant was made. This means that Cogidubnus almost certainly did not receive his citizenship before Claudius, since although Tiberius belonged to the *gens Claudia* he no longer used the *nomen* of Claudius after his adoption by Augustus; similarly, it was not used by Caligula. This narrows down the field to Claudius (Tiberius Claudius Drusus), who did not succeed through adoption. It is remotely possible, but highly unlikely, that the kingdom was granted under Claudius but the enfranchisement deferred until Nero (Nero Claudius Caesar Drusus Germanicus).

The general location of Cogidubnus' kingdom can be determined by the fact that the temple erected on his authority was located in Chichester. The question of its extent, however, has been complicated by the ambiguity of Tacitus' description of the grant: *quaedam civitates Cogidumno regi donatae*. The phrase can be taken in two ways and could mean that the *civitates* were 'given to King Cogidubnus' or were 'given to Cogidubnus to be king over'. Many scholars have assumed that the former is intended and that Tacitus' reference is not to an original appointment but to the enlargement of a kingdom already held. But the use of an 'appositional' noun (as in the latter case) is common in Latin, especially to indicate rank or office, and the notion of an enlarged kingdom involves us in two difficulties. After mentioning the granting of the *civitates*, Tacitus goes on to say that it was done because the Romans used kings as *instrumenta servitutis*. But this domination would be effected by the very fact of Cogidubnus' being king, not by the extension of a kingdom that already existed. Moreover, the reference to Cogidubnus occurs in the briefest possible summary of the first nine years of the Roman presence in Britain. The mere expansion of a kingdom (unless the original was so small as to be quite insignificant) would not have merited a reference. Professor Bogaers sees in the expression *rex magnus* the equivalent of the Greek *Megas Basileus* 'Great King', a title often associated in the east with a king who had expanded his ancestral domain by the acquisition of new territory, and one that Cogidubnus might have picked up in his youth from eastern princes staying at the court of Augustus. Final certainty is impossible, but *Megas Basileus*, with its grandiloquent eastern associations, would surely smack of megalomania if used as far west as Britain, and it is difficult to reconcile with a western king noted more for his conformity to Roman policy than his personal pretensions and who apparently did not even mint coins in his own name. It may be possible to explain the title in purely British terms as one that has nothing to do with the gaining of new territory. It has often been suggested by Celtic scholars that features of Celtic culture and society have survived from the Classical through the mediaeval period; it is possible then that *rex magnus* is a Latin version of a Celtic, rather than oriental, title,[10] reflected later in such nomenclature as 'Lord of the Isles' or Rhodri Mawr (*mawr = magnus*), and would not seem out of place in a Celtic context.[11] No special significance should be read into Tacitus' choice of the word *donatae* 'given', which could appropriately be used for the bestowal of a whole kingdom during the Julio-Claudian period. It is the type of word that accurately reflects Roman attitude to client-kings at this time; Mauretania, for instance, granted to Juba by Augustus, is described by Tacitus (*Annales* 4.5) as a *donum populi Romani* ('a gift of the Roman people').

Thus the *civitates* handed over some time before AD 52 almost certainly constituted an original kingdom. Although it must have been large enough to have merited mention in the *Agricola*, its precise size is not easy to determine. One of the most useful tools for identifying the boundaries of Celtic kingdoms in the Roman period is coin distribution.[12] Yet no coin has been securely attributed to Cogidubnus. Two silver coins with the legend C R A B are known from Hod Hill, but the possibility that the letters might stand for Cogidubnus Rex Atrebatum Britannorum, or the like, has been discounted by D.F. Allen, who believes that the inscription constitutes the first four letters of an unknown ruler, on the analogy of C A R A for Caratacus.[13] The word used by Tacitus to describe the kingdom, *civitates*, is unfortunately ambiguous. Caesar uses *civitas* of British tribes,[14] and Tacitus might similarly be speaking loosely of tribes whose groupings are now lost to us. *Civitas* is also, however, the term used for self-governing administrative units within the Roman empire, and it is possible that Tacitus was using the term anachronistically in the *Agricola*. At the time he wrote this work (AD 97/98), the old kingdom of the Atrebates was divided into three such self-governing *civitates*: the Regni (or Regini), in whose territory Chichester lay, the *civitas Atrebatum*, with its capital at Silchester, and the *civitas Belgarum* (containing also part of the Dubunni), with its capital at Winchester. Thus Cogidubnus may have received the old kingdom of the Atrebates, comprising three administrative units at the end of the century and perhaps described by Tacitus in terms appropriate to his own day.

The problem of the special role and status of Cogidubnus' kingdom is obviously closely related to the problem of *when* it was created, since the date might offer some clue to the circumstances that prompted the Romans to this unusual arrangement. We can be certain from the allusion in the *Agricola* that Cogidubnus was made king before AD 52 and the arrival of Didius Gallus, but how much before can only be inferred from events of the period. Since Tacitus contracted his narrative at this point in the *Agricola* to the briefest possible summation of important developments, the mention of the kingdom after the *colonia* at Colchester need have no chronological significance. Nor does the fact that Tacitus then introduces Didius' arrival by the phrase *mox Didius Gallus* mean that his governorship began *soon* after the creation of the kingdom, since *mox* does not strictly mean 'soon' in Latin, but rather 'afterwards' or 'next'. It simply indicates that Didius Gallus was the next governor after Scapula. One possibility is that Cogidubnus might have been created king at the very outset of the invasion, and may even have played a direct role in the invasion by supporting the Romans during a landing on the Sussex plain. This theory is based on the account of Dio (60.19–23), who informs us that Aulus Plautius' invasion force was divided into three in case a single unified landing might be prevented. This is usually understood as a tactical disposition of the three units, so that they might disembark in close proximity and then converge. As early as 1890, however, Hübner suggested that one of the forces might have sailed west and landed somewhere in Sussex.[15] This notion has been revived recently[16] and has been reinforced somewhat by excavations at Fishbourne, close to Chichester. From the earliest Roman period there are two timber military buildings, one possibly some sort of storage depot, the other almost certainly a granary, bearing similarities to granaries found in the earliest stages at Richborough, the major site of the Claudian landing. Besides this, a few items of military equipment have been found. It is of course possible that the military phase at Fishbourne should be associated not with the initial invasion but with the campaigns undertaken shortly afterwards in the south-west by *Legio II* under the command of Vespasian (Suetonius, *Vespasian* 4), in which Cogidubnus might have participated. But in any case, even if Cogidubnus did take part in some phase of the Claudian invasion and promote the Roman cause in his old ancestral area, it is highly unlikely that he could have done so in the formal capacity of king. The Romans would not have taken the risk of granting any ruler authority over a territory that had not yet been conquered. Also, Tacitus' description of Cogidubnus as an 'instrument of domination', even if we make allowances for his cynicism, better suits an appointment some time after the serious military phase was over.

The circumstances that led to the creation of Cogidubnus' kingdom may well arise from an aspect of Britain during this period that we tend to overlook. Despite flourishing commercial contacts with Rome, Britain had, before the conquest, remained relatively isolated. No Roman troops had set foot on the island for almost a century and the vast majority of Britons had probably never seen a Roman. The Atrebates seem generally to have been pro-Roman, but it must be remembered that they had experienced widespread penetration by the hostile Catuvellauni in the years before the invasion.[17] The people of southern England would in the long run prove to be very amenable to Romanization, but their loyalty could not be won overnight. There is, indeed, evidence that the Romans encountered considerable difficulties in maintaining internal stability in the civilian zone of the province. The resentment felt towards Roman authorities before Boudica's revolt is familiar to us, of course, from Tacitus.[18] But there are also indications that the Romans faced an internal rebellion in Britain some years before that, in AD 47.[19] In that year, as Tacitus (*Annales* xiv.31) tells us, the enemy launched a massive campaign against Rome's allies (*socii*) to take advantage of the winter and the inexperience of Scapula in his new post. The 'enemy' is usually taken to refer to an external hostile force, probably the Silures, but that an internal uprising was involved is suggested by the words Tacitus uses to describe the events – *turbidae res* – a phrase that he uses elsewhere of sedition or internal uprising.[20] Also, to prevent a recurrence of the disaster once the enemy assault had been crushed, Scapula, Tacitus tells us, disarmed the tribes *ne rursus conglobarentur* (so that they would not mass together again). But the tribes disarmed were located *cis Trisantonam et Sabrinam* (this side of the Trent and Severn), that is, *east*, and not west, of the Fosse Way, and thus within the *provincia*. Cogidubnus' role, then may have been to maintain a firm hand in an area where local loyalty could not be counted upon. If Cogidubnus understood his task as primarily one of establishing Roman authority over the native population (as opposed merely to providing effective government), this could explain why he might have felt it impolitic to mint coins in his own name. It is also possible that Prasutagus of the Iceni might have been expected to perform a similar role, albeit on a smaller scale. Cogidubnus' appointment would not merely have been a means for the Romans of dealing with a somewhat recalcitrant population without incurring the odium of direct rule. It was also highly economic in military terms, since troops who would otherwise have been needed to garrison large areas could be diverted to other tasks. Thus on the basis of the scanty information available, the rebellion of 47 seems to provide the most likely circumstances for the creation of the kingdom. It might have occurred after the rebellion, or, if Plautius had anticipated that there might be trouble on his departure, just before. In the latter case, Cogidubnus could have been one of the *socii* attacked.

The Roman policy towards Cogidubnus was certainly vindicated, as Tacitus notes that he *fidissimus mansit*. During the years of his reign his control over the peoples to the south of the Thames must have been a major factor in enabling Scapula to move large numbers of troops west for the Roman advance beyond the Fosse Way and for succeeding governors to continue his work. During Boudica's revolt the old Atrebatic kingdom seems to have remained loyal to the Romans. A secondary outer earthwork constructed at Silchester may even belong to the period of the revolt, although, as Boon has pointed out, it would take a long time to erect.

How long did Cogidubnus remain king? Tacitus' words *fidissimus mansit* imply that he remained in authority to the end of his life, and it has been suggested that Cogidubnus was alive well into the Flavian period. This notion is based largely on the assumption that *RIB* 91 is a Flavian inscription, which in turn relies on the old reading of *legatus Augusti* and the belief that Cogidubnus was elevated to the *legatio* and a seat in the Roman senate by Vespasian. Vespasian campaigned in the south-west after the Claudian invasion and he could well have made the acquaintance of Cogidubnus then (as noted earlier); in addition, Cogidubnus might have played some role in ensuring the support of the British legions for Vespasian during the critical period of 68/69 when Vespasian was engaged in a bitter struggle for imperial power. Thus Vespasian might have rewarded his old friend by elevating him to the Senate. It is also thought that Cogdiubnus could be associated with the famous palace built at Fishbourne some time between 75 and 80 and covering more than 10 acres in area. The west wing is particularly important in this context since it seems to contain an audience chamber with a vaulted roof. Cunliffe has suggested that the palace was intended to reflect his elevated status and the apsidal room might have been used in the discharge of his royal duties.

These reconstructions present a number of problems, however. The almost certain rejection of *legatus Augusti* from the inscription removes the basis for associating Cogidubnus with Vespasian. In any case, *RIB* 91 cannot be Flavian. The *terminus ante quem* for Cogidubnus' death must be 78, when Agricola's governorship of Britain began, since, had Cogidubnus been alive then, Tacitus would surely have said so, instead of relegating the sole mention of him to the brief introductory passage. So Cogidubnus could not have survived Vespasian. *RIB* 91, however, contains a reference to the *domus divina* 'the home of the god'. Vespasian was the first of the Flavians and could not lay claim to divine ancestry. Only after his death could the Flavian house be called divine. But since by this time Cogidubnus himself was almost certainly dead, the inscription must be Julio-Claudian. Also, while it would be impossible to prove that Cogidubnus was *not* the builder of the palace at Fishbourne, there is no primary evidence to indicate that he *was*. Indeed, if he was dead by 78 at the latest there would barely have been time for it to be built. The palace had a history of its own, long after Cogidubnus, and it is worth noting that through all the major alterations the west wing remained unchanged, so the function of the apsidal room for nearly 200 years continued to be domestic, not administrative, and this may have been the case in the early years of the building also. There is therefore no compelling reason for associating Cogidubnus with the palace. It is, of course, a remarkable building, in close proximity to Chichester, and does seem to require some explanation. However, an association between Cogidubnus and the site need not presuppose that the king lived into the Flavian period. There were two predecessors to the palace at Fishbourne, a timber house that followed the military phase, and a substantial and luxurious masonry building from the Neronian period. Either, or both, of these might have been built by Cogidubnus, and the 'palace' built as a private residence by his heirs, whose interests would be diverted from the administrative duties of governing a kingdom to the enjoyment of the material amenities of civilized life in the Roman style. The palace at Fishbourne presupposes wealth, not power, and is located in a region noted for its prosperity, as indicated by its fine villas.[21]

It is difficult to explain why the Romans would have allowed Cogidubnus to remain as king into the Flavian period. Sentimentality had little place in Roman foreign policy, and it was not the practice to allow client kings to continue to rule once they had outlived their usefulness, no matter how staunchly loyal their previous service. Polemo II, for instance, after a lifetime of service in the cause of Rome, was deprived of his kingdom of Pontus in 64/65, when it was incorporated fully into the *imperium*. Once Britain had survived the effects of Boudica's revolt the danger of internal unrest seems to have been crushed once and for all. Moreover, Tacitus' use of the superlative *fidissimus* '*most* loyal' and of the verb *mansit* 'remained' instead of the simple *erat* 'was', seems to imply that Cogidubnus faced a major test of his loyalty towards the end of his life, since the phrase *fidissimus mansit* means that he *stayed* most loyal. Boudica's revolt would provide an excellent context for such a display of loyalty.

The notion of death a short time after the revolt recieves some support from Tacitus' narrative. He says that Cogidubnus maintained his loyalty *usque ad nostram memoriam*. The latter is a common Latin expression 'down to our own time'. It is, however, extremely vague and could be applied to almost any decade in the first century. The gap between Cogidubnus' and Tacitus' time was certainly relatively short, and the expression seems almost meaningless in this particular context. It is just possible that Tacitus meant *memoria* to be taken literally rather than idiomatically. Since the historian was born in the mid-50s he could properly say that Cogidubnus had survived into the time of his (Tacitus') recollection, if had had lived until some point in the early to mid sixties.

The evidence for Cogidubnus' life and activities is shadowy, but seems to indicate that he discharged his role perfectly as a Roman client king, and that the innovation of creating a client state behind the forward military zone was an unqualified success. Cogidubnus remained loyal, and seems to have succeeded in persuading his subjects to comply with the notion that their independence was to take second place to Rome's needs. This compliance, in its turn, allowed the Roman governors to concentrate on extending the *limes*. The foundations laid by Cogidubnus were secure. When his kingdom was incorporated into the *provincia*, its people were fully ready for Romanization, and progress towards it proved to be smooth and orderly.

The Army at the Time of Claudius

The Roman provincial armies consisted basically of two main elements, the legionaries, who were all citizens, and the auxiliaries recruited from non-citizens. Some provinces had units of the Fleet, especially on large rivers like the Rhine and Danube, and Britain had its own fleet the *Classis Britannica*. The Imperial bodyguard, the Praetorian Guards and *Equites Singulares* (the Imperial mounted bodyguard) normally remained in Rome and accompanied the Emperor on his campaigns. The army was in a constant state of change, yet essential adjustments were sometimes not made until forced by internal pressure. This is well illustrated by the great mutiny on the Rhine in AD 4. Augustus had always been reluctant to alter long standing regulations and practices. He had inherited a very large number of troops of several armies, some of which had been in opposition in the civil war. The task of reducing this force to a manageable size was successfully accomplished by means of substantial land grants and the founding of *coloniae*, many financed out of his own funds. This could not continue indefinitely and he was obliged, in spite of senatorial opposition, to create in AD 6 a military chest *aerarium militare* by levying a death duty and a tax on public auctions (*Dio*, lv. 25). He earlier made an important regulation dealing with the length of service of 16 years, which could and was normally extended to 20, except for Praetorians. There was also a lump sum payment on discharge in lieu of the land grant a soldier had previously expected (Dio, liv. 24). Apart from this, Augustus left the army much as it had been from late Republican days; the mutiny of AD 4 was resolved by promises of discharges after 16 years, which were never fulfilled (*Ann*. i. 17).

It was Claudius who made the next significant changes which arose out of his determination to further the career prospects of members of the equestrian order. He also introduced a new regulation whereby all auxiliaries became citizens after 16 years honourable service, and even more important this included the grant of *conubium*, i.e. the right to marry women who were not citizens. This was to have far reaching effects on the rapid spread of citizenship in the provinces. Auxiliaries, however, still served 25 years, although this was reduced for some by Vespasian, but not until Trajan did citizenship and discharge become coincidental.[1] Vespasian also created an award of citizenship to whole units for acts of valour in the field, so that the letters *C(ivium) R(omanorum)* could be added after the title of the unit. An early example is on the tombstone of a trooper of the *Ala Hispanorum Vettonum* from Bath.[2] The formula *H(ic)S(itus)E(st)* dates it to the first century, and, at one time, it was considered as evidence of this unit having been stationed in Bath in the invasion period. If the unit had been serving in Britain, it could well have earned its honour in the northern campaigns of Cerealis or Agricola, but it seems unlikely that Bath would still have been under military control in the seventies. The recent excavations by Professor Barry Cunliffe on the sacred spring have shown that construction work began in the early Flavian period.[3] This means that the site was developed as a place of healing at this time and the earliest inscription is dated to AD 76, and bears the name of Vespasian (*RIB* 172). It is possible that the spring was taken over by the army,[4] as in the case of similar sites in Germany, but this would not have necessitated a unit being stationed there.

The Imperial army was divided into the following four sections:

1. The Legions
2. The *Auxilia*
3. The Fleets
4. The Rome Cohorts

The Legions

The legions represented the main fighting force of the army. Citizens to a man, they were heavily armoured infantry trained for close-quarter fighting, where their short swords (*gladii*) could be used more effectively. The body armour was an assemblage of horizontal steel strips with front and back plates and curved shoulder pieces, held together with leather straps (*lorica segmentata*)[5] which had been introduced probably in late Augustan or Tiberian times. The men were also equipped with two long javelins (*pila*) which they hurled at the advancing enemy, before drawing their swords and then advanced swiftly in a wedge-shaped formation, cutting great swathes of carnage into the packed barbarian hordes. The legionaries were much helped in this tactic by their large shields (*scuta*) which protected the whole of the left side of the body from chin to knee; it also had a heavy bronze boss (*umbo*) which was thrust into the enemy faces while they slid their swords into the stomach with a swift twisting movement. In a set-piece battle, the legions were highly efficient killing machines. A century of 80 men was commanded by a centurion, and 6 formed a cohort which was not normally an independent tactical unit, except for the first cohort which consist of 5 double centuries, i.e. 800 hand-picked men under 5 senior centurions (*primi ordines*), a formidable fighting unit.[6] Including this special cohort, there were 10 in the legion. The commanding officer was the *legatus legionis*, drawn from the Senatorial Order. The 6 tribunes had mainly judicial and administrative functions, the senior was a senator designate (*tribunus laticlavius*), the other 5 were equestrians (*tribuni angusticlavii*). The command and administrative structure and promotion system was highly complicated and is not fully understood.[7] The steps in the ladder of promotion are not clear-cut and this is due to the careful selection of men for advancement at an early stage of their military life. They were divided into two main categories, the potential leaders in the field and administrators; it was necessary, however, for each group to have wide experience in both areas so that any special abilities could be noted in any further advancement. This involved a complicated pattern of movement generally in an upward direction, but with many side steps. The main objective of most of the legionaries was to become a centurion. Such a man had not only to have to be a good fighter and leader, but also to understand the complicated administrative system and be literate enough to keep records, daily rosters and to write reports. But within the centurionate there were large differences in rank and those who needed special training had been picked as potential *primi ordines*, i.e. centurions of the first cohort, each of whom had well defined responsibilities in the legionary organisation. The training was mainly through the H.Q. office (*tabularium legionis*) where knowledge of the inner workings of the legionary administration could be obtained. For those destined for these appointments there was an even greater goal, to become *primus pilus*, chief centurion. This led automatically to entry into the equestrian order, an important rung in the social ladder.[8] Claudius established a well defined career structure for equestrians and an able man could rise to a very high rank in the Imperial service, the four top posts being Prefect of the Imperial Guard (*Praefectus Praetorius*), Prefect of Egypt, Prefect of the *Vigiles* and Prefect of the *Annona*.

But behind this admirable scheme lurked what would seem to us today a more corrupt element, that of patronage, but this was an integral part of Roman life. Men of wealth felt responsible for their families, tenants, servants and a great body of hangers-on, who would claim some remote connection. This large 'supporters club' was a valuable aid to a great man, since he could call on any member to do special service for him, some of a discreet, delicate or more positive nature. It penetrated every aspect of Roman life and any young ambitious man not born into the highest social rank could never hope to gain rapid promotion on his ability alone; a patron was essential. Although army promotion was largely governed by patronage and nepotism, ability certainly had its place, but it was for the most part secondary to influence from above. The highest was the patronage of the Emperor himself, and here is where the troops of the Imperial Guard were especially favoured, since they had the opportunity of coming to the Emperor's personal notice. It was normal practice for the *evocati* of the Guards, i.e. those who had served their 16 years, to be advanced into the legionary centurionate and for centurions to become the *primi ordines*. Those rising through the legionary ranks would have little hope with such competition of rising so far, but had to be content to live out their career in the ordinary centurionate, but it must be appreciated that centurions were never retired like the *miles*, but stayed until they were physically unable to continue to serve.

Another way to seek promotion was through the administrative grades and this could be achieved by becoming a *beneficiarius*. This has been translated by some as 'orderly officer', but in fact it means far more than this. The position was an attachment to a particular officer, or civil official, and the duties varied in relation to the rank and responsibility of that officer. The legionary tribunes all had *beneficiarii* and they acted as clerks and general 'dogs-bodies', but higher up the scale a soldier could become a *beneficiarius legati pro praetore* i.e. on the staff of the governor. The governor of Britain may have had as many as sixty *beneficiarii*, and they acted in a number of roles such as tax collectors, police, district officers or in the general office of the governor. Thus a legionary could become quite an important person in the civil administrative machinery, although still attached to the legion and drawing his pay from it. Such a man was Gaius Mannius Secundus, who died at Wroxeter before AD 60.[9] He may have been a kind of district officer responsible for law and order beyond the *territorium* of the legion, or he may have been there before the legion had become established. He could have controlled river traffic up and down the Severn and collected tolls, or just taxes from the Cornovii, or he could have been on special assignment for the governor. These soldiers would continue their service long after the retiring age; Mannius was 52 when he died.

Apart from all these complications, the army was full of craftsmen and artificers, all of whom were numbered along the fighting ranks. They did, however, have the considerable privilege of being exempted from heavy fatigues and they were called *immunes*. So although they received no extra pay for their skills, they could not be given many unpleasant duties which fell to the ordinary soldiers, whose only escape was to bribe the centurion, and for whom this was a considerable perk of his office. An incomplete list of these *immunes* is preserved in a law digest which dates from the mid-second century.[10] It is useful in showing the great variety of trades and skills needed by the Roman army. It includes surveyors, medical technicians, medical orderlies and dressers, ditch-diggers, farriers, architects, copper-smiths, helmet-makers, wagon-makers, horn-makers, bow-makers, plumbers, stone-cutters, lime-burners, wood-cutters, charcoal-burners, butchers, huntsmen, keepers of the sacrificial animals, grades of clerk, i.e. of the *deposita*, the granaries, estates of the deceased etc., grooms, armourers, trumpeters etc.

The *Auxilia*

The *auxilia*[11] consisted of units 500 strong, but from the Flavian period there is an increasing number of units double this size, i.e. *milliaria*. There were three categories of *auxilia* in descending order of status: (1) cavalry *ala* (literally 'wing'); (2) *cohors peditata* (infantry cohort); (3) *cohors equitata* (a cohort of mixed infantry and mounted men). The internal organisation of these units is not fully understood.[12] The size of the squadron (*turma*) of an *ala* is not known, but the most likely figure is 32, whereas that of a *turma* of a *cohors equitata* seems to have been 30. There were 4 *turmae* in this latter unit with 6 centurions, each of men of infantry. The *milliaria* cohorts, both *peditata and equitata*, had 10 centuries of infantry, but the latter consisted also of 8 *turmae*. The *ala milliaria* had 24 *turmae*, giving a total of 768 horse. Their commanders were equestrian *praefecti* with centurions in charge of the infantry centuries. The squadron (*turmae*) of cavalry were commanded by *decuriones*, under whom were *duplicarii* and *sesquiplicarii* (men with double and one and a half times pay, respectively)

The Fleet

The other arm of the Roman army was the Fleet which was considered as an inferior branch of the service.[13] Claudius saw it as a useful way employing gifted equestrians and provided important promotion steps with commands of the Mediterranean fleets. One of the most famous *praefecti* was Pliny the Elder, who commanded the *Classis Misenensis* at the time of the eruption of Vesuvius in 79 and lost his life in making too close an inspection. The British Fleet *Classis Britannica* played an important role in the invasion and the Agricolan conquest of Scotland, but its main function was to protect the long coast line.[14] There may have been a number of harbours used by the ships, but the H.Q. of the Fleet seems to have been Lympne (*Portus Lemanis*) near Hythe, and two other ports used were Dover (Portus Dubris) and Boulogne (Gesoriacum).

The Seven Sisters Hoard

This is an interesting assemblage of material which has an indirect bearing on the early conquest of Wales. Known as the Seven Sisters Hoard, it was found by children in 1875 scattered in the bed of a small stream, a tributary of the Dulais, which joins the Nedd, just above Neath. The objects had been washed out of the bank of the stream after heavy rain and flooding the same year. An interval of 29 years elapsed between the discovery and the material coming into the possession of the Cardiff Museum, so it is by no means certain that all the objects recovered in 1875 are yet known; another was, in fact, purchased by the B.M. in 1928, and others may have remained in private hands or unrecognised in other collections. The objects have been studied several times and the latest and fullest account appeared in 1976.[1] Most of the bronzes are items of mid-first-century military harness equipment from a well-accoutred trooper. But there are other objects such as five tankard handles and lumps and billets of bronze and casting-jets, which clearly indicates that the hoard belonged to a travelling bronze and casting-jets, which clearly indicate that the hoard belonged to a travelling scrap in the area. The question arises as to how he obtained possession of the Roman military items. It seems unlikely that they represented scrap discarded by an auxiliary workshop, nor does it seem that the man could have been working for the army, since the site of discovery is far from any known fort. Contracting to civil artisans was possible, but they worked under the close eye of the army staff in compounds attached to the fort. The most feasible solution seems to be that it was loot, taken by a Welsh tribesman after a successful foray or ambush, and exchanged with the bronze-smith for a brooch or similar attractive piece. In these circumstances, the smith must have been operating well clear of the Roman lines, since being found in possession of this material could have been most unfortunate for him; in any case, he would have been anxious to melt it all down so that its identity was totally lost. The probability is, therefore, that the objects came from one of the many guerilla engagements at the time of Scapula (or after his untimely death) and offers a useful assemblage of reasonably closely dated material. It is all of fine quality and some pieces beautifully decorated with red and blue enamel. Some are quite unusual, such as the remarkable strap-junction (Report No. 4), the small strap-slide (Report No. 5).[2] The so-called 'pendant hooks' (Report Nos 14 and 15) are an intrusive element, and not of Roman origin (the nearest parallel is from the Celtic hoard from Polden Hill in the B.M):[3] they possibly had some useful and decorative function on a Celtic war chariot. Another oddity is the bronze sheeting, or object with a circular base (Report No. 6): it cannot be readily seen as a piece of equipment carried in a campaign, unless it was from a box for something like military decorations (i.e. *torques* and *phalerae*).

Four Military Tombstones from Wroxeter (pl 23–26)

1. Found in 1752 in the northern cemetery about 200 yards north-east of the city defences.[1] It has a gable top surmounted by a pine cone, a symbol of everlasting life and flanked by two lions, symbols of death, and reads:
G(AIVS) MANNIVS G(AI) F(ILIVS) POL(LIA TRIBV) SECVNDVS POLLENT(IA) MIL(ES) LEG(IONIS) XX AN(N)ORV(M) LII STIP(ENDIORVM) XXXI BEN(EFICIARIVS) LEG(ATI) PR(O PRAETORE) H(IC) S(ITVS) E(ST)
Gaius Mannius Secundus, son of Gaius, of the Pollian voting tribe, a soldier of *Legio XX* from Pollentia aged 52 with 31 years service, a *beneficiarius* on the staff of the governor, lies here (*RIB* 293)
    The man had the three names of a citizen and came from Pollentia which was near Turin in N. Italy. The stone is now in the Rowley House Museum, Shrewsbury.
2. Found in 1783 near the blacksmith's shop, north of the bath-house. This is now part of the post office and since it is well within the city defences was presumably reused as a building stone at an earlier period. It reads:
TIB(ERIVS) CLAVD(IVS) TIRINTIVS EQ(VES) COH(ORTIS) [. . .] THRACVM AN(N)ORVM LVII STI[P]ENDIOR(VM) XX[. . .] H(IC) S(ITVS) E(ST)
Tiberius Claudius Tirintius, trooper of [. . .] Cohort of Thracians, aged 57 with [. . .] years of service lies here (*RIB*. 291).
    This man or his father had received his citizenship under Claudius or Nero. There is only room on the broken edge of the stone for one or at most two digits, so it may have been *Coh. VI* which was at Gloucester *c.*44–47 (*RIB*. 121).
3. Found in 1752 near No. 1. It has a gable top with floral decoration round a disc. It reads:
M(ARCVS) PETRONIVS L(VCI) F(ILIVS) MEN(ENIA TRIBV) VIC(ETIA ANN(ORVM) XXXVIII MIL(ES) LEG(IONIS) XIV GEM(INAE) MILI-TAVIT ANN(OS) XVIII SIGN(IFER) FVIT H(IC) S(ITVS) E(ST)
Marcus Petronius, son of Lucius of the Menenian voting-tribe, aged 38 with 18 years service, a soldier of *Legio XIV Gem.*, he was a standard-bearer and lies here (*RIB* 294).
    He is one of the soldiers with only two names and came from modern Vicenza in N. Italy. The legion took the title *Martia Victrix* after 61 for its part in the victory over Boudica.
4. It was seen in 1789 at the side of the road near the church and was recovered from a garden wall of 'The Cottage' and is now in the Rowley House Museum. It reads:
VA]LERI[VS . . .] F(ILIVS) GAL(ERIA TRIBV) . . . MILES . . . LEG XII]II G[EM . . .
Valerius . . . son of . . . of the Galerian voting-tribe, soldier of *Legio XIV Gem* . . . (*RIB* 296)

Place Names in Roman and Modern Forms

Roman name	*Modern name*
ABONA	Sea Mills
AD PONTEM	Thorpe-by-Newark
ALABVM	Llandovery
AQVAE ARNEMETIAE	Buxton
AQVAE SVLIS	Bath
ARGISTILLVM	N of Gloucester
ARICONIUM	Weston-under-Penyard
BOVIVM	Cowbridge
BOVIVM	Holt
BRANOGENIVM	Leintwardine
BREMIA	Llanio
BVRRIVM	Usk
CAMVLODVNVM	Colchester
CAMVLODVNVM	Slack
CICVCIVM	Y Gaer, Brecon
CONDATE	Northwich
DANVM	Doncaster
DERVENTIO	Littlechester
DEVA	Chester
DVBRIS	Dover
DVRNOVARIA (DVROTRIGVM)	Dorchester, Dorset
EBVRACVM	York
GLEVVM	Gloucester
GOBANNIVM	Abergavenny
ISCA	Caerleon
ISCA (DVMNONIORVM)	Exeter
ISCALIS	Axmouth
ISVRIVM (BRIGANTVM)	Aldborough
LAGENTIVM	Castleford, Yorks
LEMANIS	Lympne
LETOCETVM	Wall, Staffs
LEVCARVM	Loughor
LEVOBRINTA	Forden Gaer
LINDINIS	Ilchester

LONDINIVM	London
LVENTINVM	Pumpsaint
MAGNIS	Kenchester
MAMVCIVM	Manchester
MANDVESSEDVM	Mancetter
MEDIOLANVM	Whitchurch
MEDIOLANVM	Caersws
MONA	Anglesey
MORIDVNVM (DEMETARVM)	Carmarthen
NAVIO	Brough-on-Noe
NEMETIO STATIO	North Tawton
NIDVM	Neath
NOVIOMAGVS (REGNORVM)	Chichester
PENNOCRVCIVM	By the R. Penk
PETVARIA	Brough-on-Humber
RATAE (CORITANORVM)	Leicester
RIGODVNVM	Castleshaw
RVTVNIVM	Harcourt Mill, Shrops.
RVTVPIAE	Richborough
SABRINA	R. Severn
SALINAE	Droitwich
SALINAE	Middlewich, Ches.
SEGELOCVM	Littleborough
TAMARA	on the R. Tamar
TAMIVM	Cardiff
TRAIECTVS	a crossing point on the Severn Estuary
VXACONA	Red Hill, Shrops
VXELA	near Barnstaple
VENTA (SILVRVM)	Caerwent
VERNEMETVM	Willoughby-on-the-Wolds
VIROCONIVM	Wroxeter

Modern Names	*Roman Names*
Abergavenny	GOBANNIVM
Aldborough	ISVRIVM (BRIGANTVM)
Anglesey	MONA
Axmouth	ISCALIS
Bath	AQVAE SVLIS
Barnstaple (near)	VXELA
Brecon	CICVTIVM
Brough-on-Humber	PETVARIA
Brough-on-Noe	NAVIO
Buxton	AQVAE ARNEMETIAE
Caerwent	VENTA (SILVRVM)
Cardiff	TAMIVM
Carmarthen	MORIDVNVM (DEMETARVM)

Castleshaw	RIGODVNVM
Chester	DEVA
Chichester	NOVIOMAGVS (REGNORVM)
Colchester	CAMVLODVNVM
Cowbridge	BOVIVM
Doncaster	DANVM
Dorchester, Dorset	DVRNOVARIA (DVROTRIGVM)
Dover	DVBRIS
Droitwich	SALINAE
Exeter	ISCA (DVMNONIORVM)
Forden Gaer	LEVOBRINTA
Gloucester	GLEVVM
Gloucester N. of	ARGISTILLVM
Harcourt Mill, Shrops	RVTVNIVM
Holt, Denbighs.	BOVIVM
Ilchester	LINDINIS
Kenchester	MAGNIS
Leicester	RATAE (CORITANORVM)
Leintwardine	BRANOGENIVM
Littleborough-on-Trent	SEGELOCVM
Littlechester	DERVENTIO
Llandovery	ALABVM
Llanio	BREMIA
London	LONDINIVM
Loughor	LEVCARVM
Lympne	LEMANIS
Mancetter, Warks.	MANDVESSEDVM
Manchester	MAMVCIVM
Middlewich, Ches.	SALINAE
Neath	NIDVM
North Tawton	NEMETIO STATIO
Northwich	CONDATE
Penk R. by the	PENNOCRVCIVM
Pumpsaint	LVENTINVM
Red Hill, Shrops.	VXACONA
Richborough	RVTVPIAE
Sea Mills	ABONA
Severn Estuary, crossing	TRAIECTVS
Severn, R.	SABRINA
Slack	CAMVLODVNVM
Tamar, R. on the	TAMARA
Thorpe-by-Newark	AD PONTEM
Usk	BURRIVM
Wall, Staffs.	LETOCETVM
Weston-under-Penyard	ARICONIVM
Willoughby-on-the-Wolds	VERNEMETVM

Whitchurch, Shrops.   MEDIOLANVM
Wroxeter   VIROCONIVM
York   EBVRACVM

Glossary of Latin terms

ala a cavalry unit usually at this period about 500 strong divided into squadrons (*turmae*) and commanded by a *praefectus*

amphora a large pottery container for transporting commodities like wine, oil, fish sauce (*garum*) etc. to distant parts of the empire. It became a unit of liquid measure

aquila the eagle standard of the legions, considered to be a symbol of the legion and was in consequence its most precious possession; normally kept in the *sacellum* of the *principia*

as a copper coin of the first and second century, equivalent to half a *dupondius* which was made of a 'brass' alloy

auxilia the general term for the Roman allies who provided troops for the army to assist the legions. Satisfactory service led to citizenship on discharge

ballista a spring-gun of which there were several kinds and sizes used normally by legionaries. The small gun (*carro-ballista*) was mounted on a cart, was provided for each century and operated by ten men

burgus a small fortified post usually controlling a main road

centuria the smallest operational unit in a legion and auxiliary cohort consisting of 80 men commanded by a centurion and divided into eight *contubernia* (mess or tent parties)

civitas a tribe and its territory

civium romanorum title on receiving the award of Roman citizenship; when given to auxiliary units as a reward for outstanding services, it is denoted by the letters C R as part of the unit's title

Classis Britannica the fleet based on Britannia

clientela the client-patron relationship, whereby the clients owed allegiance to a patron who in turn undertook responsibility for them

cognomen the third name of the *tria nomina* of a citizen, usually peculiar to the individual

cohors a military unit of about 500 men when it was known as *quingenaria*. Those 1000 strong were *milliarii*

cohors equitata a part-mounted auxiliary unit

colonia a settlement of retired army veterans who were usually given land allotments

comites literally 'companions', but used here as members of the imperial retinue of Claudius

consilium a council or assembly of leaders

corona civica the civic crown of oak leaves awarded to soldiers for saving the life of a citizen

cos ord   the title of the two senior magistrates of Rome who entered office on the 1st January, giving their names to the year

cos suff   the title of the pairs of magistrates who became consuls after the *consulares ordinarii*, and usually holding office for three months

curator aquarum   the title of the senator in charge of the Roman water supply, normally it was a pro-consular appointment

cursus honorum   the steps in promotion open to a member of the senatorial class

denarius   the silver Roman coin, 25 of which were equivalent to the gold *aureus*

dolabra   an iron tool with a pick at one end and hoe-like blade at the other, carried by legionaries and used for digging ditches

duplicarius   a junior commander in an auxiliary *ala* in charge of a *turma*, and so-called as he was given double pay

evocatus   a soldier, often a praetorian, who continued to serve after his normal period of service

fasces   a bundle of rods bound round an axe, which became a symbol of law and authority and carried by lictors before a consul and magistrates

gemina   a title given to a legion when it was created by splitting one into two, as with *Legio XIV Gem.*

gladius   the short thrusting sword used by legionaries

hiberna   winter quarters where units spend the winter 'under canvas'

insignia triumphalia   the special *toga*, sceptre and wreath worn at a triumph

legatus   a man to whom the Emperor delegated responsibility, as with legionary commanders and provincial governors

legatus legionis   the commander of a legion

legio   a legion comprising Roman citizens and consisting of 10 cohorts, nine of which were quingenary (i.e. 500 strong) and the first, probably from the Flavian period, milliary (i.e. 1000 strong)

limes   originally a dividing path between fields, but later a name given to a frontier zone

lorica segmentata   a cuirass made of horizontal strips of steel, held together by vertical leather bands, worn by legionaries

macellum   a market-place, often for one kind of goods, such as meat or fish

miles   a soldier; sometimes the qualifying *gregarius* is used with it to indicate the common soldier or private

murus gallicus   a term used for an early type of Iron Age rampart which was laced with horizontal timbers

nemeton   a Celtic word for a shrine or temple appears as a place-name, such as Aquae Arnemetiae

nuntius   a despatch rider

oppidum   the Latin word for any native settlement, but it has usually been restricted by British archaeologists to an area protected by Gallo-Belgic dykes, as at Camulodunum

ornamenta triumphalia   insignia and awards given to victorious commanders and consuls, instead of a triumph, in imperial times

ovatio   a triumph of lesser degree than the *triumphus* itself, which was reserved for Emperors, the last person to receive the *ovatio* who was not a member of the Imperial family was Aulus Plautius (Suet. *Claudius*, 24)

pabulor   to forage, hence used for military forage parties (Caes *Bell. Civ.*i 59; pl. 4)

paludamentum   the cloak worn by commanders and senior officers to distinguish them from the *sagum* of the ordinary soldier

pax Romana   the peace imposed and held by Rome

pilum   the javelin used by legionaries. It was seven feet long mostly consisting of a wood shaft. The iron shank was left flexible but the pyramidal point was hardened

piscina   an ornamental pool usually surrounded by colonnaded walks, as distinguished from a *natatio* i.e. a swimming pool

polis   the Greek word for a city used by Ptolemy for native settlements (Rivet and Smith, 105)

praefectus   a commander of an auxiliary unit at this period

praefectus equitatus   a man with an unusual command of a force of cavalry as may have been given to Didius Gallus by Claudius in the invasion of Britain (*ILS* 970; *Epig.Stud.* 4 (1967) 65)

praefectus fabrorum   an officer in charge of ordnance and workshops

praetentura   that part of a fort or fortress in front of the *principia* and which is bisected by the *via praetoria*

praetorium   the house of the commanding officer, normally adjacent to the *principia*

primus pilus   literally 'first javelin', was the chief centurion of a legion, an office held for a year, after which he became an equestrian and he could enter a higher career structure as one of the *primipilares* (see Brian Dobson *Die Primpilares: Entwicklung und Bedeutung, Laufbahnen und Persönlichkeiten eines römischen Offiziersranges* 1978)

principia   the headquarters building in a fort or fortress and occupying the central position

quinquennium   a five-year period

retentura   that part of a fort or fortress to the rear of the *principia*

sesterius   a large bronze or 'brass' coin equivalent to 4 *asses* or a quarter of a silver *denarius*

spolium   literally the skin of an animal but used for the armour stripped from a defeated enemy and hence a general term (in the plural – *spolia*) for booty or spoils of war

terra nigra   pottery made in Gaul and imported into Britain in the Claudian-Neronian period. It was mainly in the form of platters and dishes in a grey ware with a highly polished surface and usually stamped with the maker's name. It was widely imitated in Britain

terra rubra   pottery made in Gaul and imported into Britain in the Claudian-Neronian period. It was mainly in the form of cups and bowls in a red ware with a burnished finish and often stamped with the potter's name

testudo   literally a 'tortoise', a technique developed by legionaries – a tight group holding their shields over their head to enable them to advance to a gateway or base of a wall with a battering ram (pl. 3)

tria nomina   the three names '*praenomen, nomen* and *cognomen*' normally adopted by a Roman citizen

triumvir monetalis one of those men in Republican and early Imperial times who was responsible for the mint in Rome and whose names appear on *denarii*

turma   a squadron of 32 mounted men in a quingenary *ala* and probably of 30 in a *turma* of a *cohors equitata*

via principalis   the street which crosses a fort or fortress in front of the *principia*

Glossary of Technical Terms

antefix a specially shaped imbrex fixed at the roof edge which presented a 'face', often with a moulded decoration, to the observer on the ground

barnacle bit a toothed bit used for curbing horses

campaign camp a camp enclosed by a ditch and bank in which the Roman army pitched their tents when on field duties

carrot amphora a small wine container in the shape of a carrot, used in the mid-first century

Claudian the period of the Emperor Claudius (AD 41–54)

Claudian imitation a copy of one of the bronze issues of Claudius, probably struck by the army during a shortage of coins (C.H.V. Sutherland, *Coinage and Currency in Roman Britain*, 1937, 8–13)

chlamys a long wool scarf draped over the shoulder or wrapped round the arm, used to indicate high rank

currency bar a long strip of wrought iron used by some of the southern British tribes. It was really a rough-out for a sword and could have been beaten into one, (D.F. Allen in *O S Map of Southern Britain in the Iron Age*, 1962, Map 8)

finial an ornament projecting vertically usually from a roof, but also in pottery

Flavian the period of the Flavian emperors, Vespasian, Titus and Domitian (AD 69–96)

fort the word used for a permanent Roman establishment of up to about eight acres, normally for an auxiliary unit

fortress the word used for a permanent legionary establishment

hill-fort a banked or ditched enclosure of pre-Roman times usually on a hill, following the contours

intaglio a carved design on a gemstone or moulded on paste, usually for a ring

melon bead a small ribbed blue glass bead commonly used as an amulet in the first century, especially by soldiers

millefiore a kind of decorated glass made by fusing together many small glass rods of different colours used in glass vessels, brooches and buckles

mortarium a pottery bowl with a large rim and pouring spout, used in the kitchen for pulverising vegetables etc. in food preparation. The interior surface is usually studded with small grits

motte and bailey a castle of the late Saxon and Norman periods which consisted of a conical mound surrounded by a ditch, making a strong defence position, beyond which was a ditched enclosure known as the bailey where buildings were erected

niello a black coloured inlay applied to bronzes

Punic ditch   a military ditch with a vertical outer face and a sloping inner one which made it appear easy to cross, but difficult to negotiate when retreating

samian   a red slip pottery made mainly in Gaul, both in plain and decorated forms, widely exported to Britain in the first two centuries

schutthügel   a rubbish tip shot over the edge of a cliff. The classic example is at Vindonissa, a legionary fortress on the R. Aare in Switzerland (for a study of the pottery recovered from it see E. Ettlinger and C. Simonett, 'Römische Keramik aus dem Schutthügel von Vindonissa', *Veröffentlichungen der Gesellschaft pro Vindonissa*, Band III, 1952)

triskele   a Celtic form of decoration in the shape of three 'legs' radiating from a centre

vexillation fort   a term suggested by Professor Frere (*Britannia* 1967, 71) for forts of 20–30 acres, which, it has been assumed, were occupied by a vexillation or detachment of different units, probably including one from a legion

Notes and References

Ancient Sources

Ant. It	*Antonine Itinerary*
Caesar	*de Bello Gallico*
	de Bello Civili
Cassius Dio	*Historia Romana*
Frontinus	*Strategemata*
Hygini gromatici	*liber de munitionibus castrorum*
Peutinger	*Tabula Peutingeriana*
Pliny the Elder	*Naturalis Historia*
Ptolemy	*Claudii Ptolemaei Geographia*
Ravenna	*Ravenna Cosmography*
Suetonius	*de vita Caesarum*
Tacitus	*Agricola*
	Annales
	Historiae
Vegetius	*Epitoma rei militaris*

Bibliographical References

Boudica	Graham Webster (Batsford) 1978
Camulodunum	C.F.C. Hawkes and M.R. Hull, Rep. of the Research Committee of the Soc. of Antiquaries of London, No.XIV, 1947
CIL	*Corpus Inscriptionum Latinarum*
Davies, J.L. 1980	'Roman military deployment in Wales and the Marches from Claudius to the Antonines' in *Roman Frontier Studies*, 1969 ed. W.S. Hanson and L.J.F. Keppie (BAR), 255–278
Déch.	J. Déchelette, *Les Vases céramiques ornés de la Gaule romaine*, 1904
EE	*Ephemeris Epigraphische* ix, fasc.iv, ed. Haverfield, includes British material
Greene, K. 1979	*The Pre-Flavian Fine Wares, Report on the Excavations at Usk 1965–1976*, Univ. Wales Press 1979
ILS	*Inscriptiones Latinae Selectae*

Invasion	Graham Webster, *The Roman Invasion of Britain* (Batsford) 1980
Margary, I.D. 1957	*The Roman Roads of Britain*, ii (Phoenix)
Nash-Williams, V.E. 1954	*The Roman Frontier in Wales*, (Univ. Wales Press)
Nash-Williams, V.E. 1969	*The Roman Frontier in Wales*, ed. M.G. Jarrett (Univ. Wales Press)
ORL	*Der Obergermanish-Raetische Limes*
Rivet and Smith	A.L.F. Rivet and C. Smith, *The Place Names of Roman Britain* (Batsford) 1979
samian form numbers	refer to the classification by Dragendorff and extended by others. For a brief account see Chap. XIII by B.R. Hartley in R.G. Collingwood and Ian Richmond, *The Archaeology of Roman Britain*, 2nd ed. D.R. Wilson (Methuen) 1969
Fortress	Webster, Graham (ed.), *Fortress into City*, 1988

Abbreviations of Periodicals

Antiq. J.	*Antiquaries Journal* published by the Society of Antiquaries of London
Archaeol. Camb.	*Archaeologia Cambrensis*, published by The Cambrian Association
Archaeol. J.	*Archaeological Journal*, published by The Royal Archaeological Institute
Archaeol. in Wales	*Archaeology in Wales*, an annual review of excavations and field work published CBA Group 2
BAR	*British Archaeological Reports*, published from 122 Banbury Road, Oxford
Bonn. Jhrb.	*Bonner Jahrbücher*, published by the Rheinisches Landesmuseum, Bonn
Brit.	*Britannia*, an annual publication of the Society for the Promotion of Roman Studies
Epig. Stud.	*Epigraphische Studien*, Rheinland-Verlag, Bonn
JRS	*Journal of Roman Studies*, published by the Society for the Promotion of Roman Studies
W. Midlands N.S.	*West Midlands News-Sheet*, an annual review of excavations and field work published by CBA Group 8, and up to 1980, the Department of Extra-Mural Studies of the University of Birmingham

Other Abbreviations

Acc. No.	Accession Number
Antiq.	Antiquaries or Antiquarian
Archaeol.	Archaeological
Ass.	Association
BM	British Museum
Bull.	Bulletin
Cat.	Catalogue
ed.	edited by
fn.	footnote
Hist.	Historical
ibid.	*ibidem* (the same)
Inst.	Institute
J.	Journal
Mag.	Magazine
Nat. Hist.	Natural History
NGR	National Grid Reference
op cit.	*opere citato* (work quoted)
OS	Ordnance Survey
Pap.	*Papers*
Proc.	*Proceedings*
Rec.	Records
RCHM	Royal Commission on Historical Monuments
Soc.	Society
Stud.	*Studies*
Trans.	*Transactions*

Notes to the Text

1 Introduction (pages 13–27)

1 I am most grateful for considerable help with this passage from Professor A. Birley

2 *Historia* 17 (1968), 79, based on an inscription set up by freedmen who took their names from those of their patrons

3 Only the first two consuls (*consulares ordinarii*) in the year gave their name to it, the *consulares suffecti* are the pairs which follow, holding office, sometimes for only two months

4 *Nat. Hist.* vii. 39

5 *JRS* 60 (1970), 28

6 The phase used by Tacitus in *Agricola* 14, *uterque bello egregius* referring to Plautius and Scapula, could have simply reflected their campaigns in Britain

7 The evidence for this is the discovery of a milestone which had been built into the town wall of Kenchester and which has the letters R(ES) P(VBLICA) C(IVITAS) D(OBVNNORVM) (*RIB* 2250)

8 Graham Webster, *The Cornovii* 1975, 2nd ed. 1991

9 Dr S.C. Stanford, *Archaeol. J.* 128 (1971), 82

10 The evidence is summarised by M.G. Jarrett and J.C. Mann in 'The Tribes of Wales', *The Welsh Hist. Review: Cylchgrawn Hanes Cymru* 4 (1968), No 2, 161–174; for more additional information see A.L.F. Rivet and C. Smith, *The Place Names of Roman Britain* 1979

11 Rivet and Smith, 59

12 *Ibid.* 333

13 *Ibid.* 343

14 W.F. Grimes, *Guide to the Collections illustrating the Prehistory of Wales* 1939, 21–6

15 Fn 13, 115

16 'The British Section of the Ravenna Cosmography' *Archaeologia* 93 (1948), 40, but this idea finds no favour with Rivet and Smith

17 *Archaeol. Camb.* 9 (1892), 165–6

18 *Flint, Hist. Soc.* 13 (1953), 3ff; *JRS.* 12 (1922), 283–4

19 Rivet and Smith, 365

20 S.C. Stanford, *Archaeol. J.* 127 (1970), 124

21 Jarrett and Mann, fn 10 above, 165

22 *Academy*, 28 April and 19 May 1883

23 These are long wrought-iron bars which could easily be hammered into swords;

they appear to have been used as a form of portable wealth.

24 The *corona civica*, a crown of oak leaves

25 *Ann.* xvi, 15–6. M. Ostorius Scapula, notable for his strength and skill at arms, had a distinguished military career. He was forced into suicide in 66. He may have been on his father's staff as a tribune.

26 I.A. Richmond, 'Queen Cartimandua,' *JRS* 44 (1954), 48. This is also represented by the distribution of Type VI hill-forts of J. Forde-Johnson (*Hillforts of the Iron Age in England and Wales* 1979, fig 151), although his typology is based on physical rather than cultural affinities

27 This name is, of course, post-Roman. We do not know what contemporary names, if any, was given to the main roads of Roman Britain

28 This was first observed by Arnold Baker and subsequently photographed and published by Professor St Joseph (*JRS* 63 (1973), 234–5 and pl xvii, 1; 67 (1977), 145 and fig 12). A rescue excavation by Dr S.C. Stanford on the Wrekin produced evidence of the destruction of the hill-fort at the conquest period (*W. Midlands N.S.* No 16 (1973), 9–10; later confirmed by C14 dating)

29 This has now been established by the excavation of Philip Crummy who found that the legionaries had not dismantled their barrack-blocks, but left them to be adapted by the colonists and their families, *Brit.* 8 (1977), 65–106, see also *Fortress into City*, 1988 ed. Graham Webster, pp. 24–47

30 See O.A.W. Dilke, *The Roman Land Surveyors* 1971, Chapters 12 and 13, and J. Bradford, *Ancient Landscapes* 1957, Chap IV

31 Although Commagene, the northern part of Syria, had been annexed by Tiberius in AD 17 and made into a province; it was restored by Claudius to the local dynast Antiochus IV. This is not, however, an acceptable parallel, as it was at this period a frontier province

32 This stone is slightly damaged, but it has been subject to a sad history of mis-readings over a long period, now corrected by Professor J.R. Bogaers (*Brit.* 10 (1979), 243–54)

33 H. Cleere, *Archaeol. J.* 131 (1975), 171–99; although it has not been established, this activity had started as early as the mid-first century

34 A. Barrett, *Brit.* 10 (1979), 227–42

35 This appears to receive support from Professor A. Barrett who has stressed the point that the grant was not necessarily at the time of the conquest, *ibid.* 233

36 See Rivet and Smith, 445–6

37 *Silchester: The Roman Town of Calleva* 1974, 46, 203 and fig 7, no 1.

38 Germanicus was not a title, but the name he inherited from his father Gnaeus Domitius Ahenobarbus, who became better known as Germanicus Caesar for his victories in Germany.

39 *EE.* ix, 1767; *Archaeologia* 54 (1905), 366 and fig 13

40 *Antiq. J.* 6 (1926), 75–6

41 *Agrarian Hist. of England and Wales* I, ii, 1967, 15 and 29. Professor Barrett has concluded that the king died between 61 and 78 (*Brit.* 10 (1979), 241)

42 This is the view of George Boon who dates the street plan to the Flavian period after the death of Cogidubnus, but the bath-house pre-dates it, since its portico had to be altered to accommodate the building to the new street (fn 36 above, 53)

43 *Britannia* 1974, 283

44 Dr Mike Fulford has recently shown that the outer earthwork was uncompleted

and it may have been a boundary (Report forthcoming)

45 *O.S. Map of Southern Britain in the Iron Age* 1962, map 6

46 Rivet and Smith, 267

47 P.H. Robinson, *Brit, Numis. J.* 47 (1978), 5–20

48 *The Regni* 1975, 16

49 This idea may also help to explain the mid-first century timber gate-way at Winchester (*Antiq.J.* 55 (1975), 110–12 and fig 6). The irregular sizes of the post-pits and the placing of the posts in a central position do not suggest military work. According to John Wacher, presumably on the authority of Martin Biddle, an unworn coin of Nero was found in the filling of one of the post-pits, (*The Towns of Roman Britain* 1975, 280) and this would make the work certainly post-Scapulan

2 The Last Stand of Caratacus (pages 28–39)

1 *Si auxiliaribus resisterent, gladiis ac pilis legionariorum si huc verterent, spathis et hastis auxiliarium sternebantur*

2 Cunobeline must, therefore, have had at least five sons, Togodumnus, Adminius, Caratacus and at least two more, unless sons-in-law are included

3 Corbulo had advanced beyond the Rhine and built a fort, but was ordered by Claudius to withdraw to the west bank for fear of starting a serious war against the Chauci. He complied, saying nothing except 'Happy the Roman generals of older time', but to keep the legions occupied he ordered them to dig a 23-mile canal from the Meuse to the Rhine (*Ann*, ii, 19–20)

4 *De Vita Agricolae*, R.M. Ogilvie and I.A. Richmond, 1967, 67; it has been suggested by W.S. Hanson that this may have been the work of Agricola's successor ('The First Roman Occupation of Scotland', in *Roman Frontier Studies, 1979*, 1980, 30)

5 Dio, lv. 6

6 Suet, *Aug.* 21; *Tib.* 9

7 *Praefectum castrorum et legionarias cohortes exstruendis apud Siluras praesidiis relictas circumfundunt*

8 As in *Hist.* iv. 75

9 See the description of the Seven Sisters Hoard, Appendix 4 above

10 I.e. in the ninth year of the occupation, but this could be understood as 51 or 52; it is by no means certain (R. Syme, *Tacitus*, 1958, 391, n 3)

11 According to Petrus Patricius, he wore the Greek chlamys (*Exc. Vat.* 42, 208), but it is possible that it is a confusion with another ceremony when the Fucine Lake was drained. It was then that Agrippina sat on a separate tribunal dressed in a chlamys of cloth of gold (*chlamyde aurata*) while Claudius wore the military cloak (*paludamentum*; *Ann.* xii. 56).

12 Her attendance extended to other public occasions such as the reception of ambassadors and even the normal business of state (Dio, lxi. 7)

13 *At non Caratacus aut vultu demisso aut verbis misericordiam requirens*

14 D.R. Dudley, 'The Celebration of Claudius' British Victories', *University of Birmingham Hist.J.* 7 (1959), 9–12

15 First published in 1793 and dedicated to Edmund Burke. A few slight amendments have been made

16 In particular iv. 69, 17 and 20–2. The fragments of this work which have survived are speeches and letters collected together in the second century AD as a textbook for the Schools of Rhetoric

17 See R. Syme, *Tacitus*, Chap 39

18 Donald Dudley's translation, Mentor Books, 1966

19 Plutarch, *Aemilius Paullus*, 26

3 The Scapulan Frontier: the Legionary Fortresses and the Sea Routes (pages 40–60)

1 *JRS* 42 (1951), 52–65; 43 (1953), 81–97; 48 (1958), 86–101; 51 (1961), 117–35; 55 (1965), 74–89; 59 (1969), 104–28; 63 (1973), 214–46; 67 (1977), 125–61

2 *JRS* 63 (1973), fig 23

3 'Military aspects of Roman Wales', *Trans. Hon. Soc. of Cymmrodorion* (1910), 53–187

4 *Ibid.* 63; although he thought that *Legio II Aug.* could by now have been at Caerleon

5 Due, he felt, to the inertia of the last years of Claudius and the preoccupation of Nero with the eastern frontier

6 *The Roman Occupation of Britain*, 1924, 112

7 *Y Cymmrodor*, 37 (1926)

8 This probably led to massive troop withdrawal with only small holding detachments left behind. Wales is not likely to have been neglected in the post-Boudican period once stability had been reached, and some consolidation must be expected from 65 to 75

9 Referred to below as Nash-Williams, V.E., 1954 and 1969

10 *Archaeol. Camb.* 112 (1962), 103–166; 133 (1963), 13–76; and subsequent in shortened and revised form as *Britons and the Roman Army*, 1968

11 Greene, K. 1979

12 *JRS* 63 (1973), 228–33

13 S.S. Frere and J.K. St Joseph, 'The Roman Fortress at Longthorpe', Brit. 5 (1974), 1–129 and G.B. Danell and J.P. Wild, *Longthorpe* II, *Brit. Monograph Ser.* No. 8, 1987

14 *Reliquiae Britannico Romanae* ii and in a brief note in *Archaeologia* 18 (1817), 121–3. This material is now in the BM. The items illustrated by Lysons are: axe-head sheaths (pl xv 4 and 5), the bird mount (no 10) which is similar to the one on a large pendant at Cirencester, the mess-tin (pl xvii, no 1) and coins (pl xv, nos 11 and 12)

15 Almost identical to others from Caves Inn and Broxstowe (see *Invasion* 156, 157 and fn 199)

16 *RIB* 122, for its final spot see fig 3; it tells us that the soldier belonged to the century of Livius Saturninus and had died at the age of 40, after 13 years' service

17 C. Green, 'Glevum and the Second Legion' *JRS* 32 (1942), 40–7; samian stamps are listed of: Carbonis, Masculus, Calvus, Sabinus, Primus and Vitalis; further material was published in *JRS* 33 (1943), 15–28 and pl 1; this includes early brooches, coins, a lunate pendant (pl 1, no 17) which can be paralleled from other military sites and the coarse pottery includes a pre-Flavian Hofheim type flagon (fig 5). Dr C.H.V. Sutherland has commented on the large number of high grade copies of Claudian bronze coins, *Romano-British Imitations of Bronze*

NOTES TO THE TEXT

Coins of Claudius I, Numismatic Notes and Monographs No 65, The American Numismatic Soc. 1935, 7 and 24

18 *Antiq. J.* 55 (1975), 7 and 24

19 *RIB* 121

20 Although this does not fall within the period of this study, it should be noted that that this post-Boudican event was associated with the removal of *Legio XIV* from Britain and its replacement at Wroxeter by *Legio XX*, the consequence of this was the move of *Legio II Aug.* from Exeter to Gloucester, but the fortress was constructed on the site of the later *colonia*, medieval and modern city

21 The bone handle of a legionary *gladius* and a centurion's belt mount, with millefiore inlay, *Proc. Dorset Archaeol. and Nat. Hist. Soc.* 2 (1878), 109

Invasion, 142; I am grateful to Ian Horsey for information about his excavations

22 of 1979–80; see also *Fortress into City*, 1988, p. 91

23 Mr Geoff. Dannell informs me that there is a definite overlap in the samian he has studied from Lake and Exeter

24 Rivet and Smith, 1979, 378

25 Paul T. Bidwell, *The Legionary Bath-house and Basilica and Forum at Exeter*, Exeter Archaeological Reports, Vol 1, 1979

26 *Boudica*, 1978, 95

27 Paul T. Bidwell, Roman Exeter: Fortress and Town, 1980, 12; Christopher Henderson, *Fortress into City*, 1988, Chap. 5

28 *Brit.* 7 (1976), 278–80 and pl XXV A

29 Adrian Oswald, *Trans. Birmingham Archaeol. Soc.* 79 (1964), 117–20

30 Keith Scott, *ibid.* 85 (1973), 211–13 and pl 35

31 This appears now to be confirmed with the discovery of two ditches at right angles to one another in the central area, and which cut through the legionary levels. The dating evidence suggests that this later system may be Flavian.

32 *VCH Shrops.* i, 1908, 243–4

33 L.R. Dean, *A Study of the Cognomina of Soldiers in the Roman Legion*, 1916

34 Undertaken by David Panett, to whom I am most grateful for allowing me to use the results prior to publication. His findings have since been proved by the chance discovery in 1975 of the city wall on the edge of the cliff face

35 *Archaeologia* 88 (1940), 175–224

36 See Graham Webster, 'The defences of the legionary fortress at Viroconium (Wroxeter) *c*. AD 55-90' in *Roman Frontier Studies* ed. V.A. Maxfield and M.J. Dobson, 1991, pp. 125-31; *Wroxeter* (*c*. AD 55-90) forthcoming

37 This happened under Agricola, *c*.78

38 I.A. Richmond and R.M. Ogilvy, *de Vita Agricolae*, 1967, fig 9

39 Barry Cunliffe, *Excavations at Fishbourne*, i, 1971, 74

40 M. Cotton and P. Gathercole, *Excavations at Clausentum, Southampton, 1951–1954*, 1958; G. Rogers and Lloyd R. Laing, *Gallo-Roman Pottery from Southampton*, City Museum Publication No 6, 1966; the non-samian is here dated to the Flavian period which is clearly far too late for this group. Miss Maggi Darling tells me that there is more early pottery in the Southampton Museum from Clausentum, which was not included in the report.

41 Valerie A. Maxfield, *Roman Frontier Studies, 1979*; 1980, 305–6

42 *Trans. Devonshire Ass.* 62 (1931), 119–20; 91 (1959), 81

43 Aileen Fox and W.L.D. Ravenhill 'Early Roman Outposts on the north Devon Coast, ...' *Proc. Devon Archaeol. Explor. Soc.* 24 (1966), 3–39

44   There is a useful note on navigational and tidal problems in crossing the Bristol
     Channel by Donald Moore, 'Maritime aspects of Roman Wales' in *Studien zu den
     Militärgrenzen Roms II*, 1977, 34–7
45   R.E.M. and T.V. Wheeler, *Report on the Pre-historic Roman and Post-Roman Site
     in Lydney Park, Gloucestershire*, 1932
46   Very similar ones have been found on the German frontier at Heddernheim and
     Waldmössingen (*ORL*, vi, Kastell Walmössingen, 7 and Taf III, 4) and from Great
     Chesterford (*Archaeol. J.* 115 (1960), fig 5, no 104)
47   The finest is from Dorchester, Dorset (see *The Roman Conquest of Britain*, 1965,
     pl 28); a short list is given in *Archaeol. J.* 115 (1960), 98, no 258. Since then more
     examples have been found at Wroxeter (report forthcoming)
48   Buildings found in ill-recorded excavations at Park Farm have been given the
     symbol of a villa on the OS Map, but it seems more likely that there was a
     riverside settlement with a dock, originally in the invasion period
49   V.E. Nash-Williams, 'An Early Iron Age Coastal Camp at Sudbrook near the
     Severn Tunnel, Monmouthshire', *Archaeol. Camb.* 94 (1939), 42–79; Davies,
     J.L. 1980, 260
50   S.C. Stanford, *The Welsh Marches*, 1980, 115
51   W.F. Grimes, *Guide to the Collection illustrating the Prehistory of Wales*, 1939, pl
     IX and p 119
52   I am grateful to David Zienkiewicz and Vivienne Metcalf for this information;
     a bronze saucepan recently found in a well, embossed *Ala Thracum* may indicate
     the transfer of this unit from Cirencester
53   Nash-Williams, V.E. 1969, 70–3; for recent discoveries: *Brit.* 6 (1975), 222–3; 7
     (1976), 298; 8 (1977), 360; 9 (1978), 408–9; 10 (1979), 273; 11 (1980), 349; 12
     (1981), 316; 13 (1982), 331–2
54   *Glamorgan* 1, RCHM, Wales 1976, 121–2; *Archaeol. Camb.* 124 (1976), 114f.
55   273–4
56   'An embanked rectangular enclosure' has been observed after ploughing
     (*Archaeol, in Wales*, No 16 (1976), 34) and this suggests a possible fort (Davies,
     J.L. 1980, 264); see also D. Robinson, *Cowbridge: the archaeology and topography
     of a small market town in the Vale of Glamorgan*, a survey of the Glamorgan-
     Gwent Archaeological Trust, 1981
57   Nash-Williams, V.E. 1969, 98–101
58   *Bull. Board of Celtic Stud.* 13 (1950), 239–45
59   This level continued below the S–W Gate of the later fort, *ibid.* fig 2
60   *Ibid.* fig 5, no. 4
61   Barry Cunliffe, *Excavations at Fishbourne* ii, 1971, 208
62   Fn 57 above, 99
63   *JRS* 49 (1959), 102
64   Davies J.L. 1980, 260
65   'The Roman Military Occupation of South-West England: Further Light and
     Fresh Problems' in *Roman Frontier Studies*, 1980, 292–309; see also Valerie A.
     Maxfield, 'Conquest and Aftermath' in *Research on Roman Britain 1960–1989, Brit.
     Mon. Ser.*, No. 11, 1989, pp. 25–6
66   The only hint so far is from Hembury where excavations in 1934 and 1935
     produced two military imitation coins of Claudius and sherds of
     Claudio–Neronian samian, Dorothy L. Liddell 'Report on the Excavations at
     Hembury Fort', *Proc. Devon Archaeol. Explor. Soc.* 2 for 1935, 156–9

4 The Scapulan Frontier: the Land Routes (pages 61–86)

1   *JRS* 43 (1953), 124 and pl xxiv. The rampart is said to have stood to a height of 8 feet up to 1940, when it was bulldozed. A trial hole showed that it was built of sandstone rubble which seems a little unusual for a military rampart of this period

2   *JRS* 48 (1958), 98

3   *Ibid.* 67 (1977), 125–6

4   *Brit.* 10 (1979), 255–6; the site was first recognised by C.J. Balkwill on an RAF vertical

5   *Proc. Devon Archaeol. Soc.* 34 (1976), 86–9; there is also an ancient trackway aligned to the field system

6   Nanstallon Report, p. 89

7   Two first century coins are recorded in *VCH ii Cornwall*, 1924, 36

8   Rivet and Smith, 115 and 464

9   *Ibid* 507–8

10 One of the sherds has a band of large overlapping leaves which is probably a poor drawing of a motif of Passenus, a Neronian potter (R. Knorr, *Töpfer und Fabriken verzierter Terra-Sigillata des ersten Jahrhunderts*, 1919, Taf 64. Sherds of another f.29 from the same factory were found in the excavations (Report, fig 21, no 2)). A mortarium with the stamp LESBIVS is also illustrated, but there appears to be no record of this potter

11 Interim reports appeared in *Cornish Archaeol.* 5 (1966), 28–30; 6 (1967), 32–3; 7 (1968), 40–2; 9 (1970), 99–101; and the final report in *Brit.* 3 (1971), 56–111

12 See plan in *Roman Frontier Studies, 1969*, ed. E. Birley, B. Dobson and M. Jarrett, 1974, fig 17

13 *JRS* 67 (1977), 126 and fig 1

14 Rivet and Smith, 483

15 It may be worthy of note from what is known of the street plan of the fortress (fig 4), the *principia* faces north. This is quite often the direction of the enemy, although there are notable exceptions from this idea, such as Inchtuthil

16 *Boudica*, 1978, 95

17 *Trans. Birmingham Archaeol. Soc.* 58 (1937), 68–83

18 *Ibid.* 72 (1956), 1–4

19 *Brit.* 2 (1971), 263; extensive annual notes appeared in the *W. Midlands NS* no 10 (1967) 4–5; no 11 (1968), 10–11; no 12 (1969), 24–5. I am most grateful to Trevor Rowley for discussing the site with me and for sending me copies of his plans from which I have prepared simplified versions

20 I must confess I am doubtful about this conclusion. It would make much better sense if the 14½-acre site was primary and later reduced to a 6½-acre fort. The main difficulty is the corner tower, an unusual feature in both an annexe and a campaign camp. Buildings would not be expected in a campaign camp and tent lines are difficult to recognise, especially in the very difficult sub-soil on this site

21 W.J. Watkins, *Roman Cheshire*, 1886, 214

22 I.A. Richmond and Graham Webster 'Excavations in Goss Street, Chester, 1948–49', *Chester Archaeol. Soc. J.* (1950), fig 14, no 2

23 J.C. McPeake 'The First Century AD', *New Evidence from Roman Chester*,

published by the Inst. of Extension Studies, Univ. of Liverpool, 1978, 9

24 G.D.B. Jones and P.V. Webster, 'Mediolanum: excavations at Whitchurch, 1965–66', *Archaeol. J.* 125 (1969), 193

25 As elsewhere, most of the artefacts came from demolition pits at the end of the occupation and very little, if any, came from foundation deposits

26 J.K. St Joseph, 'Roman Forts on Watling Street near Penkridge and Wroxeter', *Birmingham Archaeol. Soc. Trans.* 69 (1953), 54–6

27 Now in the village Post Office

28 *JRS* 63 (1973), 235

29 *Ibid.* 235 and pl. xvii, 2

30 *Ibid.* 235

31 *JRS* 51 (1961), 124–5

32 S.C. Stanford, 'The Roman Forts at Leintwardine and Buckton', *Trans. Woolhope Field Club* 39 (1968), 230–7

33 *Antiquity* 53 (1979) 51–5, fig 2 and pl viiia; see also *Brit.* 13 (1982), pp. 360-1; 17 (1986), pp. 292–3; 18 (1987), p. 11

34 Dr S.C. Stanford, *Croft Ambrey*, 1974

35 A possible exception is the piece of decorated iron cheek-piece (fig 76, no 6), which, although much corroded, was identified as Celtic, but the cable moulding round the edge would seem to suggest that it came from a Roman helmet

36 S.C. Stanford, 'Credenhill Camp, Herefordshire: An Iron Age Hill Fort Capital', *Archaeol. J.* 127 (1971), 122

37 Kathleen M. Kenyon, 'Excavations at Sutton Walls, Herefordshire, 1948–1961', *Archaeol. J.* 110, (1953), 66–83

38 *Ibid.* 4; 24 skeletons were found in the trenches, but it is clear that they are only a sample; six had been beheaded, but in other cases the heads seem to have been partly severed. In a detailed report Dr I.A. Cornwall (pp. 66–78), concluded that the skeletons were 'conclusively male, chiefly youths and young men in the prime of life with only two individuals over 40'. This would seem to identify them all as warriors who had been defending the fort

39 This applies even to fig 15, no 2 of which is described in the text as a 'Belgic type', but it is a much devolved form; probably second century

40 G.H. Jack, *The Romano-British Town of Magna (Kenchester) Herefordshire*, 1916; *Excavations carried out during the years 1924–25*, 1926

41 *Woolhope Club. Trans.* 32 (1949), fig 7, no 10

42 *VCH Hereford* i, 180–181: details in *Woolhope Club Trans.* (1882), 248 and (1893), 59

43 Rivet and Smith, 369

44 *Monmouth Antiq.* 2 (1971), 165–198; *Archaeol. in Wales*, no 10, 1970, 19

45 *Monmouth Antiq.* 3 (1974), 108–110

46 This important deposit, the only one known in Britain, deserves a careful and thorough investigation. The most famous example is that at the legionary fortress at Vindonissa. It was formed by tipping rubbish over the cliff top down the steep slope to the River Aare; Elisabeth Ettlinger and Christoph Simonett, *Römische Keramik aus dem Schutthügel von Vindonissa*, Gesellschaft pro Vindonissa, 3 (1952)

47 *Monmouth Antiq.* 2 (1971), 176–192

48 Described by Dr Mansel Spratling, Report 196–8. A much earlier find was a *sestertius* of Claudius (*RIC* 60, *Monmouth Antiq.* i (1963), 27)

49 W.H. Manning, *The Fortress Excavations 1968–1971*, 1981; *1972–1974*, 1989

50 Greene, K. 1979, *The Pre-Flavian Fine Wares*

51 Summarised by George Boon in *Isca, The Roman Legionary Fortress at Caerleon, Mon.* 1972, Nat. Museum of Wales

52 Recent work in this area has been carried out by David Zienkiewicz and Vivienne Metcalf and both have kindly informed me that there are a few pre-Flavian sherds in the pottery they have found

53 Nash-Williams, V.E., 1969, 81

54 G. Boon, 'The earliest samian bowl from Wales', *Monmouth Antiq.* 2 (1965) 42–51

55 *JRS* 51 (1961), 123

56 *Trans. Birmingham Archaeol. Soc.* 79 (1964), 11–23; *Lichfield and S. Staffs. Archaeol. Soc. Trans.* 5 (1964); 8 (1968), 1–38; by A.A. Round, *ibid.* 11 (1971), 7–31

57 *Trans. Birmingham Archaeol. Soc.* 69 (1953), 50–6

58 *JRS* 55 (1965), 76–7 and fig 3

59 *Ibid.* 43 (1953), 83–4; 48 (1958), 94

60 *Trans. Birmingham Archaeol. Soc.* 73 (1956), 100–108. This has been supported by a later excavation by Neville Ingrey (*W. Midlands NS*, no 16, 1973, 15)

61 I am greatly indebted to Mr Billington of Kemsey Manor for drawing my attention to this promising site and looking for surface finds after ploughing

62 *JRS* 59 (1969), 105

63 Rivet and Smith, 482

64 *JRS* 43 (1953), 84; 51 (1961), 123

65 *Trans. Shrops. Archaeol. Soc.* 57 (1964), 132–3; also an air photograph of this site by Arnold Baker, pl xxii

66 *Brit.* 5 (1974), 427–8; the full report is forthcoming

67 *Trans. Worcs. Archaeol. Soc.* 37 (1961), 41–4

68 Rivet and Smith, 257

69 P. Barker, 'The Origins of Worcester', *Trans. Worcs. Archaeol. Soc.* 3rd. ser. 2 (1976), 10–12 and fig 1

70 *Ibid.* 44–50; a V-shaped ditch found in Lich Street and which has an early Flavian samian sherd near the bottom and later Roman pottery in the upper filling could be early Roman and military, *ibid.* 48 and fig 10

71 Listed by Derek Allen in *Problems of the Iron Age in Southern Britain*, ed. S.S. Frere, Occasional paper No 11, 1978. Institute of Archaeology and Colin Haselgrove's Supplement Gazatteer of Find-Spots of Celtic coins. The provenance of few of these finds is secure, two have come from the river, one from Powick and another known only to have been purchased in Worcester. These are a very mixed collection, two are British Q types, three Dobunnic, one Durotrigian and one a Gallic type

72 For the importance of this river crossing see Martin Carver, 'Medieval Worcester' in *Trans. Worcs. Archaeol. Soc.* 7 (1980), 17–21

73 Ekwall, *Dictionary of English Place-Names*, 1936, 359; the reference is also in the *Chronicle* of Florence of Winchester in 1118

74 *Britannia*, 1675, pl 50

75 Beatrice Hopkinson, 'Archaeological Evidence of Salt-moulding at important European Salt-sites and its Relationship to the Distribution of Urnfielders', *J. Indo-European Studies*, 3 (1975), 44–6

76 D.F. Freezer, *From Saltings to Spa Town: The Archaeology of Droitwich*, Worcs. County Museum, 1979; *W. Midlands NS*, No 22 (1979), 83–91.

77 *Trans. Birmingham Archaeol. Soc.* 62 (1943), 27–31. A church and graveyard occupy the centre of this site

78 *Trans. Worcs. Archaeol. Soc.* 39 (1969), 55–8

79 This has been emphasised above (fn 56)

80 *Trans. Worcs. Archaeol. Soc.* 7 (1980). The word *straet* (fig 12), as Della Hooke points out, on some of the early maps is described as *sylweg* which indicates a construction of logs

81 *Woolhope. Nat. F.C.* 34 (1954), 283–6. It could have been one of the later military sites such as Wall Town and Buckton which show that Roman control was maintained in this area well into the second century (S.C. Stanford, *The Welsh Marches*, 1980, 135)

82 It is also known by the parish name – Neen Savage

83 *Antiq. J.* 10 (1930), 385

84 *JRS* 43 (1953) and pl IX, 3

85 B.R. Hartley, 'Dating Town Buildings and Structures' in *The Civitas Capitals of Roman Britain*, 1966, 56; J. Wacher, *The Towns of Roman Britain*, 1975, 376

86 They took place between 1899 and 1912 and brief reports appeared in *Archaeologia* 58 (1901), 119–52, 391–406; 59 (1902), 87–124, 289–310; 60 (1906), 111–30, 451–64; 61 (1909), 565–82; 62 (1910), 1–20, 405–49; 64 (1913), 437–52

87 *Trans. Bristol and Gloucs. Arch. Soc.* 109 (199), 91–8

88 *VCH Hereford*, 1908, 195

89 Arnold Baker 'Results in Herefordshire from Aerial Reconnaissance in 1969', *Trans. Woolhope Nat. FC.* 40 (1970), 45–6, pl x

90 Fn 72

91 I am grateful to Ron Shoesmith for drawing my attention to this find and to Geoff Dannell for doing a report on the samian. The earliest piece is a form 29, similar to those produced by CELADVS, *c.*55–70 The site is listed under the parish name of Stoke Prior and it is possible that the Dobunnic gold coin, inscribed EISV (*ibid.* 164; Mack 388), from Leominster, may also have been found here

92 D.B. Whitehouse, 'A Section across the Roman road between Droitwich and Greensforge near Chaddersley Corbett', *Trans. Worcs. Archaeol. Soc.* 39 (1963), 49–54

93 *William Salt Archaeol. Soc.* for 1927 (1929), 185

94 For Professor St Joseph's contribution see *JRS* 43 (1953), 44 and pl IX, 2; 48 (1958), 95; 51 (1961), 123; 59 (1969), 104–5; 63 (1973), 233; see also *Trans. Birmingham Archaeol. Soc.* 80 (1965), 82–3

95 Report forthcoming

96 It has serrated edges for curbing wayward animals

97 T.J. O'Leary and P.J. Davey, 'Excavations at Pentre Farm, Flint 1976–7', *Flints. Hist. Soc. Pub.* 27 (1976), 138–151, with references to earlier work

98 *Y Cymmrodor*, 41 (1930)

99 *Antiquity* 51 (1977), 55–60

100 *Brit.* 9 (1978), 436; 10 (1979), 296–7. A report in the 1977 excavations was issued by the Border Counties Archaeological Group

101 *JRS* 59 (1969), 119–120; 63 (1973), 235 and fig 19

102 *Ibid.* 63 (1973), 235

103 Known as 'The Ancient Road' or 'The Sarn'; Lily F. Chitty, 'The Clun-Clee Ridgeway: a Prehistoric Trackway across South Shropshire' in *Culture and Environment*, ed. I.LL. Foster and L. Alcock, 1963, 174 and fig 47. The Brompton fort is also on the line of Offa's Dyke which may be on the line of a much earlier political boundary

104 Ffridd Faldwyn was partly excavated by Bryan O'Neil in 1937–39 (*Archaeol. Camb.* 97 (1943), 1–57; 98 (1944), 147). The same excavator also worked at the Breiddin in 1933–1935 (*ibid.* 92 (1937), 16–128), to which must be added the important results of more recent work by the Clwyd-Powys Trust (full report forthcoming; brief interim reports in *Archaeol. in Wales*, No 15 (1975), 35–7; No 16 (1976), 26)

105 Although no datable finds have been made here, the site has every appearance of Roman work, *VCH Shrops.* i, 379–380; *Trans. Shrops. Archaeol. Soc.* 55, for 1955–56, 119–120

106 Fn 87 above

107 The site, postulated as such by Professor Barri Jones at the junction of the Clun and the Unk near Bicton (Nash-Williams, V.E. 1969, 77), has since been disproved

108 *Ibid.* 84–5; by the Clwyd-Powys Archaeological Trust (*Brit.* 11 (1980), 315–7)

109 *Trans. Radnorshire Soc.* 27 (1957), 68–9. A fragment of an amber-glass jug and hypocaust tiles were also found, the latter indicating the presence of a nearby bath-house

110 Nash-Williams, V.E. 1969, 200

111 *Trans. Radnorshire Soc.* 46 (1976), 78–80; before the site was bulldozed, the platform of about 5 acres was clearly visible

112 *Ibid.* 49 (1979), 10–23

113 *JRS* 48 (1958), 95

114 Nash-Williams, V.E. 1969, 77–80

115 *JRS* 59 (1969), 123

116 *Ibid.* 63 (1973), 238–9 and fig 21

117 It was also crossed by the old Hereford-Hay horse tramway which pre-dated the railway

118 Davies, J.L. 1980, 260

119 Nash-Williams, V.E. 1969, 108–10; *JRS* 67 (1977), 150

120 David Crossley, 'Excavations at Pen-y-Gaer Roman Fort, Brecknock, 1966', *Archaeol. Camb.* 117 (1968), 92–102

121 Camulodunum form 17, D.P.S. Peacock in *Pottery and Early Commerce*, 1977, 147–62, where 7 different fabrics are distinguished, the latest pieces appear to come from Inchtuthil (AD 83–87)

122 Camulodunum form 45

123 It could have been part of the Veranian advance in 58. The section through the defences on the north side (Report, fig 2) poses problems. The first rampart produced no datable material, nor any ditch system, which is very peculiar, but

the excavator pointed out that the ground slopes away very sharply on this side and there may have been no need for ditches. However, there is the profile of a very fine outer Punic ditch, but this appeared only on one side of the trench and was assumed to be a pit

5 Aulus Didius Gallus and the Northern Advance (pages 87–103)

1 Anthony R. Birley, *The Fasti of Roman Britain*, 1981
2 *ILS* 970 = *CIL* iii, 7247; two other fragments from Greece have been studied by J.H. Oliver, one includes the word BRITTAN(IA) and the other, E]QVIT[ATVS (*Revue Archaéologique* (1947), No 76, 209). Oliver links them together as parts of inscriptions relating to Gallus and, on the basis of this, proposes a new reading of *ILS* 970 (*Revue Archaéologique* (1949), No 11, 174–5). See also L. Peterson and L. Vidman (*Conf, Eirene 1972*, 656 ff) and Professor A. Birley's summary in his 'The Roman Governors of Britain', *Epig. Stud.* 4(1967), 65
3 A.T. Didius was consul in 98 BC
4 Petersen and Vidman, *op. cit.* 668
5 *De Aquis Urbis Romae*, ii, 102. 7
6 He sprang to fame as a successful accuser in the trials under Tiberius (*Ann.* iv. 52)
7 Dio, lix. 20. 3. The circumstances of this appointment, as reported, were bizarre. Afer needed all his histrionic ability to persuade Gaius that he could not compete with him in oratory, later he was elevated to the consulship after Gaius had removed those already in office, breaking their *fasces* in the process, since they had failed to provide a thanksgiving for his birthday
8 G. Alföldy 'Die Hilfstruppen in der romischen Provinz Germanis inferior', *Epig. Stud.* 6 (1968), 131–5; for examples under Vespasian (the two officers concerned had this post before they became legionary commanders)
9 *Ann.* xii. 15
10 A suggestion I owe to Professor Anthony Birley. This man was exiled by Nero for his scandalous writings and dealings in patronage (*Ann.* xiv. 50) but he survived to worm his way into the good graces of the Flavians and ended with four priesthoods (R. Syme, *Tacitus*, 1958, 4–6; the relationship with Gallus is presumed (*ibid.* fn 9, 594)
11 *Hist.* i. 64
12 Dio, lxvii. 14. 5. This is a suggestion by Professor Anthony Birley (*The People of Roman Britain*, 1979, 44), but Dio only refers to a Gaius Valens
13 This was normal practice, as pointed out, with examples, by David Breeze 'Roman Scotland during the reign of Antoninius Pius' in *Roman Frontier Studies 1979*, pt i, 1980, 45
14 E. MacNeill, 'Ancient Irish Law: Law of Status and Franchise', *Proc. R. Irish Acad.* 26 for 1921–24, Sect. C, A reference I owe to Professor A. Birley, who was given it by C.E. Stevens
15 Professor A. Birley has noted that this man could have been the elder brother of Q. Petillius Cerealis Caesius Rufus, who commanded *Legio IX* in 60 and was later to become governor of Britain (*Brit.* 4 (1973), 181). If this suggestion is valid, it offers the only evidence that these events all took place before 60 and that they

are not two separate incidents which should have been brought together by Tacitus in error (S. Mitchell, Liverpool Classical Monthly 3 (1978), 219)

16 There are indications of this from the air (see D.W. Riley, *Yorks. Archaeol. J.* 46 (1974), 183; 47 (1975), 11), but local surface geology with much frost cracking is not helpful to the formation and interpretation of crop-marks

17 R.M. Butler, ed *Soldier and Civilian in Roman Yorkshire*, 1971

18 Hermann Ramm, 'Native Settlements East of the Pennines', in *Rome and the Brigantes*, 1980, ed K. Branigan, 28–31

19 Rivet and Smith, 448

20 The little which is known about this site has been culled from the interim report of the three seasons' excavations in 1939, '46 and '47 by W.J. Varley, who did not complete a full report, but published a general paper (*Archaeol. J.* 106 (1950), 41–60)

21 'Queen Cartimandua', *JRS.* 44 (1954), 43–52

22 *The Stanwick Fortifications North Riding of Yorkshire*, 1954, Soc. of Antiq. Res. Rep. 17, 19, fn 1

23 I.A. Richmond, *Huddersfield in Roman Times*, 1925, 14

24 *The Coins of the Coritani*, 1963, 22–5

25 Barry Cunliffe, *Iron Age Communications in Britain*, 1974, Chap 13

26 *Soldier and Citizen in Roman Yorkshire*, ed R.M. Butler, 1971, 66

27 *Rome and the Brigantes*, ed. K. Branigan 1980, 28–31 and fig 4.2

28 Rivet and Smith, 448

29 *Ibid.* 295

30 *JRS* 44 (1954), 44–6

31 I.M. Stead, *The Arras Culture*, 1979

32 *Antiq. J.* 18 (1938), 262

33 J. Wacher, *The Towns of Roman Britain*, 1975, 394–5 and fig 85

34 He had been tutor to the youthful Nero

35 Most of his career had been spent in administration and finance, he was not a military man

36 Dio lxi. 4; *Ann.* xiii. 2; see also B.H. Warmington, *Nero: Reality and Legend*, 1969

37 O. Davies, *Roman Mines in Europe*, 1935; quoting Waldron fn 7, 148; for Spain *ibid.* fn 1, 106 and fn 9, 112–3

38 The richest ores of Asia Minor produced as much as 600 oz/ton (P.J. Forbes, *Metallurgy in Antiquity*, 1950, 180)

39 Malcolm Todd, *The Coritani*, 1973, 167, citing evidence from Thorpe and Margidunum

40 This attitude can be seen in other peoples unused to the operations of capitalist economy. The Spaniards had similar difficulties with the Incas of South America

41 *Italiam, et provincias inmenso faenore hauriri*

42 This is the view of G. Walser, *Rom. das Reich und die freuden Völker in der Geschichtsschreibung der frühen Kaiserzeit*, and this seems to be the judgment of R. Syme, *Tacitus*, 762–3

43 Tacitus regarded him as one of the finest of the younger writers, even equated him to Livy (*Agricola*, 10; a reference which makes it certain that he was describing Britain).

44 A suggestion I owe to Nicholas Reed in his brief note in *Arepo*, No 3 (1970) 5–8 (an Oxford Classical Journal)

45   *JRS* 67 (1977), 129 and fig 3
46   Harold Dudley, *Early Days in North-West Lincolnshire*, 1949, 149; quoting Trollope; it was removed in 1820 to improve navigation
47   *JRS* 55 (1965), 74–6, fig 2 and pl x; 59 (1969), 104; 63 (1973), 214; 67 (1977), 128–9
48   *Britannia* 1974, 87
49   *Trans. Thoroton Soc.* 62 (1959), 24–34
50   *JRS* 59 (1969) 104 and pl II, 1; 67 (1977), 129
51   *Hist.* iii. 45
52   Paul Buckland, 'A First-century Shield from Doncaster', *Brit.* 9 (1978), 247
53   I.D. Margary, *Roman Roads in Britain*, 1957, 142
54   M. Todd, *The Coritani*, 1973, 18
55   *Brit.* 11 (1980), 330–5 and fig 9
56   Also found by Dr Riley, *ibid.* 7 (1977), 119
57   *Ibid.* 11 (1980), 332 and fig 10
58   'First Century Roman Occupation at Strutts Park, Derby', *Derbyshire Archaeol. J.* 90 (1970), 22–30; 87 (1967), 162–5; 105 (1985), 15–32
59   *Brit.* 6 (1975), 244; a coin of Vespasian with little wear was also found
60   *Ibid.* 81 (1961); 87 (1967), 39–85; *Antiq.J.* 51 (1971), 36–69; *Brit.* 4 (1973), 285; 5 (1974), 419–20; 6 (1975), 242–4
61   *JRS* 43 (1963), 87
62   *Brit.* 7 (1976), 322; 8 (1977), 387; 9 (1978), 430 and fig 9; 10 (1979), 292–3, where the earlier interpretation is amended; see also a booklet by the excavator, T. Courtney, *Chesterfield: the recent archaeological discoveries*, 1975
63   Thomas May, *The Roman Forts of Templeborough, near Rotherham*, 1922
64   I am informed by Mrs Scott Anderson that the early pieces bear a striking resemblance to those from Chesterfield
65   S.S. Frere, *Britannia*, 1967, 85
66   Grace Simpson, *Britons and the Roman Army*, 1964, 11 and fig 1; 'Roman Manchester and Templeborough: The Facts and Dates Revised' in *Greeks, Celts and Romans*, ed C. and S. Hawkes, i, 1973, 69–93
67   Note pl XIV, nos 16, 17, 18; XV, no 5; they deserve closer study and possibly cleaning
68   *N. Staffs. J. of Field Stud.* 2 (1962), 37 and 52
69   A.E. Mountford, J. Gee and G. Simpson, 'The Excavation of an early Neronian pottery kiln and workshop at Trent Vale, Stoke-on-Trent', *N. Staffs J. of Field Stud.* 8 (1968), 19–38
70   It has been the subject of a special report by Professor Howard Comfort 'An Italian Sigillata Crater in Britain' in 'Hommages à Albert Grenier', *Latomus*, 58 (1962), 448–56
71   It was found on the late Neronian fort by Brian Hobley, *Trans. Birmingham and Warks. Archaeol. Soc.* 85 (1972), 63–5 and fig 16, no 158, fig 32 and pl 13 (b)
72   It would seem a little strange that someone would find a single sherd of such poor quality in the Mediterranean area and present it to the Museum.
73   F.H. Goodyear, 'The Roman Fort at Chesterton, Newcastle-under-Lyme: Report of the Excavations of 1960–71', *N. Staffs. J. of Field Stud.*, 16 (1976), 1–15
74   G.D.B. Jones, 'Excavations at Northwich', *Archaeol. J.* 128 (1972), 31–77
75   For the earliest finds see W. Thompson, *Roman Cheshire*, 1886, 260–73 and the various reports of Thomas May, *Trans. Hist. Soc. Lancs. and Chesh.* 23 (1871),

153–72; 48 (1897), 1–28; 50 (1900), 1–40; 52 (1902), 1–52; 55–6 (1903/4), 209–37; 58 (1906), 15–40. For recent work by the DOE see *Archaeol. Excavations 1976*, HMSO, 1977, 36–7; also *JRS* 21 (1931), 223; 58 (1968), 182 and Fig 10; *Brit.* 6 (1975), 240

76 G.B. Jones, 'The Romans in the North East', *Northern History*, 3 (1968), 1–26
77 *Roman Manchester*, 1974, 6 and fig 2
78 *Ibid.*
79 *Derbyshire Archaeol. J.* 26 (1904), 177–204; by I.A. Richmond and J.P. Gillam, *ibid.* 59 (1938), 53–65, but the work in 1939 remains unpublished; *JRS* 29 (1939), 206; 30 (1940), 168; as does that of Dr Petch in 1958 and 9; *ibid.* 44 (1959), 108; 50 (1961), 216
80 *Derbyshire Archaeol. J.* 85 (1965), 125–6; 86 (1966), 99–106; 87 (1967), 154–8; 88 (1968), 89–96; 89 (1969), 99–106

6 The Advance under Quintus Veranius (pages 104–118)

1 'Britain under Nero: The Significance of Q. Veranius', *Durham Univ. J.* June 1952, 88–92; also in the collected papers, *Roman Britain and the Roman Army*, 1963, 1–9
2 *Inscriptiones Graecae ad res Romanas pertinentes*, 1961, iii, 703
3 He was made a *triumvir monetalis*, a post usually reserved for patricans, but in the case of a plebeian the appointment indicated that he had chosen by the Emperor for greater than usual promotion in his service
4 Veranius and Brocchus were at that time tribunes of the plebs and were sent by the Senate to negotiate with the Emperor after he had been found by the Praetorians and hailed as Emperor (Josephus, *Antiquities of the Jews*, xix. 3. 4)
5 Arthur E. Gordon, 'Quintus Veranius, Consul AD 49', Univ. of California, Pap. in *Classical Archaeology*, 2. no 5 (1952), 231–75 (excl. appendices).
6 The Cibyrae thanked him for carrying out building works to the Emperor's instructions (fn 46, 1901, 4.902), and there are also unrecorded altars, so Professor Martin Harrison kindly informs me; and natives receiving citizenship took his name (see fn 16, 241 in A.E. Gordon's paper). There is some doubt about a coin which appears to bear a portrait of a Veranius, but this is probably that of his father (see Gordon fn 17, 241).
7 This does not seem to relate to any known celebration, but it could, as A.E. Gordon considers, have been a special unrecorded occasion which Nero chose to acknowledge.
8 *Ann.* xiv. 29; *modicis excursibus Siluras populatus, quin ultra bellum proferret, morte probibitus est*, i.e. after limited attacks against the Silures, he was prevented by death from extending the war any further. This could be interpreted that he actually died while on campaign
9 This is a seventh-century list of places which has survived in a very corrupt form. Professor Rivet has suggested that the compiler extracted the names from an actual map. Richmond and Crawford attempted to rationalise the list into a sequence of routes, but this posed considerable difficulties (*Archaeologia* 93 (1949), 1–50)
10 A suggestion made by Richmond and Crawford, but accepting the spelling Mediomano (see fn 1, 40)

11 *The Fortress Excavations 1968–71*, 1981; *The Fortress Excavations 1972–74 and Minor Excavations on the Fortress and Flavian Fort*, 1989

12 Dr Greene kindly informs me that since he published this map single sherds from Lyons have turned up at Binchester, Newstead and Camelon, which indicates that these two vessels survived even longer. Another site which has produced two vessels is Burgh-by-Woodbridge, Suffolk, which has no known military association.

13 L.P. Wenham, 'The Beginning of Roman York', in *Soldier and Civilian in Roman Yorkshire*, ed R.M. Butler, 1971, 47–51

14 *Archaeol. in Wales*, No 15 (1975), 50

15 *Brit.* 1 (1970), 273

16 H.R. Hurst, *Kingsholm*, 1985, p. 6

17 Jeffrey Davies could only place a few question marks against sites in his paper 'Roman military development in Wales and the Marches from Claudius to the Antonines' in *Roman Frontier Studies*, 1980, 255–77 and fig 17.

18 Except perhaps to some (M.G. Jarrett and J.C. Mann, 'The Tribes of Wales', in *The Welsh History Review* 4 (1968), 167)

19 *Antiq. J.* 49 (1969), 253–4

20 Interim reports by G.D.B. Jones and J.H. Little have appeared in *The Carmarthen Antiq.*, 9 (1973), 3–27; 10 (1974), 3–16

21 *JRS* 59 (1969), 198

22 Nash-Williams, V.E., 1969; 96; *JRS.* 52 (1962), 161–2; 53 (1963), 126; the first clay bank had a possible connection 'with certain pre-Flavian sherds'

23 *Brit.* 1 (1970), 270–2

24 Dr Jarrett's careful statement is 'the proportion of objects which are unlikely to have remained in circulation in the Flavian period is high enough for us to regard this as corroborated evidence of a pre-Flavian occupation', (*Archaeol. J.* 121 (1965), 28–9). Unfortunately, the excavation and its critical sherds have not yet been published.

25 *Montgomery Coll.* 61 (1971), 96; this evidence relies entirely on tile fragments being correctly identified as Roman

26 There is a 2.3 acre enclosure with a turf rampart near Caersws and known as Gaer Noddfor, 6 miles from Caersws up the valley. It is known to have been occupied in the thirteenth-century by the Knights Hospitaller of St John, and although the defences have a Roman appearance, not a sherd of Roman pottery has been found and this site can only remain a possible early campaign camp, which could fit into the Veranian scheme (Nash-Williams, V.E. 1969, 137–8; a trench through the defences was cut by W.G. Putman in 1964 and 65, *Montgomery Coll.* 62 (1973), 195–201)

27 Nash-Williams, V.E. 1969, 66–70

28 This was never published, but the pottery recovered was studied by F.N. Pryce (*Montgomery Coll.* 42 (1931), 17 ff; 46 (1940), 66 ff)

29 *Ibid.* 59 (1968), 112–5; 60 (1969), 64–6

30 *Ibid.* 59 (1968), 113; earlier finds include samian form 15/17 and polychrome

glass, the latter of which is normally pre-Flavian (Nash-Williams, V.E. 1965, 56)

31 *JRS* 48 (1958), 97

32 Nash-Williams, V.E. 1969, 66 and fig 29

33 *Ibid.* 132–5

34 *JRS* 67 (1977), 153 and fig 16

35 *Brit.* 9 (1978), 408; *Archaeol in Wales*, No 17 (1977), 31

36 J.A. Steers, *The Coastline of England and Wales*, 1946, 148–152

37 *Brit.* 10 (1979), 272; *Archaeol. in Wales*, No 18 (1978), 51; for the Pennal fort see Nash-Williams, V.E. 1969, 104–6 and *JRS* 67 (1977), 151

38 Greene, K. 1979, 87 and 100; see also his distribution map for British finds, fig 38

39 Davies, J.L. 1980, 260; but his statement 'Neither of these sites, i.e. (Pennal and Caer Gai) can ante-date the early 70s' needs reconsideration, since they could have been established by Paullinus in 59–60

40 *JRS* 67 (1977), 153; *Archaeol. in Wales*, No 16 (1967), 31

41 Nash-Williams, V.E. 1969, 113–6; the streets showed remarkable from the air in 1975 (*JRS* 67 (1977), 154–5 and pl xiv); for further excavations by Dr Davies, see *Brit.* 5 (1974), 400; 6 (1975), 222

42 Nash-Williams, V.E. 1969, 116

43 *Ibid.* 97–8 and 200; *Brit.* 1 (1970), 269; 2 (1971), 243; 3 (1972), 300; 4 (1973), 271; for the bath-house see *Archaeol. in Wales*, No 10 (1970), 15–6

44 This is the Celtic word for a female breast and thought by Richmond and Crawford to refer to the rounded contours of the site, a suggestion accepted by Rivet and Smith, 307

45 *Y Cymmrodor*, 37 (1926)

46 Dr G. Simpson, *Archaeol. Camb.* 113 (1963), 19

47 Dr D. Harden in *Camulodunum*, 1947, 293

48 *Archaeol. Camb.,* 120 (1971), 93

49 Nash-Williams, V.E. 1969, 74–9

50 *Ibid.*

51 *Archaeol. Camb.* 113 (1964), 64–96

52 Nash-Williams, V.E. 1969, 81–3

53 *Archaeol. Camb.* 112 (1963), 44

54 Margery, I.D. 1957, 70–1

55 *VCH Hereford* i, 1908, 187–190

56 *Trans. Woolhope Nat. F.C.* (1924) App.; *Antiq. J.* (1923), 68–9

57 *Trans. Woolhope Nat. F.C.* 38 (1965), 124–135

58 'The Origins of Coinage in Britain: A Reappraisal' in *Problems of the Iron Age in Southern Britain*, ed. S.S. Frere, London Institute of Archaeology, Occasional Paper No 11, 97–308

59 *Supplementary Gazetteer of Find Spots of Celtic coins in Britain, 1975; ibid.* No 11a, 1978; this includes two, said to have been found near Ross-on-Wye, and thus presumed to have come from Ariconium

60 The other 3 are of Cunobeline, of Verica and an example of British C

61 A view also expressed by Dr Stanford, *The Welsh Marches*, 1980, 160

62 *Brit. Archaeol. Ass. J.* 27 (1871), 203, pl ii, no 19; reproduced with less detail in *VCH Hereford* i, 1908, 190 and fig 13, centre brooch

63 I am very grateful to Donald Mackreth for a note on this brooch and to Dr Grace Simpson for informing me that it is now in the Gloucester City Museum (Acc. No

1618). She has also kindly listed the British parallels: from Camulodunum, two from Canterbury, Braughing and also Skeleton Green, where there appears to have been a Roman trading depôt prior to the conquest, and which has been investigated by Clive Partridge (Report forthcoming as a monograph by the Roman Soc.); there is another from an early ditch at Mildenhall (Wilts.) and an unprovenanced example in the Cheltenham Museum.

64 The coins listed in the 1924 Report (fn 48), 10 and the samian, ibid. 16, no 2 and pl 4, fig 5. See also the *Newsletter of the Dean Arch. Group*, ii, No. 3, 1989

65 Nash-Williams, V.E. 1965, 91; a bath-house was found during the construction of the railway line and station in 1852

66 Carried out in 1971 and 1973, *Archaeol. Camb.* 122 (1973), 99–146; 128 (1980), 13–39

67 The small fragment of green-glazed ware 'with horizontal ribbing and decoration' (Second Report, 33), is difficult to identify with any known form

68 *Archaeol. Camb.* 112 (1963), 38 and fig 6, no 1

69 Nash-Williams, V.E. 1969, 64–5

70 By J.M. Lewis, *Archaeol. Camb.* 115 (1966), 67–87

71 Nash-Williams, V.E. 1969, 88–91; and for full references

72 *The Roman Fort at Gellygaer*, 1903; Appendix II has a note on excavation techniques which gives a clear indication of Ward's forward thinking

73 *Archaeol. Camb.* 112 (1962), 52 and 60

74 Nash-Williams, V.E. 1969, 106–8

75 A brief note was published in *JRS* 48 (1958), 131

76 *Brit.* 11 (1980), 348; *Archaeol. in Wales*, No 18 (1978), 28; the faint crop-marks are of a rectangular enclosure, c.200m by 180m

77 Nash-Williams, V.E. 1969, 46–8; *Bull. Board of Celtic Stud.* (1958), 310–4

78 *JRS* 56 (1966), 196

79 *JRS* 67 (1977), 151; it is an enclosure c.160ft by 125ft only 600ft west of the fort

80 *JRS* 63 (1973), 241

81 C.M. Daniels and G.B.D. Jones, 'The Roman Camps on Llandrindod Common', *Archaeol. Camb.* 118 (1969), 124–33

82 It was recognised by C.J. Spurgeon of the Welsh Royal Commission, *Archaeol. in Wales*, No 14 (1971), 20–1

Appendix Two (pages 124–130)

1 The usual Roman term for these rulers was *reges socii*, although by the late Republic we find them informally referred to as 'clients', as in Cicero, *Ep.* 9.9.2

2 See A.N. Sherwin-White, *Roman Society and Roman Law in the New Testament* (Oxford 1963) 56

3 For client kings often cited as parallels, see *Britannia* 10 (1979) 236–7

4 *Britannia* 10 (1979) 244–5

5 The name of a Gallic Cogidubnus may be contained in a fragmentary inscription from Mediolanum Santonum (*CIL* 13.1040)

6 Tacitus, *Ag.*13, points out that provided they were treated fairly the British were prepared to discharge their *imperii munera* energetically

7 See, for example, A.E. Wilson, *Sussex Archaeological Collections* 114 (1956) 103 and J. Wacher, *The Towns of Roman Britain* (London 1974) 239

8   See B. Cunliffe, *Excavations at Fishbourne, 1961–9*. Vol. I: *The Site* (London 1971) 13

9   Strabo 12.6.1; Appian, BC 5.75

10   I owe this explanation to an idea originally suggested to me by my colleague J. Russel

11   There is some evidence that the Celtic equivalent of *rex* might have been used by rulers of the period on their coins; this is the usual interpretation of the legend *ricon/rigon* found on staters of Tasciovanus (Mack 184–5)

12   On the limitations of this tool, however, see J.R. Collis, *World Archaeology* 3 (1971) 71–84 and A.H.A. Hogg, *The Iron Age and its Hill-Forts*, ed. M. Jesson and D. Hill (Southamptom 1971) 105–126

13   In *Hod Hill* Vol. II (London 1968) 53–54

14   See *BG* 4.21, 5.22

15   *Römische Herrschaft in Westeuropa* (Berlin 1890) 16–20

16   B.H. St.J. O'Neil, *Archaeological Journal* 109 (1952) 28–9 and Cunliffe, *op cit.* n.8, 72–3

17   See *Archaeologia* 90 (1944) 25–7

18   *Annales* 14.31

19   See *American Journal of Philology* 100 (1979) 538–40

20   Eg. *Historiae* i.55, *Annales* iii.27

21   For examples, the villas at Angmering, Southwick, Pulborough and Eastbourne

Appendix Three (pages 131–134)

This gave rise to the practice of obtaining the *diplomata*, i.e. two bronze plates on which was inscribed the senatorial decree listing the units of a province receiving discharges. There are very valuable documents for information about auxiliary units in different provinces, see G.R. Watson, *The Roman Soldier*, 1969, 136–7; they are listed in *CIL* XVI, and the list has been up-dated by M. Roxan, *Roman Military Diplomas 1954–1977*, Institute of Archaeol. Occ. Pap. No 2 (1978)

2   *RIB* 159; see also Paul Holder, *The Auxilia from Augustus to Trajan*, BAR, 1980, 20–32

3   *Brit.* 11 (1980), 388

4   The name of the place is given by Ptolemy who may have been using a Neronian military map, as Aquae Calidae

5   Russell Robinson, *The Armour of Imperial Rome*, 1975, 174–86

6   It is not clear when this formation was created, but it was certainly in existence by 86, as exemplified by Inchtuthil, where the plan of the barrack-blocks has been established (R.M. Ogilvie and Sir Ian Richmond, *de vita Agricolae*, 1967, fig 9; see also S.S. Frere, 'Hyginus and the First Cohort', *Brit,* 11 (1980), 51–69)

7   David Breeze, 'Pay Grades and Ranks below the Centurionate', *JRS* 61 (1971), 130–5; see also 'The Organisation of the career structure of the *immunes* and *principales* of the Roman Army', *Bonner Jahrb,* 174 (1974) 247–92

8   Brian Dobson, *Die Primipilares, Beihefle der Bonner Jahrb*; see also his contribution in English in *Aufstieg und Niedergang der romischen Welt*, II. 1, 1974, 393

9   *RIB* 293; The title *Victrix* is not attached to the legion

10   The list survives as a fragment of Tarruntenus Paternus, a military jurist of the time of Commodus in the *Digest of Justinian*, 1.6.7; see also G.R. Watson, *The Roman Soldier*, 1969, 75–7

11   The best book is still G.L. Cheesman, *The Auxilia of the Roman Army*, 1914, but it is now much outdated. Paul Holder, *The Auxilia from Augustus to Trajan*, BAR, 1980, is now an essential reference book

12   See Paul Holder, 1980, *op. cit. supra*, Cap. 1

13   The only extensive study is C.G. Starr, *Roman Imperial Navy 31* BC–AD *324*, 2nd ed, 1960

14   The status of the British Fleet can be judged by the fact that a *praefectus* by the late second century was a *centenarius* (i.e. earned 100,000 *sesterces* a year) and had the title of *procurator Augusti* (see also A.R. Birley, *The People of Roman Britain*, 1979, 50–1)

Appendix Four (page 135)

1   Jeffrey L. Davies and Mansel G. Spratling 'The Seven Sisters hoard: a centenary study' in *Welsh Antiquity*, essays presented to H.N. Savory, ed. by George C. Boon and J.M. Lewis, 121–47

2   A parallel for this has been found at Ashton near Oundle in the Nene Valley (report forthcoming)

3   *Later Prehistoric Antiquities of the British Isles*, BM, 1953, 62 and pl XIII

Appendix Five (page 136)

1   This provenance is given in *VCH Shrops.* i, 1908, 244 and incorrectly recorded in *RIB* p. 99

Index